DEVOTIONAL THOUGHTS ON THE BIBLE

Charles Haddon Spurgeon

DEVOTIONAL THOUGHTS ON THE BIBLE

Charles Haddon Spurgeon

MATTHEW AND MARK

Prepared by Larry Brown

EP EVANGELICAL PRESS

Also available in this series
Devotional thoughts on the Bible: The Pentateuch
(ISBN 978 0 85234 605 1)

 EVANGELICAL PRESS

Evangelical Press
Faverdale North, Darlington, DL3 0PH England

Evangelical Press USA
P. O. Box 825, Webster NY 14580 USA

email: sales@evangelicalpress.org
www.evangelicalpress.org

All Scripture quotations are from the Holy Bible, King James Version (KJV). Public domain.

British Library Cataloguing in Publication Data available
ISBN 978 0 85234 663 1

PRINTED AND BOUND IN THE USA

To my pastors, friends, and the preservers of my soul:
Maurice, Henry, and Don

Charles Haddon Spurgeon

FOREWORD

In my early days of studying for the ministry, I asked Dr Lee Roberson, president of Tennessee Temple College, 'Would you recommend to me books or writings of the man you believe to be the greatest preacher, theologian, and student of the Word in the world?' The next day he brought me a copy of C. H. Spurgeon's 1861 sermons and said, 'Read Mr Spurgeon.' I did — and I have been reading Mr Spurgeon since that day! Indeed, throughout my sixty years of preaching the gospel, I have read and profited greatly from his writings. As someone once said, 'C. H. Spurgeon is so commanding, so simple, so humble, and so entirely *God's man*!'

In 1886 Spurgeon wrote a preface to his publication of *My Sermon Notes* in which he said, 'I know nothing but the doctrines of grace, the teachings of the cross, the gospel of salvation, and I write only that these notes may be more widely published.' I pray that this new series, Spurgeon's *Devotional Thoughts on the Bible*, will be blessed of God to the spiritual benefit of many.

Pastor Henry T. Mahan
Ashland, Kentucky, USA

Charles Haddon Spurgeon

PREFACE

Perhaps the most widely read and often quoted preacher in history is Charles Haddon Spurgeon. His published sermons, totaling sixty-three volumes, demonstrate his remarkable gifts, his understanding of the Scriptures, his theological acumen, his mastery of the English language, his ability to illustrate the profound truths of the gospel with simplicity, and his tremendous intellect.

Spurgeon preached Christ and preached Christ passionately. Without question, he was used of God for the furtherance of the gospel around the world in a remarkable way and continues to be, through his written works. Spurgeon's deep, yet simple trust and understanding of our Lord Jesus Christ, his great mercy, grace, and love is evident in his writings. His great longing was to have others come to know, trust, love, and worship our Lord. To that end he laboured tirelessly in publishing the gospel.

In addition to his volumes of sermons, Spurgeon edited *The Sword and the Trowel* magazine, wrote and published *The Golden Alphabet* (an exposition of Psalm 119), *Around the Wicket Gate, The Salt Cellars, Till He Come* (a series of communion sermons), *Words of Wisdom for Daily Life, Words of Cheer for Daily Life, All of Grace* (a four-volume autobiography),

Faith's Checkbook, Morning and Evening Devotional, Spurgeon's Devotional Bible (morning and evening expositions), *The Treasury of David* (a seven-volume exposition of the Psalms), *John Ploughman's Talks, A Catechism for Children, My Sermon Notes,* and *A Commentary on the Gospel of Matthew.* He also compiled *Our Own Hymn Book* for his congregation at the Metropolitan Tabernacle in London. All of these volumes have been reproduced many times and are still available today.

But there is another aspect of Spurgeon's preaching and writing that is hardly known: when he preached before thousands each Sunday at the Metropolitan Tabernacle, he read and gave a brief exposition of a passage of Scripture before his morning sermon. These were transcribed and possess a literary characteristic found in none of his other writings. The subject matter almost always grips you in the initial verses and comments, the language is simple, and their flow is staccato. In making spontaneous remarks on the passages, he often interrupts his readings mid-verse, mid-sentence, and in many instances, mid-phrase! It is this unique trait that makes them so easily read. When compiled and sequenced as a body of readings, the expositions are extensive enough to cover virtually the entire Bible, giving a remarkable overview of its contents. These expositions are now being published in volumes, each giving general coverage to a particular section of the Bible.

Without question, these devotionals could be the most popular published in a generation, and their value as family devotionals is beyond measure. May they be blessed of God to the good of many, for the glory of Christ.

Perhaps Charles Spurgeon expressed it best when, commenting on Psalm 90:17, he said:

> *Let not what we do for thee fall to the ground like a badly built wall! Let not our work be consumed in the great testing fire, but the work of our hands establish thou it!*

Charles Haddon Spurgeon

ACKNOWLEDGEMENTS

The draft manuscript from which these devotionals were arranged and compiled contained over 1,755,000 words, 2,700 single-spaced pages, and comments on over 1,400 expositions. The final publications would have been impossible without the generous assistance in proofing and editing from these people:

Al and Rebecca Smith, Bill and Michelle Augustine, Bill and Vicci Rolley, Bob and Carol Pruitt, Bob and Mary Lou Duff, Bob and Sally Poncer, Carter and Joyce Brown, Chris Kendziora, Daniel and Sandy Parks, David and Betty Burge, David and Celeste Peterson, Don and Shelby Fortner, Don Williams, Don and Mary Bell, Evelyn M. Wang, Gene and Judy Harmon, Geoff and Valerie Thomas, Jim and Nancy Byrd, Bobbie and Judy Estes, Tim and Debbie James, and, most of all, Carol.

Charles Haddon Spurgeon

MATTHEW

MATTHEW 2:1-12

Matt. 2:1   Now when Jesus was born in Bethlehem of Judaea in the days of Herod the king, behold, there came wise men from the east to Jerusalem,

Our Lord was born in Bethlehem, an inconsiderable village of Judaea. Its name, however, is significant; it means, 'the house of bread'. Truly Bethlehem has become, in a spiritual sense, the house of bread to all who feed on Christ. When Jesus was born in Bethlehem, there came wise men from the east to Jerusalem.

2   Saying, Where is he that is born King of the Jews? —

There was another king, of whom we have just read: 'Herod the king', but he was an Idumean, an Edomite. He had no right to the throne; but here is born the true Heir to the throne of David, and the Magi from the east have come to ask for him.

2-3   for we have seen his star in the east, and are come to worship him. When Herod the king had heard these things, he was troubled, and all Jerusalem with him.

Tidings of the arrival of these strangers in the Jewish capital, asking for the newborn King, would be sure to spread rapidly. The news soon reached the palace; and Herod, one of the most suspicious and cruel of tyrants, and therefore the most cowardly of men, 'was troubled, and all Jerusalem with him'.

4 And when he had gathered all the chief priests and scribes of the people together, he demanded of them where Christ should be born.

They could tell him if they wished to do so, for they were deeply versed in the Scriptures. The scribes copied the sacred writings. The Pharisees had counted the very letters of the Word; they could tell which was the middle letter of the Old Testament. They were great at the letter but, alas, they had missed the spirit! Men may know a great deal about the Bible, and yet really know nothing of it. The husks of Scripture yield small profit; we need to come to the kernel, the real corn, the spiritual meaning of the inspired Word.

5-7 And they said unto him, In Bethlehem of Judaea: for thus it is written by the prophet, And thou Bethlehem, in the land of Judah, art not the least among the princes of Judah: for out of thee shall come a Governor, that shall rule my people Israel. Then Herod, when he had privily called the wise men, inquired of them diligently what time the star appeared.

He half suspected that he should not see them again, so he determined to get all the information he possibly could out of them.

8 And he sent them to Bethlehem, and said, Go and search diligently for the young child; and when ye have found him, bring me word again, that I may come and worship him also.

It was like his deep, cunning spirit to try to find out where the child was, that he might kill him. He looked upon him as a rival, as one who might rob him of his throne, so he would put him to death if he could; and, meanwhile, he would pretend that he wanted to worship him.

9 When they had heard the king, they departed; and, lo, the star, which they saw in the east, went before them, till it came and stood over where the young child was.

It was probably not a star in the sense in which we use the word: that is a planet, or a fixed star; but a meteoric brightness, which moved in the sky, and so guided the wise men. They do not appear to have seen its light after they set out on their journey; it directed them to the region of Judaea so they came to the capital city, Jerusalem. When they departed from Herod, the star appeared again, and guided them to the little town of Bethlehem, where they found the Christ. God may sometimes send us stars, bright lights of joy, to guide us on our way; he may also take them away again, and then we must walk by faith. When they reappear, we shall be glad to have them once more, as the wise men were.

10-11 When they saw the star, they rejoiced with exceeding great joy. And when they were come into the house, —

For it would seem that the mother and child had moved out of the stable into a house. The town was, perhaps, not now quite so crowded, and there was more room for Mary and her blessed baby: 'When they were come into the house,' —

11 they saw the young child with Mary his mother, and fell down, and worshipped him: and when they had opened their treasures, they presented unto him gifts; gold, and frankincense and myrrh.

These were the products of their country, such as they would give to princes. Such treasures must have been of great use to Mary and Joseph to help them take care of the wondrous child who had been entrusted to their charge.

12 And being warned of God in a dream that they should not return to Herod, they departed into their own country another way.

I remember a long disquisition, by a learned man, to show that we may sometimes break our promise, if, upon further consideration, we find we did wrong in making it, saying that these wise men, though they had promised to go and tell Herod all about the young child, did not do so when warned of God by a dream. After reading his very ingenious dissertation, I turned to the text, and there discovered that the wise men never made any promise of the kind; so it was a sermon on a non-existent text. They never agreed to return. Herod told them to do so, which is one thing; they did not promise to do so; that would have been quite another thing. They broke no promise, and hence needed no excuse. They were in supernatural communication with God. He had guided them by a star and now he speaks to them in a dream and bids them go back to their own country another way. May we all be under like unerring guidance! Amen.

MATTHEW 2

Matt. 2:1 Now when Jesus was born in Bethlehem of Judaea in the days of Herod the king, behold, there came wise men from the east to Jerusalem,

Probably from that Assyria which is joined with Israel and Egypt in the remarkable prophecy in Isaiah 19:24-25: 'In that day shall Israel be the third with Egypt and with Assyria, even a blessing in the midst of the land: Whom the Lord of hosts shall bless, saying, Blessed be Egypt my people, and Assyria the work of my hands, and Israel mine inheritance.' 'Behold, there came wise men from the east to Jerusalem' —

2-3 Saying, Where is he that is born King of the Jews? for we have seen his star in the east, and are come to worship him. When Herod the king had heard these things, he was troubled, and all Jerusalem with him.

He was troubled about the kingship which he had no right to possess, for he thought that, if the 'King of the Jews' was really coming, he would be dethroned. And 'all Jerusalem was troubled with him', for the people over whom he reigned never knew what mischief he might do when once his suspicions were excited, for he was a cruel, bloodthirsty tyrant.

4-6 And when he had gathered all the chief priests and scribes of the people together, he demanded of them where Christ should be born. And they said unto him, In Bethlehem of Judaea: for thus it is written by the prophet, And thou Bethlehem, in the land of Judah, art not the least among the princes of Judah: for out of thee shall come a Governor, that shall rule my people Israel.

It was something to get a distinct declaration from the Jewish rulers that the Christ was to be born at Bethlehem, for Jesus was born there. Afterwards, they called him, 'Jesus of Nazareth'. Nazareth was the place where he was brought up, but Bethlehem was the place of his birth, in fulfilment of the prophecy given hundreds of years before the event.

7-8   Then Herod, when he had privily called the wise men, inquired of them diligently what time the star appeared. And he sent them to Bethlehem, and said, Go and search diligently for the young child; and when ye have found him, bring me word again, that I may come and worship him also.

Pretty 'worship' was that which he would render to the infant King! He intended to murder him, and in like manner, how often, under the pretense of worshipping Christ, has the very truth of Christ been murdered. Men invent new sacraments, new doctrines, new forms and Romanies, all *avowedly* for the edification of the church and for the glory of Jesus; but *really* that they may stab at the very heart of God's gospel, and put to death the living truth.

9   When they had heard the king, they departed; and, lo, the star, which they saw in the east, went before them, till it came and stood over where the young child was.

Yet it was not a wandering star, nor a shooting star; but a travelling star such as they had never seen before.

10-12   When they saw the star, they rejoiced with exceeding great joy. And when they were come into the house, they saw the young child with Mary his mother, and fell down, and worshipped him: and when they had opened their treasures, they presented unto him gifts; gold, and frankincense and myrrh. And being warned of God in a dream that they should not return to Herod, they departed into their own country another way.

Very providentially, the Magi had brought the gold with which Joseph would be able to pay the expenses incurred in journeying to the land of Egypt and in supporting his family there till he could return to his home and his business. God always takes care of his own children; and specially did he provide for his firstborn and only-begotten Son.

13-14   And when they were departed, behold, the angel of the Lord appeareth to Joseph in a dream, saying, Arise, and take the young child and his mother, and flee into Egypt, and be thou there until I bring thee word: for Herod will seek the young child to destroy him. When he arose, he took the young child and his mother by night, and departed into Egypt:

How obedient Joseph was! He was a man of a docile spirit, who willingly did as God bade him. He has, perhaps, never had his character sufficiently well set forth in the church of God, for he was eminently honoured by being the guardian of the young child and his mother; and he discharged his duty with singular humility and gentleness.

15 And was there until the death of Herod: that it might be fulfilled which was spoken of the Lord by the prophet, saying, Out of Egypt have I called my son.

Which was true first of Israel, the nation, as God's son, and now again true of Jesus, the great Son of God. It is true also of all sons of God; we have to be called out of Egypt. By the blood of the paschal Lamb we too are saved, and we are brought out of Egypt with a high hand and an outstretched arm, in the day when God delivers us from our sin.

16 Then Herod, when he saw that he was mocked of the wise men, was exceeding wroth, and sent forth, and slew all the children that were in Bethlehem, and in all the coasts thereof, from two years old and under, according to the time which he had diligently inquired of the wise men.

That was the light he put upon it: 'that he was mocked of the wise men'. He was exceeding wroth, and when he was wroth, his anger was terrible. Augustus said of him that it would be better to be Herod's sow than Herod's son, which was true, for he would not kill a sow, as he held to the Jewish faith. He did not kill swine, but he would not mind killing anybody in his passion: 'He was exceeding wroth, and sent forth, and slew all the children that were in Bethlehem, and in all the coasts thereof, from two years old and under, according to the time which he had diligently inquired of the wise men.' He took a wide range in order, so he thought, to make quite sure that he should kill the Child King whom he especially hated.

17-18 Then was fulfilled that which was spoken by Jeremiah the prophet, saying, In Rama was there a voice heard, lamentation, and weeping, and great mourning, Rachel weeping for her children, and would not be comforted, because they are not.

It must have been a very sorrowful day in Bethlehem; you can imagine the grief that filled the hearts of the mothers there. There is Herod, who acts the hypocrite and tries to slay Christ at the first, and there is

Judas at the end, who acts the hypocrite, too, and betrays his Lord. Thus is the life of Christ begun and ended in sorrow.

19-22 But when Herod was dead, behold, an angel of the Lord appeareth in a dream to Joseph in Egypt, Saying, Arise, and take the young child and his mother, and go into the land of Israel: for they are dead which sought the young child's life. And he arose, and took the young child and his mother, and came into the land of Israel. But when he heard that Archelaus did reign in Judaea in the room of his father Herod, he was afraid to go thither:

Archelaus was another chip off the old block, and a chip of very hard wood, too, equally cruel, and without his father's greatness of mind. He had all Herod's vices without his mental vigour.

22 notwithstanding, being warned of God in a dream, he turned aside into the parts of Galilee:

He did not follow his own judgement. This man, thoroughly a servant of God, waits for orders. He has his fears, but he will not even act upon them. Rather, he waits till he is warned of God in a dream and then he turns aside into the parts of Galilee.

23 And he came and dwelt in a city called Nazareth: —

Galilee was despised, but Nazareth was thought to be the worst part of Galilee. *Netzar* is a word in the Hebrew signifying a sprout or branch, and Nazareth apparently comes from the same root.

23 that it might be fulfilled which was spoken by the prophets, He shall be called a Nazarene.

This is the name commonly given to our Lord in the Old Testament. 'And there shall come forth a rod out of the stem of Jesse, and a Branch shall grow out of his roots' [Isaiah 11:1]. Jesus was the sprout, or the shoot out of the withered stem of Jesse. When the dynasty of David was like the tree cut down, and only the stem of it left, there sprang up out of it the *Netzar*, the Nazarene; so he is found dwelling in a city that is called by that name, and he also is called a Nazarene. And the name clings to him to this day; there are those who will call him by no name but 'the Nazarene'. There was one who threatened to crush the Nazarene, but when he was dying he had to cry, 'O Nazarene, thou hast triumphed', and the Nazarene will always do so. He shall be crowned King of kings and Lord of lords, and he shall reign for ever and ever. Hallelujah!

MATTHEW 3:1-12; JOHN 1:15-37; 3:22-36

We are going to read three passages relating to John the Baptist's testimony concerning Christ.

Matt. 3:1-4 In those days came John the Baptist, preaching in the wilderness of Judaea, And saying, Repent ye: for the kingdom of heaven is at hand. For this is he that was spoken of by the prophet Esaias, saying, The voice of one crying in the wilderness, Prepare ye the way of the Lord, make his paths straight. And the same John had his raiment of camel's hair, and a leathern girdle about his loins; and his meat was locusts and wild honey.

Everything connected with John the Baptist was in harmony with his message. He was the preacher of repentance, so the place where he preached was most suitable; it was in the wilderness, where there was nothing to distract his hearers' attention, as there would have been in crowded cities. His dress was striking, and everything about him, even down to the food that he ate, went to show that he was the rough pioneer preacher preparing the way for his Master. John did not teach the fulness of joy and peace; that was left for our Lord Jesus to proclaim; but John came to prepare the way of the Lord by preaching repentance.

5 Then went out to him Jerusalem, and all Judaea, and all the region round about Jordan,

There seems to have been, about that time, a widespread anticipation of the coming of the Messiah; so, no sooner did the news come that a prophet was preaching in the desert, than great multitudes went out to hear him.

6-8 And were baptized of him in Jordan, confessing their sins. But when he saw many of the Pharisees and Sadducees come to his baptism, he said unto them, O generation of vipers, who hath warned you to flee from the wrath to come? Bring forth therefore fruits meet for repentance:

Did he not speak after the style of the prophet Elijah? Yet those bold speeches of his were not at all stronger than the evils of the age required. When the self-righteous Pharisees and the skeptical Sadducees, the Ritualists and the 'modern thought' men of that day, came to him to be baptized, he welcomed them not, but bade them 'bring forth fruits meet for repentance' — *evidences* of a change of heart and life.

9 And think not to say within yourselves, We have Abraham to our father: for I say unto you, that God is able of these stones —

In the bed of Jordan, where he was baptizing —

9 to raise up children unto Abraham.

John bade them boast not of their descent from Abraham; yet that was the great thing in which they *did* glory. They despised the Gentiles as so many do outside the true fold. Note how John the Baptist really preaches the gospel to us, indirectly, while he is denouncing these people's confidence in their carnal descent. Regeneration is 'not of blood, nor of the will of the flesh, nor of the will of man, but of God' [John 1:13].

10 And now also the axe is laid unto the root of the trees: therefore every tree which bringeth not forth good fruit is hewn down, and cast into the fire.

Other teachers came, as it were, only to lop and prune the trees, but the time had come for the felling of those that were fruitless. John did this, and so did our Lord Jesus Christ, for his preaching dug up the very roots of sin, superstition and evil of every kind.

11-12 I indeed baptize you with water unto repentance. but he that cometh after me is mightier than I, whose shoes I am not worthy to bear: he shall baptize you with the Holy Ghost, and with fire: Whose fan is in his hand, and he will throughly purge his floor, and gather his wheat into the garner; but he will burn up the chaff with unquenchable fire.

Now let us turn to the Gospel according to John, where we have another account of the ministry of John the Baptist.

John 1:15 John bare witness of him, and cried, saying, This was he of whom I spake, He that cometh after me is preferred before me: for he was before me.

He was not before John in the order of human birth, yet he was truly before John, for he had an eternal pre-existence, as he was none other than the uncreated Son of God.

16-21 And of his fulness have all we received, and grace for grace. For the law was given by Moses, but grace and truth came by Jesus Christ. No man hath seen God at any time; the only begotten Son, which is in the bosom of the Father, he hath declared him. And this is the record of John, when the Jews sent priests and Levites from Jerusalem to ask him, Who art thou? And he confessed, and denied not; but confessed, I am not the Christ. And they asked him, What then? Art thou Elias? And he saith, I am not. Art thou that prophet? And he answered, No.

As they meant, 'Art thou, literally, the prophet Elijah risen from the dead?'

John said, 'I am not.'

'Art thou that prophet of whom Moses foretold?'

And he answered, 'No.' John gave short, sharp answers to these cavillers. He was not a man of dainty words and polished periods, especially in dealing with such people as they were.

22-23 Then said they unto him, Who art thou? that we may give an answer to them that sent us. What sayest thou of thyself? He said, I am the voice —

Not 'the Word' — Christ is that, but John was 'the voice'.

23-37 of one crying in the wilderness, Make straight the way of the Lord, as said the prophet Esaias. And they which were sent were of the Pharisees. And they asked him, and said unto him, Why baptizest thou then, if thou be not that Christ, nor Elias, neither that prophet? John answered them, saying, I baptize with water: but there standeth one among you, whom ye know not; He it is, who coming after me is preferred before me, whose shoe's latchet I am not worthy to unloose. These things were done in Bethabara beyond Jordan, where John was baptizing. The next day John seeth Jesus coming unto him, and saith, Behold the Lamb of God, which taketh away the sin of the world. This is he of whom I said, After me cometh a man which is preferred before me: for he was before me. And I knew him not: but that he should be made manifest to Israel, therefore am I come baptizing with water. And John bare record, saying, I saw the Spirit descending from heaven like a dove, and it abode upon him. And I knew him not: but he that sent me to baptize with water, the same said unto me, Upon whom thou shalt see the Spirit descending, and remaining on him, the same is he which baptizeth with the Holy Ghost. And I saw, and bare record that this is the Son of God. Again the next day after John stood, and two of his disciples; And looking upon Jesus as he walked, he saith, Behold the Lamb of God! And the two disciples heard him speak, and they followed Jesus.

In the third chapter of the same Gospel, we have yet another testimony by John the Baptist concerning Christ.

John 3:22-29 After these things came Jesus and his disciples into the land of Judaea; and there he tarried with them, and baptized. And John also was baptizing in Aenon near to Salim, because there was much water there: and they came, and were baptized. For John was not yet cast into prison. Then there arose a question between some of John's disciples and the Jews about puri-fying. And they came unto John, and said unto him, Rabbi, he that was with thee beyond Jordan, to whom thou barest witness, behold, the same baptizeth, and all men come to him. John answered and said, A man can receive nothing, except it be given him from heaven. Ye your-selves bear me witness, that I said, I am not the Christ, but that I am sent before him. He that hath the bride is the bridegroom: but the friend of the bridegroom, which standeth and heareth him, rejoiceth greatly because of the bridegroom's voice: this my joy therefore is fulfilled.

'I have introduced the Bridegroom; and, henceforth, it will be my part gradually to disappear from the scene.'

30   He must increase, but I must decrease.

As fades the morning star when the sun himself arises, so was it the joy of the herald of Christ to lose himself in the supreme radiance of his Lord's appearing.

31-34   He that cometh from above is above all: he that is of the earth is earthly, and speaketh of the earth: he that cometh from heaven is above all. And what he hath seen and heard, that he testifieth; and no man receiveth his testimony. He that hath received his testimony hath set to his seal that God is true. For he whom God hath sent speaketh the words of God: for God giveth not the Spirit by measure unto him.

Did not the Holy Spirit descend, and remain upon him, and that with-out measure or limit?

35-36   The Father loveth the Son, and hath given all things into his hand. He that believeth on the Son hath everlasting life: —

He has it now; and he can never lose it, or else it would not be ever-lasting. He has a life that must exist for ever and ever.

36   and he that believeth not the Son shall not see life; —

He shall not even know what spiritual life is; he shall not be able to understand it or to form any idea of it. While he is an unbeliever, he is blind to spiritual things. What a dreadful sentence that is! 'He shall not see life' —

36 but the wrath of God abideth on him.

God is ever angry with him because he has rejected his own GOD, and refused the great salvation.

MATTHEW 3

Matt. 3:1-2 In those days came John the Baptist, preaching in the wilderness of Judaea, And saying, Repent ye: for the kingdom of heaven is at hand.

There is no entering the kingdom of heaven without leaving the kingdom of darkness. We must repent of sin, or we cannot receive the blessings of salvation. Of every man, whoever he may be, whether outwardly moral or openly wicked, repentance is required. It is the door of hope; there is no other way into the kingdom: 'Repent ye: for the kingdom of heaven is at hand.'

3-4 For this is he that was spoken of by the prophet Esaias, saying, The voice of one crying in the wilderness, Prepare ye the way of the Lord, make his paths straight. And the same John had his raiment of camel's hair, and a leathern girdle about his loins; and his meat was locusts and wild honey.

His raiment and his food were like his doctrine, rough and simple. There was no mincing of words, no making of pretty phrases with John the Baptist; his message was simply, 'Repent ye: repent ye: for the kingdom of heaven is coming.' We want more of this John the Baptist teaching nowadays, that men may be plainly told their faults and warned to put away those faults that they may receive Christ Jesus as their Saviour.

5-7 Then went out to him Jerusalem, and all Judaea, and all the region round about Jordan, And were baptized of him in Jordan, confessing their sins. But when he saw many of the Pharisees and Sadducees come to his baptism, he said unto them, O generation of vipers, who hath warned you to flee from the wrath to come?

These were the influential people of the times; the Pharisees were the ritualists of that age, and the Sadducees were the rationalists of the period. Why, John, you ought to have smoothed your tongue a bit and have said some very pleasant words to these great men; for, by so doing, perhaps you might have won some of these Pharisees, or coaxed some of these Sadducees into the kingdom! Ah, no; that is not John's method! He is plain-spoken, and he deals truthfully with his hearers, for he knows that converts made by flattery are but flattering converts that are of no real value.

8-9 Bring forth therefore fruits meet for repentance: And think not to say within yourselves, We have Abraham to our father: for I say unto you, that God is able of these stones to raise up children unto Abraham.

Pointing to the stones in the River Jordan, and all along the banks, he said to the Pharisees and Sadducees, 'There is nothing, after all, in your natural descent from Abraham. God has promised that Abraham shall have a seed, but think not that he is dependent upon you for that seed; he can fulfill his promise without you. He can turn the very pebbles of the stream into children for Abraham. God is not short of men to save. If some of you will not have him, do not think that he shall have to come a-begging to you. There are others who will have him, and his rich sovereign grace will find them out. Beware, ye that are proud and think much of yourselves, for God will not humble himself to you. He hath regard to the humble and the lowly, 'but the proud he knoweth afar off' [Psalm 138:6].

10-12 And now also the axe is laid unto the root of the trees: therefore every tree which bringeth not forth good fruit is hewn down, and cast into the fire. I indeed baptize you with water unto repentance. but he that cometh after me is mightier than I, whose shoes I am not worthy to bear: he shall baptize you with the Holy Ghost, and with fire: Whose fan is in his hand, and he will throughly purge his floor, and gather his wheat into the garner; but he will burn up the chaff with unquenchable fire.

The Christ is the minister of mercy, but there is about his doctrine a searching and a trying power. Only the sincere in heart can endure Christ's winnowing fan. As for the insincere, they are blown away like the chaff on the threshing-floor, and their end is destruction. God gave us to be numbered among the wheat that Christ shall gather into his heavenly garner!

13-14 Then cometh Jesus from Galilee to Jordan unto John, to be baptized of him. But John forbad him, saying, I have need to be baptized of thee, and comest thou to me?

It seemed very strange that John, the servant, should be required to baptize Jesus, the Master.

15 And Jesus answering said unto him, Suffer it to be so now: for thus it becometh us to fulfil all righteousness. Then he suffered him.

That is to say the Teacher must himself obey the laws, which he is about to lay down; and inasmuch as he is going to bid others to be baptized, he will set the example and be himself baptized. I think also that the baptism of Christ was the picture, the type, the symbol of the work, which he afterwards accomplished. He was immersed in suffering; he died and was buried in the tomb; he rose again from the grave; and all that is set forth in the outward symbol of his baptism in the River Jordan.

16-17 And Jesus, when he was baptized, went up straightway out of the water: and, lo, the heavens were opened unto him, and he saw the Spirit of God descending like a dove, and lighting upon him: And lo a voice from heaven, saying, This is my beloved Son, in whom I am well pleased.

And we are well pleased with *him*.

MATTHEW 3:13-17; 4:1-11

Matt. 3:13-14 Then cometh Jesus from Galilee to Jordan unto John, to be baptized of him. But John forbad him, saying, I have need to be baptized of thee, and comest thou to me?

Who among us would not have felt as John did? Shall the servant baptize the Master, and such a Master, even his Lord and Saviour? But this is merely the condescension of our blessed Lord. He would do everything that he wished his people afterwards to do; and therefore, he would be baptized and set the example that he would have them all follow.

15   And Jesus answering said unto him, Suffer it to be so now: for thus it becometh us to fulfil all righteousness. Then he suffered him.

We are never to be so modest as to become disobedient to Christ's commands. We have known some who have allowed their humility to grow alone in the garden of their heart without the other sweet flowers that should have sprung up side by side with it, and thus their very humility has developed into a kind of pride. John was easily persuaded to do what his feelings at first seemed to forbid: 'Then he suffered him.'

16-17   And Jesus, when he was baptized, went up straightway out of the water: and, lo, the heavens were opened unto him, and he saw the Spirit of God descending like a dove, and lighting upon him: And lo a voice from heaven, saying, This is my beloved Son, in whom I am well pleased.

It has also happened unto the servants of Christ, as well as to their Master, that in keeping the commandments of God there has been a sweet attestation borne by the Holy Spirit. I trust that we, too, according to our measure of sonship, have heard in our hearts the voice from heaven, saying, 'This is my beloved son', and that we have experienced the descending of the dovelike Spirit, bringing us peace of mind and gentleness of nature.

Matt. 4:1   Then was Jesus led up of the Spirit into the wilderness to be tempted of the devil.

What a change it seems from the descent of the Holy Spirit to being led up into the wilderness to be tempted of the devil! Dear friends, be especially on the watch after a great spiritual joy, for it is just then that you may have some terrible temptation. Mayhap, the voice from heaven is to prepare you to do battle with the enemy. I have noticed that the Lord has two special seasons of blessing his people — sometimes, before a great trial, to prepare them for it, and at other times, after a great affliction, to remove the weakness which has been thereby occasioned. Think not that you can come up out of the waters of baptism and then live without watchfulness. Imagine not, because the Spirit has sealed you and borne witness with your spirit that you are the Lord's child, that therefore you are out of gunshot of the enemy. Oh, no! At that very time he will be preparing his most subtle temptations for you, just as Jesus was led up of the Spirit into the wilderness to be tempted of the devil immediately after his baptism and his Father's testimony: 'This is my beloved Son, in whom I am well pleased.'

2 And when he had fasted forty days and forty nights, he was afterward an hungered.

I suppose that he was not 'an hungered' during his long fast, and this renders it a fast altogether by itself. We are here told, 'He was afterward an hungered.'

3 And when the tempter came to him, he said, If thou be the Son of God, command that these stones be made bread.

'Thou canst do it if thou art indeed the Son of God. Thou art an hungered, therefore feed thyself. Thy Father has forgotten thee; his providence has failed thee; be thine own providence — work a miracle for thyself.' How little the tempter, with all his knowledge, understood the true character of Christ! Our Lord never wrought a miracle in order to supply his own needs.

4 But he answered and said, It is written, Man shall not live by bread alone, but by every word that proceedeth out of the mouth of God.

He had been attacked as a man who was hungering, so he quoted a text which evidently belonged to man: 'Man shall not live by bread alone.' It was a wilderness text; it concerned the children of Israel in the desert, so it was suitable to the position of our Lord in that wilderness. He meant to let the tempter know that, as God fed man by manna from the skies once, he could do it again. At any rate, this glorious Man, this true Son of God, was determined not to interfere with the ordinary working of providence, but he left himself and his needs in his Father's hands.

5-6 Then the devil taketh him up into the holy city, and setteth him on a pinnacle of the temple, And saith unto him, If thou be the Son of God, cast thyself down: for it is written, He shall give his angels charge concerning thee: and in their hands they shall bear thee up, lest at any time thou dash thy foot against a stone.

'It is written.' Thus the devil tried to turn Christ's own sword against himself—that two-edged sword of the Spirit which is the Word of God, and the devil can still quote Scripture to suit his own purpose. Yet it was a *misquotation* as to the letter of it, for he left out the essential words, 'to keep thee in all thy ways'; and it was a worse misquotation as to the spirit of it, for in the true meaning of the passage there is nothing to tempt us to presumption. There is a guarantee of safety when we are walking where we should walk, but not in leaping from a temple's pinnacle down into the abyss.

7 Jesus said unto him, It is written again, Thou shalt not tempt the Lord thy God.

Here was a plain, positive precept that clearly forbade Christ to tempt God by such a presumptuous action as casting himself down from the pinnacle of the temple, and we must always follow the precepts of Scripture, whatever the tempter may say.

8 Again, the devil taketh him up into an exceeding high mountain, and sheweth him all the kingdoms of the world, and the glory of them;

Notice that these temptations were in high places. Alas! high places are often full of trial, whether they be places of wealth and rank, or of eminent service in the church of God. A pinnacle is a dangerous position, even if it be a pinnacle of the temple, and on the summit of an exceeding high mountain is a perilous place, even if the view from it is not the poverty of the city nor the sin of the people, but the glory of the kingdoms of the world. Ever with such a view as that, the mountain's brow is full of danger to our weak heads.

9 And saith unto him, All these things will I give thee, if thou wilt fall down and worship me.

Why, they were Christ's already! They never belonged to Satan and, though for a while he had to some extent usurped authority over them, it was like his impudence to offer to give away what was not his own.

10 Then saith Jesus unto him, Get thee hence, Satan: for it is written, Thou shalt worship the Lord thy God, and him only shalt thou serve.

Let the bribe be what it may, thou must not worship or serve either thyself or the devil. Thy God alone claims thy homage, and if the whole earth might be thine through one act of sin, thou would not be justified in committing it.

11 Then the devil leaveth him, and, behold, angels came and ministered unto him.

What a change! When the devil goes, the angels come. Perhaps some of you are just now sorely tempted and much troubled. Oh, that you might speedily come to Mahanaim, of which we read, 'And Jacob went on his way, and the angels of God met him' [Genesis 32:1], that there you might be met by troops of angels come to minister to you, weary with the conflict with the evil one, just as they ministered to your Lord! You need them as much as he did, and therefore you are as sure to have them if you look up to him, and ask him to seal them to you.

MATTHEW 4:1-11

Matt. 4:1 Then was Jesus led up of the Spirit into the wilderness to be tempted of the devil.

He had just been baptized, the Spirit of God had descended upon him and the Father had borne witness to him, saying, 'This is my beloved Son, in whom I am well pleased.' Yet, immediately after all that, he was led into the wilderness to be tempted of the devil. So, after your times of sweetest fellowship with God, after the happiest enjoyment of gospel ordinances, after the sealing of the Spirit within your heart, you must expect to be tempted of the devil. You must not suppose that, in your Christian life, all will be sweetness — that all will be spiritual witness-bearing. You have to fight the good fight of faith, and your great adversary will not be slow to begin the encounter. You are a pilgrim in a strange land, so you must expect to find rough places on the road to heaven. Yet, since you are so much weaker than your Master was, you will do well to pray the prayer that he taught to his disciples, 'Lead us not into temptation, but deliver us from evil' [Matthew 6:13].

2-3 And when he had fasted forty days and forty nights, he was afterward an hungred. And when the tempter came to him,

See how Satan seizes opportunities. When he finds us weak, as the Saviour was through long fasting — when he finds us in trying circumstances, as the Saviour was when hungry in the desert — then it is that he comes to tempt us. This dastardly foe of ours takes every possible advantage of us, that he may, by any means, overthrow us.

3 he said, If thou be the Son of God, command that these stones be made bread.

He begins with an 'if'. He tries to cast a doubt upon the Saviour's Sonship, and this is the way that he often attacks a child of God now. He says to him, 'If thou be a son of God, do so-and-so.' He challenged Christ to work a miracle for himself — to use his divine power on his own behalf, but this the Saviour never did. He challenged Christ to distrust the providence of God and to be his own Provider, and this is still a very common temptation to God's people.

4 But he answered and said, It is written, —

That is the only sword that Christ used against Satan — 'the sword of the Spirit, which is the Word of God' [Ephesians 6:17]. There is nothing like it, and the old dragon himself knows what sharp edges this sword has. Christ said, 'It is written' —

4 Man shall not live by bread alone, but by every word that proceedeth out of the mouth of God.

God can sustain human life without the use of bread, although it is the staff of life, for bread does not sustain life unless God puts power into it to do so; and he can, if it pleases him, use that power without the outward means. Our Lord thus showed that God could provide for him in a desert without his interference with the plans of divine providence by selfishly catering for himself. So the first victory was won.

5-6   Then the devil taketh him up into the holy city, and setteth him on a pinnacle of the temple, And saith unto him, If thou be the Son of God, cast thyself down: for it is written, —

Here he plays with the Word of God, for the devil can quote Scripture when it suits his purpose to do so: 'It is written' —

6   He shall give his angels charge concerning thee: and in their hands they shall bear thee up, lest at any time thou dash thy foot against a stone.

The devil did not quote correctly from Psalm 91:11-12; he left out the most important words: 'He shall give his angels charge over thee, to keep thee in all thy ways', but it was not Christ's way to cast himself down from the pinnacle of the temple. Jesus therefore answered Satan's misquotation with a true quotation.

7   Jesus said unto him, It is written again, Thou shalt not tempt the Lord thy God.

I know some people who earn their living in employments which are very hazardous to their immortal souls. They are in the midst of evil, yet they tell me that God can keep them in safety there. I know that he *can*, but I also know that we have no right to go, voluntarily, where we are surrounded by temptation. If your calling is the wrong one, and you are continually tempted in it, you may not presume upon the goodness of God to keep you, for it is your business to get as far as you can from that which will lead you into sin. God does not put his servants on the pinnacle of the temple. It is the devil who puts them there, and if they ever are there, the best thing they can do is to get down as quickly and as safely as they can; but they must not cast themselves down; they must look to him who alone can bring them down safely. With some professors, presumption is a very common sin. They will go into worldly amusements and all sorts of frivolities, and say, 'Oh, we can be Christians and yet go there!' Can you? It may be that you can be hypocrites and go there; that is far easier than going there as Christians.

8-10 Again, the devil taketh him up into an exceeding high mountain, and sheweth him all the kingdoms of the world, and the glory of them; And saith unto him, All these things will I give thee, if thou wilt fall down and worship me. Then saith Jesus unto him, Get thee hence, Satan: for it is written, Thou shalt worship the Lord thy God, and him only shalt thou serve.

Christ will not endure any more of this talk. When it comes to a bribe, the promise that the devil will give him earth's glory if he will but fall down and worship him, Christ ends the whole matter once for all. Thrice assaulted, thrice victorious, blessed Master, enable us also to be more than conquerors through thy grace!

11 Then the devil leaveth him, and, behold, angels came and ministered unto him.

Regarding it as their highest honour to be the servants of their Lord.

MATTHEW 4:12-24; JOHN 1:19-51

Matt. 4:12 Now when Jesus had heard that John was cast into prison, he departed into Galilee;

Notice that there were at that time only two great ministers of God: John the Baptist, he must go to prison and to death; Jesus, the Son of God, he must go to the desert to be tempted of the devil. If any Christians escape temptation, they will not be the leaders of the hosts of God. Those who stand in the van (or forefront) must bear the brunt of the battle. Oh, that all who are called to such responsible positions might be as prepared to occupy them as John was, and as Jesus was!

13-16 And leaving Nazareth, he came and dwelt in Capernaum, which is upon the sea coast, in the borders of Zabulon and Nephthalim: That it might be fulfilled which was spoken by Esaias the prophet, saying, The land of Zabulon, and the land of Nephthalim, by the way of the sea, beyond Jordan, Galilee of the Gentiles; The people which sat in darkness saw great light; and to them which sat in the region and shadow of death light is sprung up.

Oh, the tender mercy of our God! Where the darkness is the deepest, there the light shines the brightest. Christ selects such dark regions as Nephthalim and Zabulon that he may dwell there and shine in all his glory.

17 From that time Jesus began to preach, and to say, Repent: for the kingdom of heaven is at hand.

He was not afraid to give an earnest exhortation to sinners and to bid men repent. He knew better than we do the inability of men concerning all that is good, yet he bade them repent.

18-23 And Jesus, walking by the sea of Galilee, saw two brethren, Simon called Peter, and Andrew his brother, casting a net into the sea: for they were fishers. And he saith unto them, Follow me, and I will make you fishers of men. And they straightway left their nets, and followed him. And going on from thence, he saw other two brethren, James the son of Zebedee, and John his brother, in a ship with Zebedee their father, mending their nets; and he called them. And they immediately left the ship and their father, and followed him. And Jesus went about all Galilee, teaching in their synagogues, and preaching the gospel of the kingdom, and healing all manner of sickness and all manner of disease among the people.

I like those words 'all manner' — that is, every kind and every sort of sickness and disease Christ met. Perhaps you, dear friend, are afflicted in your soul after a very peculiar fashion. Aye, but this great Physician heals all manner of diseases. None are excluded from the list of patients whom he can cure; twice the words 'all manner' are used: 'Healing all manner of sickness and all manner of disease among the people.'

24 And his fame went throughout all Syria: and they brought unto him all sick people that were taken with divers diseases and torments, and those which were possessed with devils, and those which were lunatick, and those that had the palsy; and he healed them.

Our Lord Jesus lived as in a hospital while he was on earth; wherever he went, the sins and sorrows of men were all open before his sympathetic gaze. But oh, what joy it must have been to him to be able to deal so well with them all! Am I addressing any who are sick in soul? Our Master is used to cases just like yours; your malady is not new to him. He has healed many like you; of all that were brought to him, it is written, 'he healed them'. Lie before him now, in all your sin and misery, and breathe the prayer, 'Thou Son of David, have mercy on me', and he will surely hear you, and heal you, for he delights to bless and save all who trust him.

John 1:19-20 And this is the record of John, when the Jews sent priests and Levites from Jerusalem to ask him, Who art thou? And he confessed, and denied not; but confessed, I am not the Christ.

'I am not the One anointed of God to save mankind.'

21 And they asked him, What then? Art thou Elias? —

'Art thou Elijah come back to earth?'

21 And he saith, I am not. —

For, though indeed he was the true spiritual Elijah who was to come as the forerunner of the Messiah, yet, in the sense in which they asked the question, the only truthful answer was, 'I am not.'

21 Art thou that prophet? —

The long-expected prophet foretold by Moses?

21-23 And he answered, No. Then said they unto him, Who art thou? that we may give an answer to them that sent us. What sayest thou of thyself? He said, I am the voice —

That is all, a voice and nothing more. John did not profess to be the Word; he was only the voice which vocalized that Word and made it audible to human ears. He came to bear witness to the Christ, but he was not himself the Christ: 'I am the voice.'

23-27 of one crying in the wilderness, Make straight the way of the Lord, as said the prophet Esaias. And they which were sent were of the Pharisees. And they asked him, and said unto him, Why baptizest thou then, if thou be not that Christ, nor Elias, neither that prophet? John answered them, saying, I baptize with water: but there standeth one among you, whom ye know not; He it is, who coming after me is preferred before me, whose shoe's latchet I am not worthy to unloose.

How wisely does God always choose and fashion his servants! John is evidently just the man for his place; he bears testimony to Christ very clearly; he earnestly turns away all attention from himself to his Master; and he has such a reverent esteem for him of whom he is the herald that he puts all honour and glory upon him.

28-30 These things were done in Bethabara beyond Jordan, where John was baptizing. The next day John seeth Jesus coming unto him, and saith, Behold the Lamb of God, which taketh away the sin of the world. This is he of whom I said, After me cometh a man which is preferred before me: for he was before me.

You know, dear friends, that Christ existed from all eternity, so, in very truth, he was *before* John; you know, too, the glory and the excellency of our divine Master's person, so that, in another sense, he was and is before John and all other creatures whom he has made.

31-34   And I knew him not: but that he should be made manifest to Israel, therefore am I come baptizing with water. And John bare record, saying, I saw the Spirit descending from heaven like a dove, and it abode upon him. And I knew him not: but he that sent me to baptize with water, the same said unto me, Upon whom thou shalt see the Spirit descending, and remaining on him, the same is he which baptizeth with the Holy Ghost. And I saw, and bare record that this is the Son of God.

The secret sign of the descent of the Spirit, in dovelike form, upon our Lord, was given to John; and as soon as he saw it, he knew of a surety that Jesus was the Sent One, the Messiah, and that he must point him out to the people.

35-36   Again the next day after John stood, and two of his disciples; And looking upon Jesus as he walked, he saith, Behold the Lamb of God!

This was the same text from which he had preached the day before, and it was the same sermon, somewhat shortened. So should it be with us.

> *His only righteousness I show,*
> *His saving truth proclaim;*
> *'Tis all my business here below*
> *To cry, 'Behold the Lamb!'*

37   And the two disciples heard him speak, and they followed Jesus.

Thus John was losing his own disciples. By his testimony to the truth, he was sending them to follow the Lord Jesus Christ, and he did it well and gracefully. There are many who would find it a hard task to reduce the number of their disciples, but it was not so with John.

38-46   Then Jesus turned, and saw them following, and saith unto them, What seek ye? They said unto him, Rabbi, (which is to say, being interpreted, Master,) where dwellest thou? He saith unto them, Come and see. They came and saw where he dwelt, and abode with him that day: for it was about the tenth hour. One of the two which heard John speak, and followed him, was Andrew, Simon Peter's brother. He first findeth his own brother Simon, and saith unto him, We have found the Messias, which is, being interpreted, the Christ. And he brought him to Jesus. And when Jesus beheld him, he said, Thou art Simon the son of Jona: thou shalt be called Cephas, which is by interpretation, A stone. The day following Jesus would go forth into Galilee, and findeth Philip, and saith unto him, Follow me. Now Philip was of Bethsaida, the city of Andrew and Peter. Philip findeth Nathanael, and saith unto him, We have found him, of whom Moses in the law, and the prophets, did write, Jesus of Nazareth, the son of Joseph. And Nathanael said unto him, Can there any good thing come out of Nazareth? Philip saith unto him, Come and see.

It was all a seeing gospel. John said, 'Behold the Lamb of God!' Then Jesus said, 'Come and see'; and now Philip says the same. Faith is that blessed sight by which we discern the Saviour. Whosoever looks to Christ by faith shall live.

47   Jesus saw Nathanael coming to him, and saith of him, Behold an Israelite indeed, in whom is no guile!

'There is no craft or deception in this man, as there was in Jacob; he is a true Israelite, like Israel at his best.'

48   Nathanael saith unto him, Whence knowest thou me? Jesus answered and said unto him, Before that Philip called thee, when thou wast under the fig tree, I saw thee.

What Nathanael had been doing there, we do not know; probably he had been meditating, or he may have been engaged in prayer. But this announcement was a proof to Nathanael that Jesus could see all things, and read men's hearts, and know what they were doing in their chosen retreats: 'When thou wast under the fig tree, I saw thee.' Christ knows all of you who came in here, tonight, in a prayerful spirit, seeking him. And whenever men are seeking him, be you sure that he is also seeking them.

49   Nathanael answered and saith unto him, Rabbi, thou art the Son of God; thou art the King of Israel.

'Thou sawest what I was doing in secret, and by that token I perceive that thou art God's own Son.'

50 Jesus answered and said unto him, Because I said unto thee, I saw thee under the fig tree, believest thou? thou shalt see greater things than these.

Those who are ready to believe Christ, on what may be thought to be slender evidence, shall 'see greater things than these'. 'Blessed are they that have not seen, and yet have believed' [John 20:29]. They shall gaze upon a wonderful sight by and by.

51 And he saith unto him, Verily, verily, I say unto you, Hereafter ye shall see heaven open, and the angels of God ascending and descending upon the Son of man.

'Thou art a true Israelite, and thou shalt have Israel's vision. Thou shalt see the same sight as thy father Jacob saw when he fell asleep with a stone for his pillow, only thy vision shall be far grander than his.' Christ always knows how to meet the needs of our hearts, and to give us something in accordance with our own expressions, and to make his answers fit our requests, only that he always far exceeds all that we ask or even think. Blessed be his holy name!

MATTHEW 5:1-12

Matt. 5:1 And seeing the multitudes, he went up into a mountain: —

For convenience, and quietude, and to be out of the way of traffic, he went up into a mountain. Elevated doctrines would seem most at home on the high places of the earth.

1 and when he was set, —

For that was the mode of Eastern teaching,

1 his disciples came unto him:

They made the inner ring around him, and others gathered around them.

2 And he opened his mouth, and taught them, —

Chrysostom says that he taught them even when he did not open his mouth; his very silence was instructive. But when he did open his mouth, what streams of wisdom flowed forth! He 'taught them'. He did not open his mouth to make an oration. He was a teacher, so his aim was to teach those who came to him; and his ministers best follow their Lord's example when they keep to the vein of teaching. The pulpit is not the place for the display of oratory and eloquence, but for real instruction: 'He opened his mouth, and taught them' —

2-3 saying, Blessed —

The Old Testament closes with the word 'curse'. The New Testament begins here, in the preaching of Christ, with the word 'blessed'. He has changed the curse into a blessing: 'Blessed' —

3 are the poor in spirit: for theirs is the kingdom of heaven.

This is a paradox that puzzles many, for the poor in spirit often seem to have nothing; yet they have the kingdom of heaven, so they have everything. He who thinks the least of himself is the man of whom God thinks the most. You are not poor in God's sight if you are poor in spirit.

4 Blessed are they that mourn: for they shall be comforted.

They are not only poor in spirit, but they are weeping, lamenting, mourning. Worldlings are frivolous, frolicsome, light-hearted, and loving everything that is akin to mirth; yet it is not said of them, but of those that mourn, 'They shall be comforted.'

5 Blessed are the meek: —

Not your high-spirited, quick-tempered men, who will put up with no insult; your hectoring, lofty ones, who are ever ready to resent any real or imagined disrespect. There is no blessing here for them. But blessed are the gentle — those who are ready to be thought nothing of.

5 for they shall inherit the earth.

Some say that the best way to get through the world is to swagger along with a coarse impudence, and to push out of your way all who may be in it; but there is no truth in that idea. The truth lies in quite another direction: 'Blessed are the meek: for they shall inherit the earth.'

6 Blessed are they which do hunger and thirst after righteousness: for they shall be filled.

The course of these beatitudes is like going downstairs. They began with spiritual poverty, went on to mourning, came down to gentle-spiritedness, and now we come to hunger and thirst. Yet we have been going up all the time, for here we read, 'They shall be filled.' What more can we have than full satisfaction?

7 Blessed are the merciful: for they shall obtain mercy.

'The merciful' are those who are always ready to forgive, always ready to help the poor and needy, always ready to overlook what they might well condemn; and 'They shall obtain mercy.'

8 Blessed are the pure in heart: for they shall see God.

When the heart is washed, the dirt is taken from the mental eye. The heart that loves God is connected with an understanding that perceives God. There is no way of seeing God until the heart is renewed by sovereign grace. It is not greatness of intellect, but purity of affection that enables us to see God.

9 Blessed are the peacemakers: —

Not only the passively peaceful, but the actively peaceful, who try to rectify mistakes, and to end all quarrels in a peaceful way.

9 for they shall be called the children of God.

They shall not only be the children of God, but men shall call them so; they shall recognize in them the likeness to the peacemaking God.

10 Blessed are they which are persecuted for righteousness' sake: for theirs is the kingdom of heaven.

They have it now, they are participating in it already; for, as Christ was persecuted, and he is again persecuted in them, as they are partakers of his sufferings, so are they sharers in his kingdom.

11-12 Blessed are ye, when men shall revile you, and persecute you, and shall say all manner of evil against you falsely, for my sake. Rejoice, and be exceeding glad: for great is your reward in heaven: for so persecuted they the prophets which were before you.

You have an elevation by persecution; you are lifted into the peerage of martyrdom. Though you occupy but an inferior place in it, yet you are in it; therefore, 'Rejoice, and be exceeding glad.'

MATTHEW 5:1-30

Matt. 5:1-2 And seeing the multitudes, he went up into a mountain: and when he was set, his disciples came unto him: And he opened his mouth, and taught them, saying, —

Our Saviour soon gathered a congregation. The multitudes perceived in him a love for them, and a willingness to impart blessing to them, and therefore they gathered about him. He chose the mountain and the open air for the delivery of this great discourse, and we should be glad to find such a place for our assemblies; but in this variable climate we cannot often do so. 'And when he was set.' The Preacher sat, and the people stood. We might make a helpful change if we were sometimes to adopt a similar plan now. I am afraid that ease of posture may contribute to the creation of slumber of heart in the hearers. There Christ sat, and 'his disciples came unto him'. They formed the inner circle that was ever nearest to him, and to them he imparted his choicest secrets; but he also spoke to the multitude, and therefore it is said that 'he opened his mouth', as well he might when there were such great truths to proceed from it, and so vast a crowd to hear them: 'He opened his mouth, and taught them, saying' —

3 Blessed are the poor in spirit: for theirs is the kingdom of heaven.

This is a gracious beginning to our Saviour's discourse: 'Blessed are the poor.' None ever considered the poor as Jesus did, but here he is speaking of a poverty of spirit, a lowliness of heart, an absence of self-esteem. Where that kind of spirit is found, it is sweet poverty: 'Blessed are the poor in spirit, for theirs is the kingdom of heaven.'

4 Blessed are they that mourn: for they shall be comforted.

There is a blessing which often goes with mourning itself; but when the sorrow is of a spiritual sort — mourning for sin — then is it blest indeed.

> *Lord, let me weep for nought but sin,*
> *And after none but thee;*
> *And then I would — oh, that I might —*
> *A constant mourner be!*

5 Blessed are the meek: —

The quiet-spirited, the gentle, the self-sacrificing.

5 for they shall inherit the earth.

It looks as if they would be pushed out of the world, but they shall not be, 'for they shall inherit the earth'. The wolves devour the sheep, yet there are more sheep in the world than there are wolves, and the sheep continue to multiply and to feed in green pastures.

6 Blessed are they which do hunger and thirst after righteousness: —

Pining to be holy, longing to serve God, anxious to spread every righteous principle — blessed are they.

6-7 for they shall be filled. Blessed are the merciful: —

Those who are kind, generous, sympathetic, ready to forgive those who have wronged them — blessed are they.

7-8 for they shall obtain mercy. Blessed are the pure in heart: —

It is a most blessed attainment to have such a longing for purity as to love everything that is chaste and holy, and to abhor everything that is questionable and unhallowed: blessed are the pure in heart —

8 for they shall see God.

There is a wonderful connection between hearts and eyes. A man who has the stains of filth on his soul cannot see God, but they who are purified in heart are purified in vision too: 'They shall see God.'

9 Blessed are the peacemakers: —

Those who always end a quarrel if they can, those who lay themselves out to prevent discord.

9-10 for they shall be called the children of God. Blessed are they which are persecuted for righteousness' sake: for theirs is the kingdom of heaven.

They share the kingdom of heaven with the poor in spirit. They are often evil spoken of, they have sometimes to suffer the spoiling of their goods, many of them have laid down their lives for Christ's sake, but they are truly blessed, for 'theirs is the kingdom of heaven'.

11 Blessed are ye, when men shall revile you, and persecute you, and shall say all manner of evil against you falsely, for my sake.

Mind, it must be said falsely, and it must be for Christ's sake, if you are to be blessed; but there is no blessing in having evil spoken of you truthfully, or in having it spoken of you falsely because of some bitterness in your own spirit.

12 Rejoice, and be exceeding glad: for great is your reward in heaven: for so persecuted they the prophets which were before you.

You are in the true prophetic succession if you cheerfully bear reproach of this kind for Christ's sake. You prove that you have the stamp and seal of those who are in the service of God.

13 Ye are the salt of the earth: —

Followers of Christ, 'ye are the salt of the earth'. You help to preserve it, and to subdue the corruption that is in it.

13 but if the salt have lost his savour, wherewith shall it be salted? —

A professing Christian with no grace in him, a religious man whose very religion is dead, what is the good of him? And he is himself in a hopeless condition. You can salt meat, but you cannot salt salt.

13   it is thenceforth good for nothing, but to be cast out, and to be trodden under foot of men.

There are people who believe that you can be children of God today, and children of the devil tomorrow; then again children of God the next day and children of the devil again the day after; but, believe me, it is not so. If the work of grace be really wrought of God in your soul, it will last through your whole life, and if it does not so last, that proves that it is not the work of God. God does not put his hand to this work a second time. There is no regeneration twice over. You can be born again, but you cannot be born again and again and again, as some teach. There is no note in Scripture of that kind. Hence I do rejoice that regeneration once truly wrought of the Spirit of God, is an incorruptible seed which liveth and abideth for ever. But beware, professor, lest you should be like salt that has lost its savour, and that therefore is good for nothing.

14   Ye are the light of the world. —

Christ never contemplated the production of secret Christians — Christians whose virtues would never be displayed, pilgrims who would travel to heaven by night and never be seen by their fellow pilgrims or anyone else.

14-15   A city that is set on an hill cannot be hid. Neither do men light a candle, and put it under a bushel, but on a candlestick; and it giveth light unto all that are in the house.

Christians ought to be seen, and they ought to let their light be seen. They should never even attempt to conceal it. If you are a lamp, you have no right to be under a bushel, or under a bed; your place is on the lampstand where your light can be seen.

16   Let your light so shine before men, that they may see your good works, and glorify your Father which is in heaven.

Not that they may glorify you, but that they may glorify your Father who is in heaven.

17-18 Think not that I am come to destroy the law, or the prophets: I am not come to destroy, but to fulfil. For verily I say unto you, Till heaven and earth pass, one jot or one tittle shall in no wise pass from the law, till all be fulfilled.

No cross of a 't' and no dot of an 'i' shall be taken from God's law. Its requirements will always be the same; immutably fixed, and never to be abated by so little as 'one jot or one tittle'.

19-20 Whosoever therefore shall break one of these least commandments, and shall teach men so, he shall be called the least in the kingdom of heaven: but whosoever shall do and teach them, the same shall be called great in the kingdom of heaven. For I say unto you, That except your righteousness shall exceed the righteousness of the scribes and Pharisees, —

Who seemed to have reached the very highest degree of it; indeed, they themselves thought they went rather *over* the mark than under it, but Christ says to his disciples, 'Unless your righteousness goes beyond that'.

20 ye shall in no case enter into the kingdom of heaven.

These are solemn words of warning. God grant that we may have a righteousness which exceeds that of the scribes and Pharisees — a righteousness inwrought by the Spirit of God, a righteousness of the heart and of the life!

21 Ye have heard that it was said by them of old time, Thou shalt not kill; and whosoever shall kill shall be in danger of the judgment:

Antiquity is often pleaded as an authority; but our King makes short work of 'them of old time'. He begins with one of their alterations of his Father's law. They added to the saved oracles. The first part of the saying which our Lord quoted was divine; but it was dragged down to a low level by the addition about the human court, and the murderer's liability to appear there. It thus became rather a proverb among men than an inspired utterance from the mouth of God. Its meaning, as God spake it, had a far wider range than when the offence was restrained to actual killing, such as could be brought before a human judgement seat. To narrow a command is measurably to annul it. We may not do this even with antiquity for our warrant. Better the whole truth newly stated than an old falsehood in ancient language.

22 But I say unto you, That whosoever is angry with his brother without a cause shall be in danger of the judgment: and whosoever shall say to his brother, Raca, shall be in danger of the council: but whosoever shall say, Thou fool, shall be in danger of hell fire.

Murder lies within anger, for we wish harm to the object of our wrath, or even wish that he did not exist, and this is to kill him in desire. Anger 'without a cause' is forbidden by the command which says, 'Thou shalt not kill', for unjust anger is killing in intent. Such anger without cause brings us under higher judgement than that of Jewish police-courts. God takes cognizance of the emotions from which acts of hate may spring and calls us to account as much for the angry feeling as for the murderous deed. Words also come under the same condemnation: a man shall be judged for what he 'shall say to his brother'. To call a man Raca, or 'a worthless fellow', is to kill him in his reputation, and to say to him, 'Thou fool', is to kill him as to the noblest characteristics of a man. Hence all this comes under such censure as men distribute in their councils; yes, under what is far worse, the punishment awarded by the highest court of the universe, which dooms men to 'hell fire'. Thus our Lord and King restores the law of God to its true force, and warns us that it denounces not only the overt act of killing, but every thought, feeling and word that would tend to injure a brother, or annihilate him by contempt.

23-24 Therefore if thou bring thy gift to the altar, and there rememberest that thy brother hath aught against thee; Leave there thy gift before the altar, and go thy way; first be reconciled to thy brother, and then come and offer thy gift.

The Pharisee would urge as a cover for his malice that he brought a sacrifice to make atonement, but our Lord will have forgiveness rendered to our brother first, and then the offering presented. We ought to worship God thoughtfully, and if in the course of that thought we remember that our brother hath aught (or anything) against us, we must stop. If we have wronged another, we are to pause, cease from the worship, and hasten to seek reconciliation. We easily remember if we have aught against our brother, but now the memory is to be turned the other way. Only when we have remembered our wrongdoing and made reconciliation can we hope for acceptance with the Lord. The rule is: first, peace with man and then, acceptance with God. The holy must be traversed to reach the Holiest of all. Peace being made with our brother, then let us conclude our service towards our Father, and we shall do so with lighter heart and truer zeal. I would anxiously desire to be at peace with all men before I attempt to worship God, lest I present to God the sacrifice of fools.

25-26 Agree with thine adversary quickly, whiles thou art in the way with him; lest at any time the adversary deliver thee to the judge, and the judge deliver thee to the officer, and thou be cast into prison. Verily I say unto thee, Thou shalt by no means come out thence, till thou hast paid the uttermost farthing.

In all disagreements be eager for peace. Leave off strife before you begin. In lawsuits, seek speedy and peaceful settlements. Often in our Lord's days, this was the most gainful way, and usually it is so now. Better lose your rights than get into the hands of those who will only fleece you in the name of justice, and hold you fast so long as a semblance of a demand can stand against you, or another penny can be extracted from you. In a country where 'just fee' meant robbery, it was wisdom to be robbed, and to make no complaint. Even in our own country, a lean settlement is better than a fat lawsuit. Many go into the court to get wool, but come out closely shorn. Carry on no angry suits in courts, but make peace with the utmost promptitude.

27-28 Ye have heard that it was said by them of old time, Thou shalt not commit adultery: But I say unto you, That whosoever looketh on a woman to lust after her hath committed adultery with her already in his heart.

In this case our King again sets aside the glosses of men upon the commands of God, and makes the law to be seen in its vast spiritual breadth. Whereas tradition had confined the prohibition to an overt act of unchastity, the King shows that it forbade the unclean desires of the *heart*. Here the divine law is shown to refer, not only to the *act* of criminal conversation, but even to the *desire, imagination or passion* which would suggest such an infamy. What a King is ours, who stretches his sceptre over the realm of our inward lusts! How sovereignly he puts it: 'But, I say unto you'! Who but a divine Being has authority to speak in this fashion? His Word is law. So it ought to be, seeing he touches vice at the fountainhead and forbids uncleanness in the heart. If sin were not allowed in the mind, it would never be made manifest in the body. This, therefore, is a very effectual way of dealing with the evil. But how searching! How condemning! Irregular looks, unchaste desires and strong passions are of the very essence of adultery; and who can claim a life-long freedom from them? Yet these are the things which defile a man. Lord, purge them out of my nature, and make me pure within!

29　And if thy right eye offend thee, pluck it out, and cast it from thee: for it is profitable for thee that one of thy members should perish, and not that thy whole body should be cast into hell.

That which is the cause of sin is to be given up as well as the sin itself. It is not sinful to have an eye or to cultivate keen perception; but if the eye of speculative knowledge leads us to offend by intellectual sin, it becomes the cause of evil and must be mortified. Anything, however harmless, which leads me to do or think or feel wrongly, I am to get rid of as much as if it were in itself an evil. Though to have done with it would involve deprivation, yet must it be dispensed with, since even a serious loss in one direction is far better than the losing of the whole man. Better a blind saint than a quick-sighted sinner. If abstaining from alcohol caused weakness of body, it would be better to be weak, than to be strong and fall into drunkenness Since vain speculations and reasonings land men in unbelief, we will have none of them. To 'be cast into hell' is too great a risk to run, merely to indulge the evil eye of lust or curiosity.

30   And if thy right hand offend thee, cut it off, and cast it from thee: for it is profitable for thee that one of thy members should perish, and not that thy whole body should be cast into hell.

The cause of offence may be rather active, as the hand, than intellectual, as the eye, but we had better be hindered in our work than drawn aside into temptation. The most dexterous hand must not be spared if it encourages us in doing evil. It is not because a certain thing may make us clever and successful that therefore we are to allow it. If it should prove to be the frequent cause of our falling into sin, we must have done with it, and place ourselves at a disadvantage for our life-work, rather than ruin our whole being by sin. Holiness is to be our first object; everything else must take a very secondary place. Right eyes and right hands are no longer right if they lead us wrong. Even hands and eyes must go that we may not offend our God by them. Yet, let no man read this literally, and therefore mutilate his body, as some foolish fanatics have done. The real meaning is clear enough.

MATTHEW 5:13-26

Matt. 5:13 Ye are the salt of the earth: —

The earth would go putrid if there were no salt of grace to preserve it. So, dear friends, if God's grace is in you, there is a pungent savour about you which fends to preserve others from going as far into sin as otherwise they would have done. 'Ye are the salt of the earth' —

13   but if the salt have lost his savour, wherewith shall it be salted?

If the God-given grace could be taken from you altogether, if you had no sanctifying power about you at all, what could be done with you? You would be like salt that has lost its savour.

13   it is thenceforth good for nothing, but to be cast out, and to be trodden under foot of men.

Mark this, then, either the saints must persevere to the end, or else the grace of God has done nothing for them effectually. If they do not continue to be saints and to exercise a saintly influence, there is no hope for them. There cannot be two new births for the same person; if the divine work has failed once, it will never be begun again. If they really have been saved, if they have been made the children of God, and if it be possible for them to lose the grace which they have received, they can never have it again. The Word of God is very emphatic upon that point: 'If they shall fall away, (it is impossible) to renew them again unto repentance' [Hebrews 6:6]. Falling may be retrieved, but falling away never can be happy. There are countries where there is found salt from which the pungency has completely gone. It is an altogether useless article; and if there are men who ever did possess the grace of God and who were truly God's people, if the divine life could go out of them, they would be in an utterly hopeless case. Perhaps there are no powers of evil in the world greater than apostate churches. Who can calculate the influence for evil that the Church of Rome exercises in the world today?

14   Ye are the light of the world. —

The Bible is not the light of the world, it is the light of the church; but the world does not read the Bible, the world reads Christians: 'Ye are the light of the world.'

14   A city that is set on an hill cannot be hid.

You Christians are like a city built upon a hilltop — you must be seen. As you will be seen, mind that you are worth seeing.

15   Neither do men light a candle, and put it under a bushel, but on a candlestick; and it giveth light unto all that are in the house.

God's intent is, first, to light you; and, secondly, to put you in a conspicuous position, where men can see you.

16 Let your light so shine before men, that they may see your good works, and glorify your Father which is in heaven.

Let the light of your purity and your good works be as bright as possible, yet let not the light be to your own praise and glory; but let it be clearly seen that your good works are the result of sovereign grace, for which all the glory must be given to 'your Father which is in heaven'.

17-18 Think not that I am come to destroy the law, or the prophets: I am not come to destroy, but to fulfil. For verily I say unto you, Till heaven and earth pass, one jot or one tittle shall in no wise pass from the law, till all be fulfilled.

See how the great Lord of the New Testament confirms the Old Testament. He has not come to set up a destructive criticism that will tear in pieces the Book of Deuteronomy, or cut out the very heart of the Psalms, or grind Ezekiel to powder between his own wheels; but Christ has come to establish yet more firmly than before all that was written aforetime, and to make it stand fast as the everlasting hills.

19 Whosoever therefore shall break one of these least commandments, and shall teach men so, he shall be called the least in the kingdom of heaven: but whosoever shall do and teach them, the same shall be called great in the kingdom of heaven.

A true man may make mistakes, and so he may teach men to violate some one or other of the divine commandments. If he does so, he shall not perish, for he was honest in his blunder; but he shall be among the least in the kingdom of heaven. But he who earnestly, perseveringly and conscientiously teaches all that he knows of the divine will, 'the same shall be called great in the kingdom of heaven'.

20 For I say unto you, That except your righteousness shall exceed the righteousness of the scribes and Pharisees, ye shall in no case enter into the kingdom of heaven.

Christ does not teach a lower kind of morality than the Pharisees taught. They were very particular about little things, jots and tittles; but we must go further than they went; we must have more righteousness of life than they had, although they seemed to their fellow-men to be excessively precise. Christ aims at perfect purity in his people, and we must aim at it too, and we must really attain to more holiness than the best outward morals can produce.

21   Ye have heard that it was said by them of old time, Thou shalt not kill; and whosoever shall kill shall be in danger of the judgment:

God had said, 'Thou shalt not kill', but the remainder of the verse was the gloss of the rabbis, a true one, yet one that very much diminishes the force of the divine command.

22   But I say unto you, That whosoever is angry with his brother without a cause shall be in danger of the judgment: —

And a far higher judgement than that of men.

22   and whosoever shall say to his brother, Raca, —

A word of very uncertain meaning, a kind of snubbing word, a word of contempt which men used to one another, meaning that there was nothing in them: 'Whosoever shall say to his brother, Raca' —

22   shall be in danger of the council: but whosoever shall say, Thou fool, shall be in danger of hell fire.

Christ will not have us treat men with anger or with contempt, which is a very evil form of hate, akin to murder, because we as good as say, 'That man is nobody'. That is, we make nothing of him, which is morally to kill him. We must not treat our fellow men with contempt and derision nor indulge an angry temper against them, for anger is of the devil, but 'love is of God'.

23-24   Therefore if thou bring thy gift to the altar, and there rememberest that thy brother hath aught against thee; Leave there thy gift before the altar, and go thy way; first be reconciled to thy brother, and then come and offer thy gift.

Note that this injunction is addressed to the man who has *offended* against his brother; why is this? Because he is the least likely to try to make up the quarrel. It is the man who has been offended who usually exhibits the nobler spirit; but the offender is almost always the last to seek a reconciliation, and therefore the Saviour says to him, 'If thy brother hath aught against thee, it is but right that thou shoulder be the first to seek reconciliation with him. Leave thy gift, go away from the prayer-meeting, turn back from the Lord's table, and go and first be reconciled to thy brother.'

25 Agree with thine adversary quickly, —

Always be ready to make peace — not peace at any price; but, still, peace at any price except the sacrifice of righteousness.

25-26 whiles thou art in the way with him; lest at any time the adversary deliver thee to the judge, and the judge deliver thee to the officer, and thou be cast into prison. Verily I say unto thee, Thou shalt by no means come out thence, till thou hast paid the uttermost farthing.

And there are some debts of which we cannot pay the uttermost farthing; and there is a prison out of which no man shall come, for the uttermost farthing demanded there shall never be paid. God grant that we may, none of us, ever know what it is to be shut up in that dreadful dungeon!

MATTHEW 5:31-42

Matt. 5:31-32 It hath been said, Whosoever shall put away his wife, let him give her a writing of divorcement: But I say unto you, That whosoever shall put away his wife, saving for the cause of fornication, causeth her to commit adultery: and whosoever shall marry her that is divorced committeth adultery.

This time our King quotes and condemns a permissive enactment of the Jewish state. Men were wont to bid their wives 'begone' and a hasty word was thought sufficient as an act of divorce. Moses insisted upon 'a writing of divorcement', that angry passions might have time to cool and that the separation, if it must come, might be performed with deliberation and legal formality. The requirement of a writing was to a certain degree a check upon an evil habit, which was so ingrained in the people that to refuse it altogether would have been useless, and would only have created another crime. The law of Moses went as far as it could practically be enforced; it was because of the hardness of their hearts that divorce was tolerated; it was never approved. But our Lord is more heroic in his legislation. He forbids divorce except for the one crime of infidelity to the marriage vow. She who commits adultery does by that act and deed in effect sunder the marriage bond, and it ought then to be formally recognized by the state as being sundered; but for nothing else should a man be divorced from his wife. Marriage is for life and cannot be loosed, except by the one great crime which severs its bond, whichever of the two is guilty of it. Our Lord would never have tolerated the wicked laws of certain of the American states, which allow married men and women to separate on the merest pretext. A woman divorced for any cause but adultery, and marrying again, is committing adultery before God, whatever the laws of man may call it. This is very plain and positive; and thus a sanctity is given to marriage which human legislation ought not to violate. Let us not be among those who take up novel ideas of wedlock and seek to deform the marriage laws under the pretense of reforming them. Our Lord knows better than our modern social reformers. We had better let the laws of God alone, for we shall never discover any better.

33-37 Again, ye have heard that it hath been said by them of old time, Thou shalt not forswear thyself, but shalt perform unto the Lord thine oaths: But I say unto you, Swear not at all; neither by heaven; for it is God's throne: Nor by the earth; for it is his footstool: neither by Jerusalem; for it is the city of the great King. Neither shalt thou swear by thy head, because thou canst not make one hair white or black. But let your communication be, Yea, yea; Nay, nay: for whatsoever is more than these cometh of evil.

False swearing was forbidden of old, but every kind of swearing is forbidden now by the Word of our Lord Jesus. He mentions several forms of oath and forbids them all and then prescribes simple forms of affirmation or denial as all that his followers should employ. Notwithstanding much that may be advanced to the contrary, there is no evading the plain sense of this passage, that every sort of oath, however solemn or true, is forbidden to a follower of Jesus. Whether in court of law or out of it, the rule is: 'Swear not at all.' Yet, in this Christian country we have swearing everywhere, and especially among lawmakers. Our legislators begin their official existence by swearing. By those who obey the law of the Saviour's kingdom, all swearing is set aside, that the simple word of affirmation or denial, calmly repeated, may remain as a sufficient bond of truth. A bad man cannot be believed on his oath, and a good man speaks the truth without an oath; to what purpose is the superfluous custom of legal swearing preserved? Christians should not yield to an evil custom, however great the pressure put upon them; but they should abide by the plain and unmistakable command of their Lord and King.

38 Ye have heard that it hath been said, An eye for an eye, and a tooth for a tooth:

The law of an eye for an eye, as administered in the proper courts of law was founded in justice, and worked far more equitably than the more modern system of fines; for that method allows rich men to offend with comparative impunity, but when the *lex talionis* came to be the rule of daily life, it fostered revenge, and our Saviour would not tolerate it as a principle carried out by individuals. Good law in court may be very bad custom in common society. He spoke against what had become a proverb and was heard and said among the people, 'Ye have heard that it hath been said'. Our loving King would have private dealings ruled by the spirit of love and not by the rule of law.

39 But I say unto you, That ye resist not evil: but whosoever shall smite thee on thy right cheek, turn to him the other also.

Non-resistance and forbearance are to be the rule among Christians. They are to endure personal ill-usage without coming to blows. They are to be as the anvil when bad men are the hammers, and thus they are to overcome by patient forgiveness. The rule of the judgement seat is not for common life; but the rule of the cross and the all-enduring

Sufferer is for us all. Yet how many regard all this as fanatical, utopian, and even cowardly! The Lord, our King, would have us bear and forbear and conquer by mighty patience. Can we do it? How are we the servants of Christ if we have not his spirit?

40   And if any man will sue thee at the law, and take away thy coat, let him have thy cloak also.

Let him have all he asks and more. Better lose a suit of cloth than be drawn into a suit in law. The courts of our Lord's day were vicious, and his disciples were advised to suffer wrong sooner than appeal to them. Our own courts often furnish the surest method of solving a difficulty by authority, and we have known them resorted to with the view of preventing strife. Yet even in a country where justice can be had, we are not to resort to law for every personal wrong. We should rather endure to be put upon than be for ever crying out, 'I'll bring an action.' At times this very rule of self-sacrifice may require us to take steps in the way of legal appeal, to stop injuries which would fall heavily upon others; but we ought often to forego our own advantage, yea, always when the main motive would be a proud desire for self-vindication. Lord, give me a patient spirit, so that I may not seek to avenge myself, even when I might righteously do so!

41   And whosoever shall compel thee to go a mile, go with him twain.

Governments in those days demanded forced service through their petty officers. Christians were to be of a yielding temper, and bear a double exaction rather than provoke ill words and anger. We ought not to evade taxation, but stand ready to render to Caesar his due. 'Yield' is our watchword. To stand up against force is not exactly our part; we may leave that to others. How few believe the long-suffering, non-resistant doctrines of our King!

42   Give to him that asketh thee, and from him that would borrow of thee turn not thou away.

Be generous. A miser is no follower of Jesus. Discretion is to be used in our giving, lest we encourage idleness and beggary; but the general rule is, 'Give to him that asketh thee.' Sometimes a loan may be more useful than a gift. Do not refuse it to those who will make right use of it. These precepts are not meant for fools, they are set before us as our general rule; but each rule is balanced by other scriptural commands, and there is the teaching of a philanthropic common-sense to guide us. Our spirit is to be one of readiness to help the needy by gift or loan, and we are not exceedingly likely to err by excess in this direction; hence the boldness of the command.

MATTHEW 5:41 – 6:8

Matt. 5:41   And whosoever shall compel thee to go a mile, go with him twain.

If you can do him any service, do it cheerfully, do it readily. Do what he wants of you.

42   Give to him that asketh thee, and from him that would borrow of thee turn not thou away.

This is the spirit of the Christian — to live with the view of doing service.

43-46   Ye have heard that it hath been said, Thou shalt love thy neighbour, and hate thine enemy. But I say unto you, Love your enemies, bless them that curse you, do good to them that hate you, and pray for them which despitefully use you, and persecute you; That ye may be the children of your Father which is in heaven: for he maketh his sun to rise on the evil and on the good, and sendeth rain on the just and on the unjust. For if ye love them which love you, what reward have ye? —

You have done what anybody would do.

46-48   do not even the publicans the same? And if ye salute your brethren only, what do ye more than others? do not even the publicans so? Be ye therefore perfect, even as your Father which is in heaven is perfect.

Rise out of ordinary manhood. Get beyond what others might expect of you. Have a high standard. 'Be ye therefore perfect, even as your Father which is in heaven is perfect.'

Matt. 6:1 Take heed that ye do not your alms before men, to be seen of them: otherwise ye have no reward of your Father which is in heaven.

Our blessed Lord does not tell his disciples to give alms, but he takes it for granted that they do that. How could they be his disciples if they did not so? But he tells them to take care that they do not do this in order to get honour and credit from it. Oh! How much is done in this world that would be very good, but it is spoiled in the doing through the motive done to be seen of men. 'Ye have no reward of your Father which is in heaven.'

2 Therefore when thou doest thine alms, do not sound a trumpet before thee, as the hypocrites do in the synagogues and in the streets, that they may have glory of men. Verily I say unto you, They have their reward.

So that they will never have another. They have been paid once for it by the approbation of their fellow men. They will never have any further reward.

3-5 But when thou doest alms, let not thy left hand know what thy right hand doeth: That thine alms may be in secret: and thy Father which seeth in secret himself shall reward thee openly. And when thou prayest, —

He does not tell his disciples to pray, but again takes it for granted that they do so, and he cannot be a Christian who does not pray. 'A prayerless soul is a Christless soul.' 'When thou prayest' —

5 thou shalt not be as the hypocrites are: for they love to pray standing in the synagogues and in the corners of the streets, that they may be seen of men. Verily I say unto you, They have their reward.

All they will ever get. People say, 'What a wonderfully pious man he is to pray up at the street corner.' Aye, but that is the reward. The prayer will die where it was offered.

6 But thou, when thou prayest, enter into thy closet, —

Get into some quiet nook — some secret place, no matter where.

6 and when thou hast shut thy door, —

So that nobody can hear you — not wishing anybody to know even that you are at prayer. 'When thou hast shut thy door.'

6-8 pray to thy Father which is in secret; and thy Father which seeth in secret shall reward thee openly. But when ye pray, use not vain repetitions, as the heathen do: for they think that they shall be heard for their much speaking. Be not ye therefore like unto them: for your Father knoweth what things ye have need of, before ye ask him.

Prayers are never measured by the yard in heaven. They are estimated by their weight. If there is earnestness in them, truth, sincerity, God accepts them, however brief they are. Indeed, brevity is often an excellence in prayer. Let us never, therefore, use vain repetitions.

MATTHEW 5:43 – 6:4

Matt. 5:43 Ye have heard that it hath been said, Thou shalt love thy neighbour, and hate thine enemy.

In this case a command of Scripture had a human antithesis fitted on to it by depraved minds, and this human addition was mischievous. This is a common method, to append to the teaching of Scripture. Something which seems to grow out of it, or to be a natural inference from it, which something may be false and wicked. This is a sad crime against the Word of the Lord. The Holy Spirit will only father his own words. He owns the precept, 'Thou shalt love thy neighbour' but he hates the parasitical growth of 'hate thine enemy'. This last sentence is destructive of that out of which it appears legitimately to grow, since those who are here styled enemies are, in fact, neighbours. Love is now the universal law; and our King, who has commanded it, is himself the pattern of it. He will not see it narrowed down and placed in a setting of hate. May grace prevent any of us from falling into this error!

44-45 But I say unto you, Love your enemies, bless them that curse you, do good to them that hate you, and pray for them which despitefully use you, and persecute you; That ye may be the children of your Father which is in heaven: for he maketh his sun to rise on the evil and on the good, and sendeth rain on the just and on the unjust.

Ours it is to persist in loving, even if men persist in enmity. We are to render blessing for cursing, prayers for persecutions. Even in the cases of cruel enemies, we are to 'do good to them, and pray for them'. We are no longer enemies to any, but friends to all. We do not merely cease to hate and then abide in a cold neutrality, but we love where hatred seemed inevitable. We bless where our old nature bids us curse, and we are active in doing good to those who deserve to receive evil from us. Where this is practically carried out, men wonder, respect and admire the followers of Jesus. The theory may be ridiculed, but the practice is reverenced and is counted so surprising that men attribute it to some Godlike quality in Christians and own that they are the children of the Father who is in heaven. Indeed, he is a child of God who can bless the unthankful and the evil; for in daily providence, the Lord is doing this on a great scale, and none but his children will imitate him. To do good for the sake of the good done, and not because of the character of the person benefitted, is a noble imitation of God. If the Lord only sent the fertilizing shower upon the land of the saintly, drought would deprive whole leagues of land of all hope of a harvest. We also must do good to the evil, or we shall have a narrow sphere, our hearts will grow contracted and our sonship towards the good God will be rendered doubtful.

46 For if ye love them which love you, what reward have ye? do not even the publicans the same?

Any common sort of man will love those who love him; even tax gatherers and the scum of the earth can rise to this poor, starving virtue. Saints cannot be content with such a groveling style of things. 'Love for love is manlike' but 'love for hate' is Christlike. Shall we not desire to act up to our high calling?

47 And if ye salute your brethren only, what do ye more than others? do not even the publicans so?

On a journey or in the streets or in the house, we are not to confine our friendly greetings to those who are near and dear to us. Courtesy should be wide, and none the less sincere because general. We should speak kindly to all and treat every man as a brother. Anyone will shake hands with an old friend, but we are to be cordially courteous towards every being in the form of man. If not, we shall reach no higher level than mere outcasts. Even a dog will salute a dog.

48 Be ye therefore perfect, even as your Father which is in heaven is perfect.

Or, 'Ye shall be perfect.' We should reach after completeness in love, fulness of love to all around us. Love is the bond of perfectness; and if we have perfect love, it will form in us a perfect character. Here is that which we aim at: perfection like that of God. Here is the manner of obtaining it; namely, by abounding in love; and this suggests the question of how far we have proceeded in this heavenly direction and, also, the reason why we should persevere in it even to the end, because as children we ought to resemble our Father. Scriptural perfection is attainable. It dies rather in proportion than in degree. A man's character may be perfect and entire, wanting nothing; and yet such a man will be the very first to admit that the grace which is in him is at best in its infancy, and though perfect as a child in all its parts, it has not yet attained to the perfection of full-grown manhood. What a mark is set before us by our perfect King, who, speaking from his mountain-throne, saith, 'Be ye perfect, even as your Father which is in heaven is perfect'! Lord, give what thou dost command; then both the grace and the glory will be thine alone.

Matt. 6:1 Take heed that ye do not your alms before men, to be seen of them: otherwise ye have no reward of your Father which is in heaven.

'You cannot expect to be paid twice. If therefore you take your reward in the applause of men, who give you a high character for generosity, you cannot expect to have any reward from God.' We ought to have a single eye to God's accepting what we give, and to have little or no thought of what man may say concerning our charitable gifts.

2 Therefore when thou doest thine alms, do not sound a trumpet before thee, as the hypocrites do in the synagogues and in the streets, that they may have glory of men. Verily I say unto you, They have their reward.

And they will have no more; there is, in their case, no laying up of any store of good works before God. Whatever they may have done, they have taken full credit for it in the praise of men.

3 But when thou doest alms, let not thy left hand know what thy right hand doeth:

'Do it so by stealth as scarcely to know it thyself; think so little of it with regard to thyself that thou shalt scarcely know that thou hast done it. Do it unto God; let him know it.'

4 That thine alms may be in secret: and thy Father which seeth in secret himself shall reward thee openly.

There is a blessed emphasis upon that word 'himself' for, if God shall reward us, what a reward it will be! Any praise from his lips, any reward from his hands, will be of priceless value. Oh, to live with an eye to that alone!

MATTHEW 6:1-24; 1 CORINTHIANS 3:1-16

Matt. 6:1 Take heed that ye do not your alms before men, to be seen of them: otherwise ye have no reward of your Father which is in heaven.

The motive which leads a man to give, will form the true estimate of what he does. If he gives to be seen of men then when he is seen of men he has the reward he sought for, and he will never have any other. Let us never do our alms before men, to be seen of them.

2-5 Therefore when thou doest thine alms, do not sound a trumpet before thee, as the hypocrites do in the synagogues and in the streets, that they may have glory of men. Verily I say unto you, They have their reward. But when thou doest alms, let not thy left hand know what thy right hand doeth: That thine alms may be in secret: and thy Father which seeth in secret himself shall reward thee openly. And when thou prayest, thou shalt not be as the hypocrites are: for they love to pray standing in the synagogues and in the corners of the streets, that they may be seen of men. Verily I say unto you, They have their reward.

I have heard very great commendation given to certain Easterns, because at the hour of the rising of the sun, or the hour when the sound is heard from the summit of the mosque, wherever they may be, they put themselves in the posture of prayer. God forbid I should rob them of any credit they deserve, but far be it from us ever to imitate them. We are not to be ashamed of our prayers, but they are not things for the public street. They are intended for God's eye and God's ear.

6-7 But thou, when thou prayest, enter into thy closet, and when thou hast shut thy door, pray to thy Father which is in secret; and thy Father which seeth in secret shall reward thee openly. But when ye pray, use not vain repetitions, as the heathen do: for they think that they shall be heard for their much speaking.

It is not very easy to repeat the same words often without it becoming a vain repetition. A repetition, however, is not forbidden, but a 'vain' repetition. And how greatly do they err who measure prayers by the yard. They think they have prayed so much because they have prayed so long, whereas it is the work of the heart — the true pouring out of the desire before God — that is the thing to be looked at. Quality, not quantity: truth, not length. Oftentimes the shortest prayers have the most prayer in them.

8-9 Be not ye therefore like unto them: for your Father knoweth what things ye have need of, before ye ask him. After this manner therefore pray ye: —

And then he gives us a model of prayer, which never can be excelled, containing all the parts of devotion. They do well who model their prayers upon this.

9-13 Our Father which art in heaven, Hallowed be thy name. Thy kingdom come, Thy will be done in earth, as it is in heaven. Give us this day our daily bread. And forgive us our debts, as we forgive our debtors. And lead us not into temptation, but deliver us from evil: For thine is the kingdom, and the power, and the glory, for ever. Amen.

Our Saviour now makes a remark upon this prayer, and on one particular part of it which has stumbled a great many.

14-15   For if ye forgive men their trespasses, your heavenly Father will also forgive you: But if ye forgive not men their trespasses, neither will your Father forgive your trespasses.

There are some who have altered this, and pray in this fashion, 'Forgive us our debts as we *desire* to forgive our debtors.' It will not do. You will have to desire God to forgive you, and desire in vain, if you pray in that fashion. It must come to this point of literal, immediate, completed forgiveness of every offence committed against you if you expect God to forgive you. There is no wriggling out of it. The man who refuses to forgive, refuses to be forgiven. God grant that we may, none of us, tolerate malice in our hearts. Anger glances in the bosom of wise men: it only burns in the heart of the foolish. May we quench it and feel that we do freely and fully and heartily forgive, knowing that we are forgiven.

16   Moreover when ye fast, be not, as the hypocrites, of a sad countenance: for they disfigure their faces, that they may appear unto men to fast. Verily I say unto you, They have their reward.

Simpletons praise them — think much of them, and they plume themselves thereon and think themselves the very best of men. They have their reward.

17-18   But thou, when thou fastest, anoint thine head, and wash thy face; That thou appear not unto men to fast, but unto thy Father which is in secret: and thy Father, which seeth in secret, shall reward thee openly.

Yet have I heard persons speak of certain emaciated ecclesiastics as being such wonderfully holy men. 'How they must have fasted! They look like it. You can see it in their faces.' Probably produced by a fault in their digestion much more likely, than by anything else and if not — if we are to suppose that the spareness of a person is to be the token of his holiness — then the living skeleton was a saint to perfection. But we are not beguiled by such follies as these. The Christian man fasts, but he takes care that no one shall know it. He wears no ring or token even when his heart is heavy. Full often he puts on a cheerful air, lest by any means he should communicate unnecessary sorrow to others, and he will be cheerful and happy, apparently, in the midst of company, to prevent their being sad, for it is enough for him to be sad himself, and sad before his Father's face.

19-21 Lay not up for yourselves treasures upon earth, where moth and rust doth corrupt, and where thieves break through and steal: But lay up for yourselves treasures in heaven, where neither moth nor rust doth corrupt, and where thieves do not break through nor steal: For where your treasure is, there will your heart be also.

There is many a way of sending your treasure before you to heaven. God's poor are his money boxes — his exchequer. You can pass your treasure over to heaven by their means. And the work of evangelizing the world by the labours of God's servants in the ministry of the gospel — you can help this also. Thus also ye can pass your treasure over into the King's exchequer, and your heart will follow it. I have heard of one who said his religion did not cost him a shilling a year, and it was remarked that very probably it would have been expensive at the price. You will find people form a pretty accurate estimate of the value of their own religion by the proportion which they are prepared to sacrifice for it.

22 The light of the body is the eye: if therefore thine eye be single, —

If thy motive be single; if thou hast only one motive, and that a right one — the master one of glorifying God. 'If thy eye be single' —

22-23 thy whole body shall be full of light. But if thine eye be evil, thy whole body shall be full of darkness. If therefore the light that is in thee be darkness, how great is that darkness!

When a man's highest motive is himself, what a dark and selfish nature he has; but when his highest motive is his God, what brightness of light will shine upon all.

24 No man can serve two masters: —

He can serve two persons very readily. For the matter of that, he can serve twenty, but not two masters. There cannot be two master principles in a man's heart, or master passions in a man's soul. 'No man can serve two masters.'

24   for either he will hate the one, and love the other; or else he will hold to the one, and despise the other. Ye cannot serve God and mammon.

Though some men's lives are a long experiment of how far they can serve the two.

1 Cor. 3:1   And I, brethren, could not speak unto you as unto spiritual, but as unto carnal, even as unto babes in Christ.

The church at Corinth consisted of persons of large education and great abilities. It was one of those churches that had given up the one-man system, where everybody talked as he liked — a very knowing church, and a church of Christians, too; but for all that, Christian babies. And though they thought themselves to be so great, yet the apostle says that he never spoke to them as to spiritual: he kept to the simple elements, regarding the carnal part as being too much in them as yet, to be able to drink down spiritual things.

2   I have fed you with milk, and not with meat: for hitherto ye were not able to bear it, neither yet now are ye able.

How grateful we ought to be that there is milk and that this milk does feed the soul — that the simplest truths of Christianity contain in them all that the soul wants, just as milk is a diet upon which the body could be sustained, without anything else. Yet how we ought to desire to grow, that we may not always be upon milk diet but that we may be able to digest the strong meat — the high doctrine of the deep things of God. These are for men, not for babes. Let the babes be thankful for the milk, but let us aspire to be strong men that we may feed on meat.

3   For ye are yet carnal: for whereas there is among you envying, and strife, and divisions, are ye not carnal, and walk as men?

A united church, you may conclude, is a growing church — perhaps a grown church; but a disunited church, split up into factions where every man is seeking position and trying to be noted, such a church is a church of babes. They are carnal and walk as men.

4 For while one saith, I am of Paul; and another, I am of Apollos; are ye not carnal?

Instead of that, they should all have striven together for the defense of the common faith of Jesus Christ. There is no greater symptom of mere infancy in true religion than the setting up of the names of leaders or the preference for this or that peculiar form of doctrine, instead of endeavouring to grasp the whole of truth wherever one can find it.

5-6 Who then is Paul, and who is Apollos, but ministers by whom ye believed, even as the Lord gave to every man? I have planted, Apollos watered; but God gave the increase.

Let God, then, have all the glory. Be grateful for the planter, and grateful for the waterer, aye, and grateful to them as well; but, still, let the stress of your gratitude be given to him without whom watering and planting would be in vain.

7-8 So then neither is he that planteth any thing, neither he that watereth; but God that giveth the increase. Now he that planteth and he that watereth are one: —

They are pursuing the same design; and Apollos and Paul were one in heart. They were true servants of one Master.

8-9 and every man shall receive his own reward according to his own labour. For we are labourers together with God: ye are God's husbandry, ye are God's building.

The church is built up. God is he who builds it up — the Master of the work, but he employs his ministers under him to be builders.

10-13 According to the grace of God which is given unto me, as a wise masterbuilder, I have laid the foundation, and another buildeth thereon. But let every man take heed how he buildeth thereupon. For other foundation can no man lay than that is laid, which is Jesus Christ. Now if any man build upon this foundation gold, silver, precious stones, wood, hay, stubble; Every man's work shall be made manifest: for the day shall declare it, because it shall be revealed by fire; and the fire shall try every man's work of what sort it is.

Very easy to build up a church quickly. Very easy to make a great excitement in religion and become very famous as a soul-winner. Very easy.

But time tries everything. If there were no other fire than the mere fire of time, it would suffice to test a man's work. And when a church crumbles away almost as soon as it is got together, when a church declines from the doctrines which it professed to hold, when the teaching of the eminent teacher is proved, after all, to have been fallacious and to have been erroneous in practical results, then what he has built comes to nothing! O dear friends, what little we do we ought to aspire to do for eternity. If you shall never lay the brush to the canvas but once, make an indelible stroke with it. If only one work of sort shall come from the statuary's workshop, let it be something that will live all down the ages.

But we are in such a mighty hurry: we make a lot of things that die with us — ephemeral results. We are not careful enough as to what we build with. May God grant that this truth may sink into our minds. Let us remember that, if it is hard building with gold and silver, and harder still building with precious stones, yet what is built *will stand the fire*. It is easy building with wood, and easier still with hay and stubble, but then there will be only a handful of ashes left of a whole lifework, if we build with these.

14-15   If any man's work abide which he hath built thereupon, he shall receive a reward. If any man's work shall be burned, he shall suffer loss: but he himself shall be saved; yet so as by fire.

If he meant right — if he did endeavour to serve God as a worker, though he may have uttered many errors and have been mistaken — (and which of us has not been?) — he shall be saved, though his work must be burnt.

16   Know ye not that ye are the temple of God, and that the Spirit of God dwelleth in you?

Do you know it? He says, 'Know ye not?' but I might leave out the 'not' and say, 'Know ye that ye are the temple of God?' What a wonderful fact it is! Within the body of the saint, God dwells, as in a temple. How do some men injure their bodies or utterly despise them, though they would not so do if they understood that they are the temple of God, and that the Spirit of God dwelleth in them.

MATTHEW 6:5-34

Matt. 6:5 And when thou prayest, thou shalt not be as the hypocrites are: for they love to pray standing in the synagogues and in the corners of the streets, that they may be seen of men. —

We ought to pray in the synagogue, and we may pray at the corners of the streets; but the wrong is to do it to 'be seen of men', that is, to be looking for some present reward in the praises that fall from human lips.

5-7 Verily I say unto you, They have their reward. But thou, when thou prayest, enter into thy closet, and when thou hast shut thy door, pray to thy Father which is in secret; and thy Father which seeth in secret shall reward thee openly. But when ye pray, use not vain repetitions, as the heathen do: for they think that they shall be heard for their much speaking.

They seem to attribute a sort of power to a certain form of words, as if it were a charm, and they repeat it over and over again. Not only do the poor Mohammedans and heathens 'use vain repetitions' but the members of the Romish and other churches that I might name do the same thing; words to which they attach but very slight meaning, and into which they put little or no heart, are repeated by them again and again, as if there could be some virtue in the words themselves. Let it not be so with you beloved. Pray as long as you like in secret, but do not pray long with the idea that God will hear you simply because you are a long while at your devotions.

8 Be not ye therefore like unto them: for your Father knoweth what things ye have need of, before ye ask him.

He does not need to be informed nor even to be persuaded. Mere words are of no value in his ears. If you must needs use many words, ask men to lend you their ears, for they may have little else to do with them; but God careth not for words alone, it is the thought, the desire of the heart to which he ever hath regard.

9 After this manner therefore pray ye: —

Here is a model prayer for you to copy as far as it is suited to your case.

9-13 Our Father which art in heaven, Hallowed be thy name. Thy kingdom come, Thy will be done in earth, as it is in heaven. Give us this day our daily bread. And forgive us our debts, as we forgive our debtors. And lead us not into temptation, but deliver us from evil: For thine is the kingdom, and the power, and the glory, for ever. Amen.

And then, as if there was one part of the prayer that would be sure to arrest the attention of his hearers, namely, that concerning forgiving our debtors, the Saviour makes the following remarks:

14-15 For if ye forgive men their trespasses, your heavenly Father will also forgive you: But if ye forgive not men their trespasses, neither will your Father forgive your trespasses.

Therefore, in order to succeed in prayer, we must have a heart purged from a spirit of revenge and from all unkindness. We must ourselves be loving and forgiving, or we cannot expect that God will hear our supplications when we come to crave his forgiveness.

16 Moreover when ye fast, be not, as the hypocrites, of a sad countenance: for they disfigure their faces, that they may appear unto men to fast. —

They seemed to say to everyone who looked at them, 'We have been so engrossed with our devotions that we have not found time even to wash our faces.' But the Saviour says to his followers, 'Do not imitate those hypocrites; do not make public your private religious exercises, perform them unto God, and not unto men.' As for those hypocrites —

16 Verily I say unto you, They have their reward.

And a poor reward it is.

17-18 But thou, when thou fastest, anoint thine head, and wash thy face; That thou appear not unto men to fast, but unto thy Father which is in secret: and thy Father, which seeth in secret, shall reward thee openly.

May God give us that modest, unselfish spirit which lives unto him, and does not want to walk in the sham light of men's esteem! What matters it, after all, what men think of us? The hypocrite proudly boasts if he wins a little praise from his fellows — but what is it except so much wind? If all men should speak well of us, all that we should gain would be this, 'Woe unto you, when all men shall speak well of you! for so did their fathers to the false prophets' [Luke 6:26].

19-20 Lay not up for yourselves treasures upon earth, where moth and rust doth corrupt, and where thieves break through and steal: But lay up for yourselves treasures in heaven, where neither moth nor rust doth corrupt, and where thieves do not break through nor steal:

Christ here first teaches us how to pray and then teaches us how really to live. He turns our thoughts from the object in life which allures and injures so many, but which is, after all, an object unworthy of our search; and he bids us seek something higher and better: 'Lay up for yourselves treasures in heaven' —

21 For where your treasure is, there will your heart be also.

It is sure to be so: your heart will follow your treasure. Send it away therefore up to the everlasting hills, lay up treasure in that blessed land before you go there yourself.

22-23 The light of the body is the eye: if therefore thine eye be single, thy whole body shall be full of light. But if thine eye be evil, thy whole body shall be full of darkness. If therefore the light that is in thee be darkness, how great is that darkness!

If thine eye be brooked up with gold dust, or if thou art living for self and this world, thy whole life will be a dark life, and the whole of thy being will dwell in darkness. 'But', says someone, 'may I not live for this world and the next too?' Listen:

24 No man can serve two masters: —

He may serve two individuals, who have conflicting interests but they cannot both be his masters.

24 for either he will hate the one, and love the other; or else he will hold to the one, and despise the other. Ye cannot serve God and mammon.

Either the one or the other will be master, they are so opposed to each other that they will never agree to a divided service. 'Ye cannot serve God and mammon.' It is the Lord Jesus Christ who says this, so do not attempt to do what he declares is impossible.

25 Therefore I say unto you, Take no thought for your life, —

It should be: 'Take no distracting thought for your life' —

25 what ye shall eat, or what ye shall drink; nor yet for your body, what ye shall put on. Is not the life more than meat, and the body than raiment?

You are obliged to leave your life with God, why not leave with him all care about your food and your raiment?

26 Behold the fowls of the air: for they sow not, neither do they reap, nor gather into barns; yet your heavenly Father feedeth them. Are ye not much better than they?

Do you believe that, after all your earnest labour and your industry, God will permit you to starve, when these creatures, that labour not, yet are fed?

27-29 Which of you by taking thought can add one cubit unto his stature? And why take ye thought for raiment? Consider the lilies of the field, how they grow; they toil not, neither do they spin: And yet I say unto you, That even Solomon in all his glory was not arrayed like one of these.

Christ asks then whether, by taking thought, they can add a single cubit to their lives, for I take his question to mean, whether they could, by any means, make the standard of existence any longer than it was. They could not do so, they could shorten it, and very often, carking care has brought men to their graves. Then Christ bade them note how the lilies grow, so that even Solomon could not excel them for beauty.

30-33 Wherefore, if God so clothe the grass of the field, which to day is, and to morrow is cast into the oven, shall he not much more clothe you, O ye of little faith? Therefore take no thought, saying, What shall we eat? or, What shall we drink? or, Wherewithal shall we be clothed? (For after all these things do the Gentiles seek:) for your heavenly Father knoweth that ye have need of all these things. But seek ye first the kingdom of God, and his righteousness; and all these things shall be added unto you.

If you want string and brown paper, you need not go into a shop to buy them, but if you buy certain articles, you get string and brown paper in the bargain. So, when you go to God, seeking first his kingdom and his righteousness; these other things, which are but the packing, as it were, the string and the brown paper, are given to you in the bargain. He who giveth you the golden treasures of heaven will not allow you to want for the copper treasures of earth.

34 Take therefore no thought for the morrow: for the morrow shall take thought for the things of itself. Sufficient unto the day is the evil thereof.

You cannot live in tomorrow, so do not fret about tomorrow. You live in today, so think of today, spend today to God's glory, and leave the care about tomorrow until tomorrow comes.

MATTHEW 7

Matt. 7:1-2 Judge not, that ye be not judged. For with what judgment ye judge, ye shall be judged: and with what measure ye mete, it shall be measured to you again.

Some people are of a censorious disposition; they see nothing in others to praise, but everything to blame, and such people generally find that they are condemned according to their own wicked rule. Other people begin to judge those who are so fond of judging. If they are so wise, and so discriminating, others expect more from them; and not finding it, they are not slow to condemn them. It is an old proverb that chickens come home to roost, and so they do. If you judge ill of others, that judgement will, sooner or later, come home to yourself.

3-5 And why beholdest thou the mote that is in thy brother's eye, but considerest not the beam that is in thine own eye? Or how wilt thou say to thy brother, Let me pull out the mote out of thine eye; and, behold, a beam is in thine own eye? Thou hypocrite, first cast out the beam out of thine own eye; and then shalt thou see clearly to cast out the mote out of thy brother's eye.

At the bottom of all censoriousness lies hypocrisy. An honest man would apply to himself the judgement which he exercises upon others, but it usually happens that those who are so busy spying out other people's faults have no time to see their own; and what is this, at the bottom, but insincerity and hypocrisy?

6 Give not that which is holy unto the dogs, neither cast ye your pearls before swine, lest they trample them under their feet, and turn again and rend you.

Zeal should always be tempered by prudence. There are times when it would be treason to truth to introduce it as a topic of conversation — when men are in such a frame of mind that they will be sure rather to cavil at it than to believe it. Not only speak thou well, but speak thou at the right time, for silence is sometimes golden. See that thou hast thy measure of golden silence as well as of silver speech.

7 Ask, and it shall be given you; seek, and ye shall find; knock, and it shall be opened unto you:

Here is a three-fold encouragement to us to pray. When we cannot use one style of prayer, let us use another, for each shall be successful at the right time. O child of God, let nothing keep thee from prayer! It has been well said that a Christian may be hedged in, but he cannot be roofed in; there is always a passageway upwards to the throne of the great Father; and asking, knocking, seeking, he shall be sure to be successful with his suit.

8 For every one that asketh receiveth; and he that seeketh findeth; and to him that knocketh it shall be opened.

Ask the people of God whether it is not so. Go among them, and question them upon this matter. They know the power of prayer, so let them tell you whether they have been deceived or not. Well then, as it has been so with them, let this encourage you to expect that it shall be the same with you also.

9-12 Or what man is there of you, whom if his son ask bread, will he give him a stone? Or if he ask a fish, will he give him a serpent? If ye then, being evil, know how to give good gifts unto your children, how much more shall your Father which is in heaven give good things to them that ask him? Therefore all things whatsoever ye would that men should do to you, do ye even so to them: for this is the law and the prophets.

Is there a connection between this conduct on our part and answers to our prayer? Undoubtedly it is so from the position of the text. If we will never grant the requests of those who need our help, in cases where we should expect to be ourselves helped, how can we go to God with any confidence and ask him to help us? I doubt not that many a man has received no answer to his prayer because that prayer has come out of a heart hard and untender, which would not permit him to grant the requests of others. O child of God, do thou to others as thou wouldst that they should do to thee, then canst thou go to thy God in prayer with the confidence that he will hear and answer thee!

13 Enter ye in at the strait gate: —

Do not be ashamed of being called Puritanical, precise and particular: 'Enter ye in at the narrow gate.'

13 for wide is the gate, and broad is the way, that leadeth to destruction, —

Do not choose that way.

13-21 and many there be which go in thereat: Because strait is the gate, and narrow is the way, which leadeth unto life, and few there be that find it. Beware of false prophets, which come to you in sheep's clothing, but inwardly they are ravening wolves. Ye shall know them by their fruits. Do men gather grapes of thorns, or figs of thistles? Even so every good tree bringeth forth good fruit; but a corrupt tree bringeth forth evil fruit. A good tree cannot bring forth evil fruit, neither can a corrupt tree bring forth good fruit. Every tree that bringeth not forth good fruit is hewn down, and cast into the fire. Wherefore by their fruits ye shall know them. Not every one that saith unto me, Lord, Lord, shall enter into the kingdom of heaven; but he that doeth the will of my Father which is in heaven.

That still remains as the great test of the true heir of heaven — the doing of the divine will. All the talking, thinking and posturing in the world will not save a man. There must be in him such a faith as produces holiness.

22-25 Many will say to me in that day, Lord, Lord, have we not prophesied in thy name? and in thy name have cast out devils? and in thy name done many wonderful works? And then will I profess unto them, I never knew you: depart from me, ye that work iniquity. Therefore whosoever heareth these sayings of mine, and doeth them, I will liken him unto a wise man, which built his house upon a rock: And the rain descended, and the floods came, and the winds blew, and beat upon that house; —

Whoever you are, and whatever you build, it will be tried. No matter how firm is the rock beneath you, the winds will blow, and the rains will pour down upon your building. Whether you are in a palace or in a hovel, trial and testing must and will come to you: 'The floods came, and the winds blew, and beat upon that house' —

25 and it fell not: —

There is the mercy: 'It fell not.'

25-27 for it was founded upon a rock. And every one that heareth these sayings of mine, and doeth them not, shall be likened unto a foolish man, which built his house upon the sand: And the rain descended, and the floods came, and the winds blew, and beat upon that house; —

Even if you live to the world, or live unto Satan, you will not live without trial. The ungodly, who have their portion in this life, have to eat some bitter herbs with it, and have to dip their morsel in vinegar quite as much as believers do. 'The floods came, and the winds blew, and beat upon that house' —

27 and it fell: —

Just when the tenant most needed shelter, it fell. He did not need it so much till the floods came, and the winds blew; but now, when he would fain have crouched down beneath his roof-tree, and have been at peace from the howling hurricane, then, 'It fell.'

27 and great was the fall of it.

The fall was so great because he could never build again.

28-29 And it came to pass, when Jesus had ended these sayings, the people were astonished at his doctrine: For he taught them as one having authority, and not as the scribes.

Not quoting Rabbi So-and-so to show how well he was acquainted with his writings, but speaking as One who knew what he had to say, and who spoke, out of the fulness of his heart, truth that was evidently inspired; and his hearers felt the force of the solemn message which he thus delivered.

MATTHEW 7

While we are reading, let us also be adoring at the same time, for the words of Christ have a gracious divinity about them; they are infinite; they are omnipotent. There is a kind of life in them — a life which communicates itself to those who hear them. Our Saviour did not preach sermons, he preached texts; all his sermons are full of golden sentences, not hammered gold leaf like those of men, but they are ingots of solid gold, and the gold of that land is good, the most fine gold; there is none like it. Thus he preaches in the seventh chapter of Matthew.

Matt. 7:1 Judge not, that ye be not judged.

Set not up for critics, especially in the act of worship. Probably there is no greater destroyer of profit in the hearing of the Word than is the spirit of carping criticism.

Matt. 7:2 For with what judgment ye judge, ye shall be judged: and with what measure ye mete, it shall be measured to you again.

When the Lord comes in judgement, he might almost decline to mount the throne, for he might say, 'These men have already tried and condemned each other; let their sentences abide.' If he were to judge us as we have judged others, who amongst us would stand? But we may rest assured that our fellow men will usually exercise towards us much the same judgement that we exercise towards them.

3 And why beholdest thou the mote that is in thy brother's eye, but considerest not the beam that is in thine own eye?

It is a beam. You do not see it because it is in your own eye. How is it that you can be so severe towards that which is in another, and so lenient towards yourself?

4-5 Or how wilt thou say to thy brother, Let me pull out the mote out of thine eye; and, behold, a beam is in thine own eye? Thou hypocrite, first cast out the beam out of thine own eye; and then shalt thou see clearly to cast out the mote out of thy brother's eye.

There may be, dear friends, a great deal of hypocrisy about us, of which we are not aware, for when a man sees a fault in another, and tells him of it, he says, 'You know I am a very plain-spoken person; there is no hypocrisy about me.' Well, but there is, and, according to the Saviour's description, this may be sheer hypocrisy because meanwhile in your own eye there is something else worse than you see in your fellow, and this you pass over. This is simply untruthful dealing, and it amounts to hypocrisy. If you were really so zealous to make people see, you would begin by being zealous to see *yourself*, and if you were so concerned to have all eyes cleansed from impurity, you would begin by cleansing your own, or seeking to have them cleansed.

6 Give not that which is holy unto the dogs, neither cast ye your pearls before swine, lest they trample them under their feet, and turn again and rend you.

It is a pity to talk about some of the secrets of our holy faith in any and every company. It would be almost profane to speak of them in the company of profane men. We know that they would not understand us; they would find occasion for jest and ridicule, and therefore our own reverence for holy things must cause us to lay a finger on our lips when we are in the presence of profane persons. Do not let us, however, carry out one precept to the exclusion of others. There are dogs that eat of the crumbs that fall from the master's table. Drop them a crumb. And there are even swine that may yet be transformed, to whom the sight of a pearl might give some inkling of a better condition of heart. Cast not the pearls before them, but you may show them to them sometimes when they are in as good a state of mind as they are likely to be in. It is ours to preach the gospel to *every* creature — that is a precept of Christ — and yet all creatures are not always in the condition to hear the gospel. We must choose our time. Yet even this I would not push too far. We are to preach the gospel 'in season and out of season' [2 Timothy 4:2]. Oh, that we may be able to follow precepts as far as they are meant to go, and no further.

7 Ask, and it shall be given you; seek, and ye shall find; knock, and it shall be opened unto you:

This is the simplest form of prayer. Follow up your prayer by the effort. 'Knock, and it shall be opened unto you.' Add force to your petitions and to your prayers. If the door blocks the way, knock until it is opened.

8 For every one that asketh receiveth; and he that seeketh findeth; and to him that knocketh it shall be opened.

One way or another you will get the blessing if you are but persevering, and blessed is the man who is a master of the art of asking but does not forget the labour of seeking an entrance through the importunity of knocking.

9-10 Or what man is there of you, whom if his son ask bread, will he give him a stone? Or if he ask a fish, will he give him a serpent?

Our Lord will give us the *real* thing. Sometimes we should be quite satisfied with the imitation of it. And sometimes we have to wait and be prepared for the reception of the real thing; it is infinitely better for us to wait for months than immediately to get a stone; better to wait for a fish than the next moment to have a scorpion. There were some in the wilderness who asked to be satisfied, and they were so, with the flesh of quails. They got their stones; they got their scorpions. But the Lord's people may sometimes find that they have to wait a while. God will not give to them that which is other than good for them.

11-12 If ye then, being evil, know how to give good gifts unto your children, how much more shall your Father which is in heaven give good things to them that ask him? Therefore all things whatsoever ye would that men should do to you, do ye even so to them: for this is the law and the prophets.

Wonderful condensation of the two tables of the law! God help us to remember it. This is a golden rule, and he that follows that shall lead a golden life.

13-14 Enter ye in at the strait gate: for wide is the gate, and broad is the way, that leadeth to destruction, and many there be which go in thereat: Because strait is the gate, and narrow is the way, which leadeth unto life, and few there be that find it.

Do not be ashamed of being called narrow. Do not be ashamed of being supposed to lead a life of great precision and exactness. There is nothing very grand about breadth, after all. And I have noticed one thing, the broadest men I have ever met in the best sense have always kept to the narrow way, and the narrowest people I know are those who are so fond of the broad way. I could indicate some literature which professes to be exceedingly liberal; it is liberal indeed in finding fault with everybody who holds the gospel, but its tone is bitterness itself towards all the orthodox. Wormwood and gall are honey compared with what the liberal people generally pour out upon those who keep close to the truth. I prefer to cultivate a broad spirit to a narrow heart, and then to talk about the breadth of the way.

15 Beware of false prophets, —

But so long as he is a prophet, people will respect him; do not find fault with him, he is a clever man.

15-25   which come to you in sheep's clothing, but inwardly they are ravening wolves. Ye shall know them by their fruits. Do men gather grapes of thorns, or figs of thistles? Even so every good tree bringeth forth good fruit; but a corrupt tree bringeth forth evil fruit. A good tree cannot bring forth evil fruit, neither can a corrupt tree bring forth good fruit. Every tree that bringeth not forth good fruit is hewn down, and cast into the fire. Wherefore by their fruits ye shall know them. Not every one that saith unto me, Lord, Lord, shall enter into the kingdom of heaven; but he that doeth the will of my Father which is in heaven. Many will say to me in that day, Lord, Lord, have we not prophesied in thy name? and in thy name have cast out devils? and in thy name done many wonderful works? And then will I profess unto them, I never knew you: depart from me, ye that work iniquity. Therefore whosoever heareth these sayings of mine, and doeth them, I will liken him unto a wise man, which built his house upon a rock: And the rain descended, and the floods came, and the winds blew, and beat upon that house; and it fell not: for it was founded upon a rock.

For the best man will be tried, and perhaps all the more because he is such.

26-29   And every one that heareth these sayings of mine, and doeth them not, shall be likened unto a foolish man, which built his house upon the sand: And the rain descended, and the floods came, and the winds blew, and beat upon that house; and it fell: and great was the fall of it. And it came to pass, when Jesus had ended these sayings, the people were astonished at his doctrine: For he taught them as one having authority, and not as the scribes.

MATTHEW 8:1-27

Matt. 8:1-2 When he was come down from the mountain, great multitudes followed him. And, behold, there came a leper —

You see that particular mention is made of this one special case and, in any congregation, while it may be recorded that so many people came together, the special case that will be noted by the recording angel will be that of anyone who comes to Christ with his own personal distresses, and who thereby obtains relief from them: 'Behold, there came a leper' —

2-3 and worshipped him, saying, Lord, if thou wilt, thou canst make me clean. And Jesus put forth his hand, and touched him, saying, I will; be thou clean. And immediately his leprosy was cleansed.

His faith was not as strong as it might have been. There was an 'if' in it; but, still, it was genuine faith, and our loving Lord fixed his eye upon the faith rather than upon the flaw that was in it. And if he sees in you, dear friend, even a trembling faith, he will rejoice in it and bless you because of it. He will not withhold his blessing because you are not as strong in faith as you should be. Probably, you will have a greater blessing if you have greater faith; but even little faith gets great blessings from Christ. The leper said to him, 'If thou wilt, thou canst make me clean'; so Christ answered to the faith that he did possess, and touched him, saying, 'I will; be thou clean. And immediately his leprosy was cleansed.'

4-7 And Jesus saith unto him, See thou tell no man; but go thy way, shew thyself to the priest, and offer the gift that Moses commanded, for a testimony unto them. And when Jesus was entered into Capernaum, there came unto him a centurion, beseeching him, And saying, Lord, my servant lieth at home sick of the palsy, grievously tormented. And Jesus saith unto him, I will come and heal him.

He had not asked Christ to 'come and heal him'. He wished his servant to be healed, but he considered that it was too great an honour for Christ to come to him. I am not sure, but I think that this man's judgement is correct — that, for Christ to come to a man is better than for

81

healing to come to him. Indeed, brethren and sisters, all the gifts of Christ fall far short of himself. If he will but come, and abide with us, that means more than all else that he can bestow upon us.

8-9 The centurion answered and said, Lord, I am not worthy that thou shouldest come under my roof: but speak the word only, and my servant shall be healed. For I am a man under authority, having soldiers under me: and I say to this man, Go, and he goeth; and to another, Come, and he cometh; and to my servant, Do this, and he doeth it.

From his own power over his soldiers and servants, he argued that Christ must have at least equal power over all the forces of nature. And, as a centurion did not need to go and do everything himself, but gave his orders to his servant and he did it, so, surely, there could be no need for the great Commander to whom he was speaking to honour the sick man with his own personal presence. He had simply to utter the command and it would be obeyed, and the centurion's servant would be healed. Do you think this is an ingenious argument? It is so, certainly, but it is also a very plain and very forcible one. I have read or heard many ingenious arguments for unbelief, and I have often wished that half the ingenuity thus vainly spent could be exercised in discovering reasons for believing. So, I am pleased to notice that this commander of 100 Roman soldiers did but argue from his own position, and so wrought in his mind still greater confidence in Christ's power to heal his sick servant. Is there not something about yourself, from which, if you would look at it in the right light, you might gather arguments concerning the power of the Lord Jesus Christ?

10 When Jesus heard it, he marvelled, and said to them that followed, Verily I say unto you, I have not found so great faith, no, not in Israel.

'Not in Israel' — where the light and the knowledge were, there was not such faith as this centurion possessed. This Roman soldier, rough by training and experience, who was more familiar with stern fighting men than with those who could instruct him concerning Christ, had more faith than Jesus had so far found 'in Israel'.

11-12 And I say unto you, That many shall come from the east and west, and shall sit down with Abraham, and Isaac, and Jacob, in the kingdom of heaven. But the children of the kingdom shall be cast out into outer darkness: there shall be weeping and gnashing of teeth.

This is a strange thing, yet it is continually happening still, despite its strangeness. That the persons who are placed in such positions of privilege that you naturally expect that they would become believers, remain unbelievers, while others, who are placed at a terrible disadvantage, nevertheless often come right out from sin and right away from ignorance and become believers in Christ. Oh, that none of us who sit under the sound of the gospel from Sabbath to Sabbath might be sad illustrations of this truth, while others, unaccustomed to listening to the Word, may be happy instances of the way in which the Lord still takes strangers and adopts them into his family.

13 And Jesus said unto the centurion, Go thy way; and as thou hast believed, so be it done unto thee. And his servant was healed in the selfsame hour.

Jesus will treat all alike according to this rule: 'As thou hast believed, so be it done unto thee'. If thou canst believe great things *of* him, thou shalt receive great things *from* him. If thou dost think him good and great and mighty, thou shalt find him to be so. If thou canst conceive greater things of him than anyone else has ever done, thou shalt find him equal to all thy conceptions, and thy greatest faith shall be surpassed. It is a law of his kingdom, from which Christ never swerves: 'According to thy faith, be it unto thee.'

14-15 And when Jesus was come into Peter's house, he saw his wife's mother laid, and sick of a fever. And he touched her hand, and the fever left her: and she arose, and ministered unto them.

That was, perhaps, the most remarkable thing of all; for, when a fever is cured, it usually leaves great weakness behind it. Persons recovered of fever cannot immediately leave their bed and begin at once to attend to household matters, but Peter's wife's mother did this. Learn, hence, that the Lord Jesus can take away from us not only the disease of sin but all the effects of it as well. He can make the man who has been worn out in the service of Satan, to become young again in the service of the Lord; and when it seems as if we never, even if converted, could be of any use to him, he can take away the consequences of evil habits and make us into bright and sanctified believers. What is there that is impossible to him? In the olden time, kings claimed to have the power of healing with a touch. That was a superstition; but this King can do it! All glory to his blessed name! May he lay his gracious hand upon many of you; for, if it could heal before it was pierced, much more can it now heal every sin-stricken soul it touches.

16-18 When the even was come, they brought unto him many that were possessed with devils: and he cast out the spirits with his word, and healed all that were sick: That it might be fulfilled which was spoken by Esaias the prophet, saying, Himself took our infirmities, and bare our sicknesses. Now when Jesus saw great multitudes about him, he gave commandment to depart unto the other side.

For he neither loved nor courted popularity, but did his utmost to shun it. It followed him like his shadow, but he always went before it; he never followed it or sought after it: 'When Jesus saw great multitudes about him, he gave commandment to depart unto the other side.'

19 And a certain scribe came, and said unto him, Master, I will follow thee whithersoever thou goest.

How bold he is with his boasting! But Jesus knows that the fastest professors are often just as fast deserters, so he tests him before he takes him into the band of his followers.

20 And Jesus saith unto him, The foxes have holes, and the birds of the air have nests; but the Son of man hath not where to lay his head.

Christ means — 'Can you follow the Son of man when there is no reward except himself — not even a place for your head to rest upon, or a home wherein you may find comfort? Can you cleave to him when the lone mountainside shall be the place where he spends whole nights in prayer while the dew falls heavily upon him? Can you follow him then?' This is a test of love which makes many to be 'found wanting'.

21-22 And another of his disciples said unto him, Lord, suffer me first to go and bury my father. But Jesus said unto him, Follow me; and let the dead bury their dead.

It must be Christ first and father afterwards. We pay no disrespect to our dearest relatives and friends when we put them after Christ; that is their proper place. To put them before Christ, to prefer the creature to the Creator, is to be traitors to the King of kings. Whoever may come next, Christ must be first.

23-26 And when he was entered into a ship, his disciples followed him. And, behold, there arose a great tempest in the sea, insomuch that the ship was covered with the waves: but he was asleep. And his disciples came to him, and awoke him, saying, Lord, save us: we perish. And he saith unto them, Why are ye fearful, O ye of little faith? Then he arose, and rebuked the winds and the sea; and there was a great calm.

Probably no calm is so profound as that which follows the tempest of the soul which Jesus stills by his peace-speaking Word. The calm of nature, the calm of long-continued prosperity, the calm of an easy temper — these are all deceitful, and are apt to be broken by sudden and furious tempests. But, after the soul has been rent to its foundations — after the awful ground swell, and the Atlantic billows of deep temptation — when Jesus gives peace, there is 'a great calm'.

27 But the men marvelled, saying, What manner of man is this, that even the winds and the sea obey him!

We have often marvelled in the same way, but we know that it is not any 'manner of man' alone, but that he, who was truly man, who was also 'very God of very God', the God-man, the man Christ Jesus, the Mediator between God and men.

MATTHEW 8:1-27

Matt. 8:1-2 When he was come down from the mountain, great multitudes followed him. And, behold, there came a leper and worshipped him, —

Great multitudes often count for nothing; it is here or there one who

is the notable individual. There may be a great company come up outwardly to worship, but it is the soul that comes into contact with Christ
that is the most worthy of observation. There is no 'Behold!' when the
great multitudes are mentioned by Matthew; but there is a 'Behold!'
before the record of the leper coming to Christ: 'Behold, there came a
leper and worshipped him.' Let us all be of the leper's mind. Let us
worship Christ. Surely we may do so, if only out of gratitude for having
escaped from so dire a disease; but, inasmuch as, spiritually, by nature
that disease is upon us, we have good reason to come to Jesus as the
'leper came, and worshipped him' —

2-3 saying, Lord, if thou wilt, thou canst make me clean. And Jesus put forth his hand, and
touched him, saying, I will; be thou clean. And immediately his leprosy was cleansed.

Come, then, to Christ, even though your faith be very incomplete.
There may be, as there was with the leper, an 'if' about it, and an 'if'
about a very vital point, namely, concerning the Master's willingness,
but he will shut his eye to that imperfection and only look at that part
of your faith which is acceptable to him — that is, your faith in his
power. 'Thou canst make me clean', said the leper; and Christ dealt
with him upon the terms of that 'thou canst'. And as to the 'if thou
wilt', he blotted that out by saying, 'I will; be thou clean.' So, sinner,
come to Jesus, even though the doubting phrase 'if thou wilt' shall still
linger on thy lip. If the leprosy shall show itself even there, in thine
unbelief as to Christ's willingness to cleanse thee, yet come to him, and
he will say to thee, 'I will; be thou clean.' And it shall be with you as it
was with the leper: 'Immediately his leprosy was cleansed.'

4 And Jesus saith unto him, See thou tell no man; —

He will never say that to you, or to me; but while he was here on earth,
our Lord was very modest and retiring. He wished to conceal himself
as much as possible. He did not strive, nor cry, nor cause his voice to
be heard in the streets. He sets us an example of what true power is;

for true power does not flaunt itself before the eyes of men, or advertise itself at every corner of the street. Rather, it longs to conceal itself, being well aware that it will have all the publicity that is needful, for such wonders cannot be hid.

4 but go thy way, shew thyself to the priest, and offer the gift that Moses commanded, for a testimony unto them.

The man was to make his cleansing known in the legal way. Our Lord Jesus Christ was very scrupulous to observe the law while it still stood; and we also should take care not to observe that ceremonialism which has passed away, but diligently to keep that which still is of divine authority and of present force.

5 And when Jesus was entered into Capernaum, there came unto him a centurion, —

There came, doubtless, a great number of people when Jesus was entered into Capernaum, but Matthew does not mention them; yet he does say, 'There came unto him a centurion.' Notice how these individuals are brought out by the scriptural narrative — 'a leper' — 'a centurion'. May there not also be some here who will come to Jesus, and prove in their own persons, or in the persons of others for whom they shall pray, his power to bless and save? The Lord grant it!

5-8 beseeching him, And saying, Lord, my servant lieth at home sick of the palsy, grievously tormented. And Jesus saith unto him, I will come and heal him. The centurion answered and said, Lord, I am not worthy that thou shouldest come under my roof: —

What a blessed thing it is to have that sense of unworthiness! Some are very flippant in the expression of their piety; after they have heard half-a-dozen sermons, they attain to perfect holiness! I wish that they were half as deeply humbled, and knew half as much of themselves as this centurion did. 'Lord, I am not worthy.' That is a good lesson for anyone to learn. Still, when we can say, 'Lord, we are not worthy', do not let us therefore think that Christ may not come to us. Let us ask him to come whatever we may be, for our want of worthiness must not stint or limit the condescension of our divine Master. However, in this case, albeit that the centurion seemed almost to decline the privilege of having Christ come under his roof, yet he gave to Jesus high honour by believing in the power of his word even without his presence

8-9   but speak the word only, and my servant shall be healed. For I am a man under authority, —

He was, therefore, only a subordinate officer, for he was subject to his superiors.

9   having soldiers under me: and I say to this man, Go, and he goeth; and to another, Come, and he cometh; and to my servant, Do this, and he doeth it.

He left the Saviour to infer what he meant, namely, that Christ, who acted under the authority of God, could readily speak to palsies and fevers and say to them, 'Go', and they would go, just as quickly as a soldier would obey his officer's command. Brother, thou art a Christian, and thou hast known the Lord for twenty years — hast thou as much faith as this Roman centurion had? Dost thou believe that thy Master's word can remove sickness, that he can clear difficulties, that he can supply needs, that he can break bonds, that he can send, by whichsoever angel or man he chooses, whatsoever blessing he pleases? Oh, that we did all believe as truly as this man did!

10-12   When Jesus heard it, he marvelled, and said to them that followed, Verily I say unto you, I have not found so great faith, no, not in Israel. And I say unto you, That many shall come from the east and west, and shall sit down with Abraham, and Isaac, and Jacob, in the kingdom of heaven. But the children of the kingdom shall be cast out into outer darkness: there shall be weeping and gnashing of teeth.

Some of the rank outsiders shall be brought in by rich mercy, while others, piously trained, nursed at the very gates of the church, shall, nevertheless, for want of faith in Christ, be utterly cast away.

13   And Jesus said unto the centurion, Go thy way; and as thou hast believed, so be it done unto thee. And his servant was healed in the selfsame hour.

Oh! Pray for your friends, pray for your children, pray for your servants; and if you have faith like that of the centurion, according to your faith, so shall it be done unto you.

14-15 And when Jesus was come into Peter's house, he saw his wife's mother laid, and sick of a fever. And he touched her hand, and the fever left her: and she arose, and ministered unto them.

Peter had a wife, you see. Romanists say that he was the first pope, therefore the first pope had a wife; and, mark you, if other popes had had wives, there would not have been any declaration of infallibility, for there is no man who will believe himself to be infallible if he has someone near enough to remind him that he is not. But one evil usually goes with another; so it is recorded here that Peter had a wife as a kind of incidental rebuke of the sin of compulsory celibacy that was yet to be committed by priests and popes.

16 When the even was come, they brought unto him many that were possessed with devils: and he cast out the spirits with his word, and healed all that were sick:

Was not that centurion a kind of prophet? He had not long spoken about Christ's command over this man and that, before Christ had an opportunity of putting his words to the test. Jesus cast out devils and cast out sicknesses.

17 That it might be fulfilled which was spoken by Esaias the prophet, saying, Himself took our infirmities, and bare our sicknesses.

That is a singular quotation, and it teaches us that Christ has power to heal because he 'himself took our infirmities, and bare our sicknesses'. Am I not to understand from the connection here, that Jesus Christ's power is to be seen in his sufferings, in his humiliation and, especially, in his wounds and in his death? He would have had no power to meet our maladies if he had not himself been compassed with infirmities for our sake. O blessed Master, thou dost teach us where power lies — not in grandeur, but in self-sacrifice; not in personal glory, but in personal humiliation.

18-24 Now when Jesus saw great multitudes about him, he gave commandment to depart unto the other side. And a certain scribe came, and said unto him, Master, I will follow thee whithersoever thou goest. And Jesus saith unto him, The foxes have holes, and the birds of the air have nests; but the Son of man hath not where to lay his head. And another of his disciples said unto him, Lord, suffer me first to go and bury my father. But Jesus said unto him, Follow me; and let the dead bury their dead. And when he was entered into a ship, his disciples followed him. And, behold, there arose a great tempest in the sea, —

We may go where Christ goes, and yet we may get into danger. Never judge the rightness of your path by the providence which attends it. You may have safe sailing to the port of destruction, and you may have a rough voyage when you are bound for heaven. 'When he was entered into a ship, his disciples followed him. And, behold, there arose a great tempest in the sea' —

24 insomuch that the ship was covered with the waves: but he was asleep.

Weary with his toil, he lay down to rest. There was his humanity: serenely confident, and therefore sleeping through the storm. There was the glory of his innocence: 'He was asleep.' And there was also the majesty of his deity, only waiting for the moment when he should arise and still the tumult of the winds and waves.

25-27 And his disciples came to him, and awoke him, saying, Lord, save us: we perish. And he saith unto them, Why are ye fearful, O ye of little faith? Then he arose, and rebuked the winds and the sea; and there was a great calm. But the men marvelled, saying, What manner of man is this, that even the winds and the sea obey him!

Glory be to his blessed name! Amen.

MATTHEW 8:23 – 9:13

Matthew's Gospel is the Gospel of the Kingdom and of the King. Here you see the King amid the storms of nature.

Matt. 8:23-24 And when he was entered into a ship, his disciples followed him. And, behold, there arose a great tempest in the sea, insomuch that the ship was covered with the waves: but he was asleep.

In the quiet confidence of faith, resting upon his God.

25-26 And his disciples came to him, and awoke him, saying, Lord, save us: we perish. And he saith unto them, Why are ye fearful, O ye of little faith? Then he arose, and rebuked the winds and the sea; and there was a great calm.

As great a calm as there had been tempest. After great trouble, expect deep, delightful rest and peace, if you are a child of God.

27 But the men marvelled, saying, What manner of man is this, that even the winds and the sea obey him!

Now see the King in conflict with the powers of darkness.

28-31 And when he was come to the other side into the country of the Gergesenes, there met him two possessed with devils, coming out of the tombs, exceeding fierce, so that no man might pass by that way. And, behold, they cried out, saying, What have we to do with thee, Jesus, thou Son of God? art thou come hither to torment us before the time? And there was a good way off from them an herd of many swine feeding. So the devils besought him, —

How the demons crouched at his feet! The dogs of hell knew the power of his tongue; that was a whip whose lash they had felt before.

31-32 saying, If thou cast us out, suffer us to go away into the herd of swine. And he said unto them, Go. —

He never wastes words on demons.

32-34 And when they were come out, they went into the herd of swine: and, behold, the whole herd of swine ran violently down a steep place into the sea, and perished in the waters. And they that kept them fled, and went their ways into the city, and told every thing, and what was befallen to the possessed of the devils. And, behold, the whole city came out to meet Jesus: and when they saw him, they besought him that he would depart out of their coasts.

A sad prayer; yet Jesus granted their request. Men may once too often ask the Holy Spirit to depart from them. They may grieve him once more, and then he will have done with them for ever. Now we shall see the King in conflict with the diseases of mankind, and with human sin.

Matt. 9:1-2 And he entered into a ship, and passed over, and came into his own city. And, behold, they brought to him a man sick of the palsy, lying on a bed: and Jesus seeing their faith —

The faith of the bearers, and the faith of the palsied man himself —

2 said unto the sick of the palsy; Son, be of good cheer; thy sins be forgiven thee.

It was remarked, by a mediaeval writer, that we do not find Christ calling any of the apostles, not even the very chief of them, by the name that he gave to this palsied man, 'Son'. This is the title that he gives to a sin-sick sinner, lying on a bed before him, waiting to be healed. Oh, the tenderness of Christ to sin and misery! He puts a kind of sonship upon this man which he had not possessed before.

3 And, behold, certain of the scribes said within themselves, This man blasphemeth.

'He arrogates to himself the prerogative of God. Who can forgive sins but God only?'

4-8 And Jesus knowing their thoughts said, Wherefore think ye evil in your hearts? For whether is easier, to say, Thy sins be forgiven thee; or to say, Arise, and walk? But that ye may know that the Son of man hath power on earth to forgive sins, (then saith he to the sick of the palsy,) Arise, take up thy bed, and go unto thine house. And he arose, and departed to his house. But when the multitudes saw it, they marvelled, and glorified God, which had given such power unto men.

They rightly saw in this miracle, wrought by Christ, power given to man. For, as you observe, Christ said, 'The Son of man hath power on earth to forgive sins'; and these people magnified God that one Man should have such power granted to him. There is an elevation to the whole of manhood in the alliance of Christ with it; through him the Lord hath given great power unto men.

9 And as Jesus passed forth from thence, —

The King is now going to show his power over the human will.

9 he saw a man, named Matthew, sitting at the receipt of custom: and he saith unto him, Follow me. And he arose, and followed him.

Everything bows before him. Is he not King of kings, and Lord of lords? Have we ever comprehended the true measure of his divine and human nature? Even when he was on earth, and known as the Son of man, what gleams of his divine glory shone forth in these truly royal acts of his! Yet how condescending was our King! Where is his court? Who are his attendants? Listen —

10   And it came to pass, as Jesus sat at meat in the house, behold, many publicans and sinners came and sat down with him and his disciples.

Lord of the sea. Conqueror of demons. Healer of the sick. Forgiver of sin. And now he has for his company publicans and sinners! When the Pharisees saw it, they did not see condescension in it, but they saw wickedness in it.

11   And when the Pharisees saw it, they said unto his disciples, Why eateth your Master with publicans and sinners?

Ah! why, indeed? You and I know; that is a secret that has made us love him better than almost anything beside.

12   But when Jesus heard that, he said unto them, They that be whole need not a physician, but they that are sick.

He has come here on purpose that he might heal our sicknesses. Oh, you who feel tonight sick with sin and sick of sin, come and sit down with him! He adds, 'Him that cometh to me, I will in no wise cast out'. And he will not cast you out, notwithstanding your sinnership, if you come unto him by faith.

13   But go ye and learn what that meaneth, I will have mercy, and not sacrifice: for I am not come to call the righteous, but sinners to repentance.

Let us never forget that Jesus is the sinner's Saviour. He does not come to save saints; he comes to save sinners, and the saints who are saved are kept from becoming sinners by his almighty love.

May God bless this reading of the Scriptures to us! Amen.

MATTHEW 9:1-17

Matt. 9:1-2 And he entered into a ship, and passed over, and came into his own city. And, behold, they brought to him a man sick of the palsy, lying on a bed: and Jesus seeing their faith said unto the sick of the palsy; Son, be of good cheer; thy sins be forgiven thee.

Our Lord dealt first with the greater evil, for sin is worse than even such a dreadful disease as the palsy. Forgiveness of sin is an even greater mercy than the healing of sickness.

3-7 And, behold, certain of the scribes said within themselves, This man blasphemeth. And Jesus knowing their thoughts said, Wherefore think ye evil in your hearts? For whether is easier, to say, Thy sins be forgiven thee; or to say, Arise, and walk? But that ye may know that the Son of man hath power on earth to forgive sins, (then saith he to the sick of the palsy,) Arise, take up thy bed, and go unto thine house. And he arose, and departed to his house.

Jesus first proved his divinity by reading the secret thoughts of the caviling scribes, and then gave a further evidence of it by working this very notable miracle.

8-9 But when the multitudes saw it, they marvelled, and glorified God, which had given such power unto men. And as Jesus passed forth from thence, he saw a man, named Matthew, sitting at the receipt of custom: and he saith unto him, Follow me. And he arose, and followed him.

This was another notable miracle, and equally set forth the power of divine grace.

10-11 And it came to pass, as Jesus sat at meat in the house, behold, many publicans and sinners came and sat down with him and his disciples. And when the Pharisees saw it, they said unto his disciples, Why eateth your Master with publicans and sinners?

He was more at home with publicans and sinners than with scribes and Pharisees, and they were more likely to welcome him as their Lord and Saviour.

12-13 But when Jesus heard that, he said unto them, They that be whole need not a physician, but they that are sick. But go ye and learn what that meaneth, I will have mercy, and not sacrifice: for I am not come to call the righteous, but sinners to repentance.

If he had come to call the righteous, where would he have found them? His call was not likely to be heeded by the self-righteous, but sinners heard it with joy and so were made righteous by him.

14 Then came to him the disciples of John, saying, Why do we and the Pharisees fast oft, but thy disciples fast not?

We must not suppose that, because a thing is proper for ourselves, it must therefore be binding upon everybody else. It might be fit and right that the disciples of John should fast often, their circumstances might require it; but it might be quite wrong for the disciples of Christ to fast, as they might be in very different circumstances.

15   And Jesus said unto them, Can the children of the bridechamber mourn, as long as the bridegroom is with them? —

Could Christ's disciples fast while Christ fed them with heavenly foods? While his presence was to them like heaven begun below, it would have been inconsistent for them to be mourning and fasting.

15   but the days will come, when the bridegroom shall be taken from them, and then shall they fast.

And nobody would say that they were turncoats if, when their circumstances had so greatly altered, they acted in harmony with their changed circumstances. The disciples could not mourn while Christ was with them; can you, believer, fast while Christ is with you? It cannot be; but when he has gone from you, then you will sorrow fast enough. So we must neither judge others by ourselves nor judge ourselves at one time by what we were at some other time.

16   No man putteth a piece of new cloth unto an old garment, for that which is put in to fill it up taketh from the garment, —

When it shrinks —

16   and the rent is made worse.

There must be a fitness about things; do not impose fasting upon a joyful heart, or the singing of joyful hymns upon a sad spirit.

17   Neither do men put new wine into old bottles: else the bottles break, and the wine runneth out, and the bottles perish: but they put new wine into new bottles, and both are preserved.

Do not expect from a young beginner that which would be unsuitable to him, even though it should be most comely and seemly in an aged Christian; and do not expect to see in an aged Christian all the vigour and alertness of spirit that you look for in ardent souls in all the fervour of their first love to Christ. Let us mind the relations of things.

MATTHEW 9

Matt. 9:1 And he entered into a ship, and passed over, and came into his own city.

Our Lord had given these Gergesenes an opportunity of becoming his disciples, the kingdom of God had come very near to them, but as they accounted themselves unworthy of it and besought him to depart out of their coasts, he did not force himself upon them. Take heed, dear friends, if you do but hear the gospel once, that you do not reject it, for you may never have the opportunity of hearing it again.

2 And, behold, they brought to him a man sick of the palsy, lying on a bed: and Jesus seeing their faith said unto the sick of the palsy; Son, be of good cheer; thy sins be forgiven thee.

He saw the faith of the one man who was brought to him, and also the faith of the four bearers who had let him down through the roof.

3-4 And, behold, certain of the scribes said within themselves, This man blasphemeth. And Jesus knowing their thoughts said, Wherefore think ye evil in your hearts?

His knowledge of the thoughts of their hearts ought to have convinced them that he was divine and that therefore he had the right to forgive sins. They were not, however, in a condition to learn anything, for they thought that they already knew everything.

5 For whether is easier, to say, Thy sins be forgiven thee; or to say, Arise, and walk?

Each of these actions needed divine power; but divinity being present, there was no difference as to the manifestation of this power between the forgiveness of sins and the healing of sickness.

6-7 But that ye may know that the Son of man hath power on earth to forgive sins, (then saith he to the sick of the palsy,) Arise, take up thy bed, and go unto thine house. And he arose, and departed to his house.

Carrying the mattress whereon he had lain. Would he keep that bed stored, think you, for a memorial? Or if he used it in future to sleep upon would he not by night upon his bed wake up and praise the Lord for what he had done for him? I think that we should treasure up in our memory the deeds of Christ on our behalf, if indeed we know his great salvation. I should not wonder if there is a mattress that you have somewhere at home, a bed, or a book, or something with which there is connected the remembrance of some deed of infinite love and almighty grace.

8 But when the multitudes saw it, they marvelled, and glorified God, which had given such power unto men.

They did not think deeply enough and go really to the bottom of the matter, but they concluded that it was a wonderful thing that any man — that any *men*, as they put it — should have such power given unto them.

9 And as Jesus passed forth from thence, he saw a man, named Matthew, sitting at the receipt of custom: —

Notice how Matthew describes himself: 'As Jesus passed forth from thence, he saw a man, named Matthew, sitting at the receipt of custom.'

9 and he saith unto him, Follow me. And he arose, and followed him.

See how everything is obedient to Christ. Paralysis leaves the palsied man, and hardness of heart departs from the tax-gatherer.

10 And it came to pass, as Jesus sat at meat in the house, behold, many publicans and sinners came and sat down with him and his disciples.

Note the modesty of these early recorders: Matthew does not say that it was his own house where this gathering took place, nor that he was the giver of the feast. Mark and Luke supply this information.

11-13 And when the Pharisees saw it, they said unto his disciples, Why eateth your Master with publicans and sinners? But when Jesus heard that, he said unto them, They that be whole need not a physician, but they that are sick. But go ye and learn what that meaneth, I will have mercy, and not sacrifice: —

God prefers the doing of good to all outward ritual and ordinances, even the best of them: 'I will have mercy, and not sacrifice.'

13-22 for I am not come to call the righteous, but sinners to repentance. Then came to him the disciples of John, saying, Why do we and the Pharisees fast oft, but thy disciples fast not? And Jesus said unto them, Can the children of the bridechamber mourn, as long as the bridegroom is with them? but the days will come, when the bridegroom shall be taken from them, and then shall they fast. No man putteth a piece of new cloth unto an old garment, for that which is put in to fill it up taketh from the garment, and the rent is made worse. Neither do men put new wine into old bottles: else the bottles break, and the wine runneth out, and the bottles perish: but they put new wine into new bottles, and both are preserved. While he spake these things unto them, behold, there came a certain ruler, and worshipped him, saying, My daughter is even now dead: but come and lay thy hand upon her, and she shall live. And Jesus arose, and followed him, and so did his disciples. And, behold, a woman, which was diseased with an issue of blood twelve years, came behind him, and touched the hem of his garment: For she said within herself, If I may but touch his garment, I shall be whole. But Jesus turned him about, and when he saw her, he said, Daughter, be of good comfort; thy faith hath made thee whole. And the woman was made whole from that hour.

See how he scatters mercy all around. He is charged to the full with the divine electricity of health, and whoever comes in his way gets a blessing. Oh, for the presence of that full and overflowing Christ in the midst of every worshipping assembly, for there are still many sick folk who need a Saviour as much as these people did in the days of Jesus!

23 And when Jesus came into the ruler's house, and saw the minstrels and the people making a noise,

They were gathered together for the funeral of this young girl.

24 He said unto them, Give place: for the maid is not dead, but sleepeth. And they laughed him to scorn.

They did not understand his expression; yet, apparently, sleep only differs from death in this respect, that the sleeper wakes again, and returns to consciousness. The Lord Jesus Christ did not mean that the maiden was not dead; but he meant that, as she was soon coming to life again, it was, as it were, only like the image of death. To her, death was not a cul-de-sac, a dark cave without an opening at the further end; it was rather a tunnel through which she was passing back again into life.

25-26 But when the people were put forth, he went in, and took her by the hand, and the maid arose. And the fame hereof went abroad into all that land.

And well it might; this was the marvel of marvels that he should even raise the dead.

27 And when Jesus departed thence, two blind men followed him, crying, and saying, Thou son of David, have mercy on us.

See, my brethren, how miracle follows upon miracle, how the way of Christ is, as it were, paved with mercy upon mercy.

28 And when he was come into the house, the blind men came to him: and Jesus saith unto them, Believe ye that I am able to do this? —

It is a great thing to have faith about the particular point that most concerns us: 'Believe ye that I am able to do this?' Some can believe everything except the one thing for which faith is most needed.

28 They said unto him, Yea, Lord.

Can you, dear friend, say, 'Yes, Lord', about yourself?

29-31 Then touched he their eyes, saying, According to your faith be it unto you. And their eyes were opened; and Jesus straitly charged them, saying, See that no man know it. But they, when they were departed, spread abroad his fame in all that country.

This was very wrong of them, for they ought to have obeyed Christ's orders. They were doing much mischief, although, no doubt, they thought they were doing good. The Saviour, first of all, was modest and did not wish his cures reported. In the next place, he wanted to have an opportunity of doing more good, and the reporting of this cure brought him immense crowds who encumbered him and also excited the animosity of the Pharisees, who would the more persecute him. Moreover, our Lord did not wish the Pharisees to think that he cured people that they might simply advertise him. I do think that we often err in imagining that making known every little thing that happens, and even every great thing, is the best course to pursue. There is a way of walking in wisdom towards them that are without, and Christ knew that way; and these blind men whose eyes he had opened should not have disobeyed him.

32 As they went out, behold, they brought to him a dumb man possessed with a devil.

'As they went out'. Do notice what a succession of mercies Christ dispersed; it was a sort of tempest of blessing, peal upon peal, following almost without intermission.

33-34 And when the devil was cast out, the dumb spake: and the multitudes marvelled, saying, It was never so seen in Israel. But the Pharisees said, He casteth out devils through the prince of the devils.

How does Christ answer this wicked taunt?

35 And Jesus went about all the cities and villages, teaching in their synagogues, and preaching the gospel of the kingdom, and healing every sickness and every disease among the people.

That is the best answer to give to cavillers, do more good than ever. There is no stopping the barking of dogs, so go you on your way; as the moon shines, let the hounds bay as they may. Oh, the glory of the Master! Like a cloud that dispenses showers of blessing wherever it moves, so did he continue to do his life-work.

36-38 But when he saw the multitudes, he was moved with compassion on them, because they fainted, and were scattered abroad, as sheep having no shepherd. Then saith he unto his disciples, The harvest truly is plenteous, but the labourers are few; Pray ye therefore the Lord of the harvest, that he will send forth labourers into his harvest.

Or, 'that he will *thrust* forth labourers into his harvest'. He who does the most is always the one who wants to see more done. This blessed Christ, with his hands so full of holy work, is the one who bows his knee, and cries to the great Lord of the harvest to thrust forth labourers into his harvest. Let us imitate him both in the working and in the praying.

MATTHEW 9:27-38

Matt. 9:27-28 And when Jesus departed thence, two blind men followed him, crying, and saying, Thou son of David, have mercy on us. And when he was come into the house, —

I suppose the house at Capernaum, where he was wont to stay.

28 the blind men came to him: —

Forced their way in. They must be attended to. Hunger breaks through stone walls, they say, and an earnest heart will follow after what it seeks.

28-29 and Jesus saith unto them, Believe ye that I am able to do this? They said unto him, Yea, Lord. Then touched he their eyes, saying, According to your faith be it unto you.

That is, 'If you do not believe, you shall not see, but if there be faith in you, behold you shall have sight.'

30-32 And their eyes were opened; and Jesus straitly charged them, saying, See that no man know it. But they, when they were departed, spread abroad his fame in all that country. As they went out, behold, they brought to him a dumb man possessed with a devil.

Here we have had the dead, those that were bleeding to death, the blind, and the dumb, and the possessed of a devil.

33 And when the devil was cast out, the dumb spake: and the multitudes marvelled, saying, It was never so seen in Israel.

No, but Jesus does wonders. Something off the common, and altogether out of the ordinary way, his work of grace must be.

34 But the Pharisees said, He casteth out devils through the prince of the devils.

There is always somebody or other who has got an ugly word to put in. It matters not how much God may bless the gospel, there is no stopping the sneers and objections, but the mercy is that it does not matter much. Our Lord was not hurt, and the work went on, notwithstanding all the cavilling of the Pharisees.

35 And Jesus went about all the cities and villages, teaching in their synagogues, and preaching the gospel of the kingdom, and healing every sickness and every disease among the people.

That was the answer to the Pharisees. Christian activity, fervent devotion to the cause of God, is the best answer that can be given to cavillers of any sort or every sort. In your work hold on, my brother, and those who cavil at thee now may come to honour thee one of these days.

36-37 But when he saw the multitudes, he was moved with compassion on them, because they fainted, and were scattered abroad, as sheep having no shepherd. Then saith he unto his disciples, The harvest truly is plenteous, but the labourers are few;

We are all loiterers, but where are the labourers? Where are they with the sharp sickle that can cut down the wheat and, with a ready hand, can bind it and, with a strong shoulder, carry it? Alas! in this great city, the harvest truly is plenteous, but the labourers are few!

38 Pray ye therefore the Lord of the harvest, that he will send forth labourers into his harvest.

MATTHEW 10:1-27

Matt. 10:1-4 And when he had called unto him his twelve disciples, he gave them power against unclean spirits, to cast them out, and to heal all manner of sickness and all manner of disease. Now the names of the twelve apostles are these; The first, Simon, who is called Peter, and Andrew his brother; James the son of Zebedee, and John his brother; Philip, and Bartholomew; Thomas, and Matthew the publican; James the son of Alphaeus, and Lebbaeus, whose surname was Thaddaeus; Simon the Canaanite, and Judas Iscariot, who also betrayed him.

The lesson to be learned from these names are, first, that these men are mentioned in couples, and I think that, as a rule, God's servants work best in pairs. In other senses than the matrimonial one, it is not good that man should be alone. Moses needs Aaron; Peter needs Andrew; James needs John. It is well to be of such a temperament and disposition that you can work harmoniously with another of your Lord's servants. If ye cannot, pray God to alter you. Notice that expression, in the third verse, 'and Bartholomew'. I think there is not a single instance in the New Testament where Bartholomew is mentioned without the word 'and' before or after his name — 'and Bartholomew' or 'Bartholomew and' someone else. Perhaps he was not a man who ever began any work by himself, but he was a grand man to join in and help it on when somebody else had started it. So, dear friend, if you are not qualified to be a leader in the church of Christ, be willing to be number two; but do serve the Master, in some capacity or other, with all your might. Be a brother who carries an 'and' with him wherever he goes; be like a horse, that has his harness on and is ready to be hooked into the team. That is the lesson of the two words 'and Bartholomew'. The last lesson from the names is at the end of the fourth verse: 'and Judas Iscariot, who also betrayed him'. He preached of Christ, he worked miracles in the name of Christ, he was ordained as one of the apostles of Christ, yet he was 'the son of perdition'. Oh! let none of us be content merely with our official position, or trust in the good which we hope we have done, or in any gifts with which the Master has entrusted us. Judas Iscariot had all these marks of distinction, yet he betrayed his Lord. God grant that no one among us may turn out to be a Judas Iscariot!

5-6 These twelve Jesus sent forth, and commanded them, saying, Go not into the way of the Gentiles, and into any city of the Samaritans enter ye not: But go rather to the lost sheep of the house of Israel.

The gospel is now to be preached to every creature in all the world; but, in those days, it was to be proclaimed first to the Jews, then to the Samaritans, and afterwards to the Gentiles as a whole. The largeness of our commission to 'preach the gospel to every creature' need not prevent our following providential directions to make it known in one place rather than in another. It is well for the servants of Christ always to ask their Master where they are to go. You know how it is recorded, in the Acts of the Apostles, that Paul and Silas 'assayed to go into Bithynia: but the Spirit suffered them not' [Acts 16:7]. Ask the Lord, therefore, where thou shalt work, as well as what thy work shall be, for thy Master knows how thou canst best serve him.

7 And as ye go, preach, saying, The kingdom of heaven is at hand.

That blessed kingdom, which is now set up among men, of which Christ is the King, and I hope many of us are the subjects. That kingdom was then 'at hand'.

8 Heal the sick, cleanse the lepers, raise the dead, cast out devils: freely ye have received, freely give.

'Exercise your healing arts most freely. They cost you nothing; let them not cost anything to those who receive the benefit of them.'

9-10 Provide neither gold, nor silver, nor brass in your purses, Nor scrip for your journey, neither two coats, neither shoes, nor yet staves: for the workman is worthy of his meat.

They were to 'quarter on the enemy', as we say. Wherever they went, they would be furnished with food and raiment and shelter, if they faithfully executed the commission with which their Master had entrusted them.

11-13 And into whatsoever city or town ye shall enter, inquire who in it is worthy; and there abide till ye go thence. And when ye come into an house, salute it. And if the house be worthy, let your peace come upon it: but if it be not worthy, let your peace return to you.

How about your houses, dear friends. Are they 'worthy' houses, in this New Testament sense? If an apostle came there, could he bring 'peace' to it? Or would he have to take the peace away with him to some other house that was more worthy to receive it?

14-15 And whosoever shall not receive you, nor hear your words, when ye depart out of that house or city, shake off the dust of your feet. Verily I say unto you, It shall be more tolerable for the land of Sodom and Gomorrha in the day of judgment, than for that city.

Despised and rejected privileges make the fiercest fuel for the fires of hell. They who might have heard the gospel, and would not hear it, shall find the hand of God more heavy upon them than it will be even upon the accursed Sodomites. Woe, then, unto such as live in London, yet who will not hear the Word of the Lord, or, when they do hear it, will not accept it!

16-17 Behold, I send you forth as sheep in the midst of wolves: be ye therefore wise as serpents, and harmless as doves. But beware of men: —

'Do not trust yourselves with them'.

17-19 for they will deliver you up to the councils, and they will scourge you in their synagogues; And ye shall be brought before governors and kings for my sake, for a testimony against them and the Gentiles. But when they deliver you up, take no thought how or what ye shall speak: for it shall be given you in that same hour what ye shall speak.

'Let it not fret you that you are not orators, that you are not men of culture; speak what God the Holy Spirit shall teach you to say, and leave the result with him.'

20 For it is not ye that speak, but the Spirit of your Father which speaketh in you.

Oh! That is grand — when a man has so communed with God that the very Spirit of the Father has entered into him. Then shall there be a wondrous power about his speech; men may not understand whence it came, but they will be obliged to feel the force of it.

21   And the brother shall deliver up the brother to death, and the father the child: and the children shall rise up against their parents, and cause them to be put to death.

Read the martyrologies, and see whether it was not exactly as our Lord foretold that it would be. In martyr times, men often burst all the bonds of natural affection, and betrayed even their own fathers or children to death. Yet the saints quaffed not; they were content to let every earthly tie be snapped so that the tie of their heavenly and eternal relationship might be confirmed. So may it be with us also!

22-27   And ye shall be hated of all men for my name's sake: but he that endureth to the end shall be saved. But when they persecute you in this city, flee ye into another: for verily I say unto you, Ye shall not have gone over the cities of Israel, till the Son of man be come. The disciple is not above his master, nor the servant above his lord. It is enough for the disciple that he be as his master, and the servant as his lord. If they have called the master of the house Beelzebub, how much more shall they call them of his household? Fear them not therefore: for there is nothing covered, that shall not be revealed; and hid, that shall not be known. What I tell you in darkness, that speak ye in light: and what ye hear in the ear, that preach ye upon the housetops.

God help us so to do, for Christ's sake! Amen.

MATTHEW 10:16-23

Matt. 10:16   Behold, I send you forth as sheep in the midst of wolves: be ye therefore wise as serpents, and harmless as doves.

It is a strange errand that you are sent upon — not as dogs to fight with the wolves. Yet you are to fight with them, but you are to go as lambs in the midst of wolves. Expect, therefore, that they will rend you. Bear much, for ever confident in that you shall conquer. If they kill you, you shall be honoured in your death. As I have often said, the fight looks very unequal between sheep and wolves, yet at the present moment there are vastly more sheep in the world than wolves, the sheep having outlived the wolves. In this country at any rate, the last wolf is gone, and the sheep, with all their weaknesses, continue to multiply. 'That is due', you say, 'to the Shepherd.' And to him shall your safety and your victory be due. He will take care of you. 'I send you forth as sheep among wolves.' But do not, therefore, provoke the wolves. 'Be wise as serpents.' Have a holy prudence. 'Be as harmless as doves', but not as silly as doves

17-19 But beware of men: for they will deliver you up to the councils, and they will scourge you in their synagogues; And ye shall be brought before governors and kings for my sake, for a testimony against them and the Gentiles. But when they deliver you up, take no thought how or what ye shall speak: for it shall be given you in that same hour what ye shall speak.

And very remarkable were the answers given by the martyrs to those who persecuted them. In some cases they were altogether unlettered men, feeble women, unused to the quibbles and the catches which ungodly wise men use, and yet with his holy ability they answered all their adversaries and often stopped their mouths. It is wonderful what God can make of the weakest of men when he dwelleth in them, and speaks through them.

20-21 For it is not ye that speak, but the Spirit of your Father which speaketh in you. And the brother shall deliver up the brother to death, and the father the child: and the children shall rise up against their parents, and cause them to be put to death.

Strange venom of human nature. It never grows so angry against anything as against God's truth. Why is this? False religions will tolerate one another but they will not tolerate the religion of Christ. Is not this all accounted for by that old dark saying at the gates of Eden, 'I will put enmity between thee and the woman; and between thy seed and her seed' [Genesis 3:15]. That enmity is sure to come up as long as the world stands.

22-23 And ye shall be hated of all men for my name's sake: but he that endureth to the end shall be saved. But when they persecute you in this city, flee ye into another: for verily I say unto you, Ye shall not have gone over the cities of Israel, till the Son of man be come.

They had not been able to get all through Palestine before the destruction of Jerusalem. Perhaps we shall scarcely have been able to preach the gospel in every part of the world before our Master's speedy footsteps shall be heard.

MATTHEW 10:24-42

Our Lord had been sending forth his twelve apostles to preach the gospel of the kingdom, and to work miracles in his name. Having given them their commission, he warned them of the treatment they must expect to receive, and then fortified their minds against the persecutions they would have to endure.

Matt. 10:24-25 The disciple is not above his master, nor the servant above his lord. It is enough for the disciple that he be as his master, and the servant as his lord. If they have called the master of the house Beelzebub, how much more shall they call them of his household?

The name Beelzebub, or Beelzebul, meaning the god of filth, or as some say, the god of flies, was applied by the Jews to the very worst of the evil spirits. They supposed that there were some devils worse than others, and the very head and master of them all they called Beelzebub — and now they supplied this title to our Lord Jesus himself. Well then, if men should give us ill names and evil characters, need we marvel? Shall Christ be spit upon and despised, and shall you and I be honoured and exalted? You have heard of Godfrey de Bouillon, the Crusader, who entered Jerusalem in triumph but who refused to have a golden crown put upon his head because he said he never would be crowned with gold where Christ was crowned with thorns. So do you expect to be honoured in the world where your Lord was crucified?

26 Fear them not therefore: for there is nothing covered, that shall not be revealed; and hid, that shall not be known.

'They will misrepresent you, slander you, and speak evil of you; but if your good name be covered up now, it shall be revealed one of these days, perhaps in this life; but if not in this life, certainly at the day of judgement, when the secrets of all hearts shall be made known.' It really is marvellous how sometimes in this life, misrepresented men suddenly obtain a refutation of their calumniators (or slanderers), and then it seems as if the world would serve them as the Greeks did their successful runners or wrestlers when they lifted them upon their shoulders and carried them in triumph.

27 What I tell you in darkness, that speak ye in light: and what ye hear in the ear, that preach ye upon the housetops.

This is what we are to preach, what Christ tells us, and this is how we are to get the matter of our discourses, be alone with Christ, let him talk to us in the darkness, in the quietude of the closet where we commune with him in prayer. Then this is where we are to preach, 'upon the housetops'. We cannot literally do this here in this land upon our slanting roofs, but in the East, 'the housetops' were the most public places in the city, and all of them flat, so that anyone proclaiming anything from the housetops would be sure of an audience, and especially at certain times of the day. Preach ye, then, ye servants of God, in the most public places of the land. Wherever there are people to hear, let there not be any lack of tongues to speak for God.

28 And fear not them which kill the body, but are not able to kill the soul: but rather fear him which is able to destroy both soul and body in hell.

A philosopher — Anaxarchus, I think it was — was wont to say when a certain tyrant had threatened to kill him, 'You cannot kill me; you may crush this body, but you cannot touch Anaxarchus.' So fear not those who cannot kill the soul. If that be safe, you are safe. Even Seneca frequently asserted that it was not in the power of any man to hurt a good philosopher, 'for', said he, 'even death is gain to such a man'; and certainly it is so to the Christian. For him to die is indeed gain. But oh! fear that God who can destroy the soul, for then the body also is destroyed with a terrible and tremendous destruction: 'fear him'.

29-30 Are not two sparrows sold for a farthing? and one of them shall not fall on the ground without your Father. But the very hairs of your head are all numbered.

So, then, God takes more care of us than we take of ourselves. You never heard of a man who numbered the hairs of his head. Men number their sheep and their cattle, but the Christian is so precious in God's esteem that he takes care of the meanest parts of his frame, and numbers even the hairs of his head.

31-32 Fear ye not therefore, ye are of more value than many sparrows. Whosoever therefore shall confess me before men, him will I confess also before my Father which is in heaven.

What a glorious promise is this! 'I will confess him to have been bought with my blood. I will confess him to have been my faithful follower and friend. I will confess him to be my brother, and in so doing I will favour him with a share of my glory.' Have you confessed Christ before men? If you have trusted him as your Saviour, but have not publicly professed your faith in him, however sincere you may be, you are living in the neglect of a known duty, and you cannot expect to have this promise fulfilled to you if you do not keep the condition that is appended to it. Christ's promise is to confess those who confess him. Be ye then, avowedly on the Lord's side. 'Come out from among them, and be ye separate, saith the Lord' [2 Corinthians 6:17]. Without the camp the Saviour suffered, and without the camp must his disciples follow him, bearing his reproach.

33 But whosoever shall deny me before men, him will I also deny before my Father which is in heaven.

Not to confess Christ is practically to deny him; not to follow him is to go away from him; not to be with him is to be against him. Looking at this matter of confessing Christ in that light, there is cause for solemn self-examination by all who regard themselves as his disciples.

34 Think not that I am come to send peace on earth: I came not to send peace, but a sword.

Do not misunderstand the Saviour's words. Christ's usually spoke in a very plain manner, and plainness is not always compatible with guardedness. Christ did come to make peace — this is the ultimate end of his mission. But for the present, Christ did not come to make peace. Wherever Christianity comes, it causes a quarrel, because the light must always quarrel with the darkness, and sin can never be friendly with righteousness. It is not possible that honesty should live in peace with theft; it cannot be that there should be harmony between God's servants and the servants of the devil. In this sense, then, understand our Saviour's words.

35-36 For I am come to set a man at variance against his father, and the daughter against her mother, and the daughter in law against her mother in law. And a man's foes shall be they of his own household.

This is always the case, and I suppose will be to the end of the chapter. Whenever true religion comes into a man's heart and life, those who are without the grace of God, however near and dear they may be to him, will be sure to oppose him.

37-39 He that loveth father or mother more than me is not worthy of me: and he that loveth son or daughter more than me is not worthy of me. And he that taketh not his cross, and followeth after me, is not worthy of me. He that findeth his life shall lose it: and he that loseth his life for my sake shall find it.

In the days of the martyrs, one man was brought before the judges, and through fear of the flames he recanted and denied the faith. He went home, and before the year was ended his own house caught fire, and he was miserably consumed in it, having had to suffer quite as much pain as he would have had to endure for Christ's sake but having no consolation in it. He found his life, yet he lost it. Now, in a higher degree, all who, to save themselves, shun the cross of Christ, only run into the fire to escape from the sparks. They shall suffer more than they would otherwise have done; but whosoever is willing to give up every-thing for Christ shall learn that no man is ever really a loser by Christ in the long run. Sooner or later, if not in this life, certainly in the next, the Lord will abundantly make up to every man all that he has ever suffered for his sake. Now comes a very delightful passage —

40 He that receiveth you receiveth me, and he that receiveth me receiveth him that sent me.

When, therefore, you are kind to the poor, when you help the people of God in their difficulties and necessities, you are really helping Christ in the person of his poor but faithful followers.

41 He that receiveth a prophet in the name of a prophet —

That is, not as a gentleman nor merely as a man nor as a talented indi-vidual, but as a prophet of God.

41 shall receive a prophet's reward; and he that receiveth a righteous man in the name of a righteous man shall receive a righteous man's reward.

Just the same reward which God gives to prophets and righteous men, he will give to those who receive them in the name of a prophet or of a righteous man. A prophet's reward must be something great, and such shall be the reward of those who generously receive the servants of God.

42 And whosoever shall give to drink unto one of these little ones a cup of cold water only in the name of a disciple, verily I say unto you, he shall in no wise lose his reward.

There have been times, even in our own country when to give 'a cup of cold water' has been to run the risk of suffering death. In the dark days of persecution, some who were called heretics were driven out into the fields in the depth of winter to perish by the cold, the king's subjects being forbidden, upon pain of death, to give them anything either to eat or to drink. Now, in such a case as that, giving 'a cup of cold water' would mean far more than if you or I simply gave a cup of water to someone who happened to be thirsty, but our Lord Jesus Christ here promises to reward any who, for his servants' sake, will dare to risk any consequences that may fall upon themselves.

MATTHEW 11

Matt. 11:1-3   And it came to pass, when Jesus had made an end of commanding his twelve disciples, he departed thence to teach and to preach in their cities. Now when John had heard in the prison the works of Christ, he sent two of his disciples, And said unto him, Art thou he that should come, or do we look for another?

Had John's faith begun to waver? It is possible that it had. Elijah had his times of trembling and depression; then, why might not the second Elijah have the same sort of experience? Possibly, John wished to strengthen the faith of his followers, and therefore he sent two of his leading disciples to Jesus, that they might make the enquiry for themselves as to whether he was the Christ or not.

4   Jesus answered and said unto them, Go and shew John again those things which ye do hear and see:

For the works of Christ are the proofs of his Messiahship. His teaching and his action must ever be the seals of his mission.

5   The blind receive their sight, and the lame walk, the lepers are cleansed, and the deaf hear, the dead are raised up, and the poor have the gospel preached to them.

This is the last, but not the least, of the signs of his Messiahship, that Jesus Christ preached so that the poor understood him and delighted to follow him wherever he went. Many despised his preaching for this reason, but the Saviour mentioned this among the signs of his being sent of God: 'The poor have the gospel preached to them.'

6-11   And blessed is he, whosoever shall not be offended in me. And as they departed, Jesus began to say unto the multitudes concerning John, What went ye out into the wilderness to see? A reed shaken with the wind? But what went ye out for to see? A man clothed in soft raiment? behold, they that wear soft clothing are in kings' houses. But what went ye out for to see? A prophet? yea, I say unto you, and more than a prophet. For this is he, of whom it is written, Behold, I send my messenger before thy face, which shall prepare thy way before thee. Verily I say unto you, Among them that are born of women there hath not risen a greater than John the Baptist: notwithstanding he that is least in the kingdom of heaven is greater than he.

His position was a very high one; he was the evening star of the old dispensation and the morning star of the new; but the light which shines after the sun has risen is brighter than any that the morning star can bring. He who has the gospel to preach has a greater thing to do than John the Baptist, who did but herald the coming of the Saviour.

12-15   And from the days of John the Baptist until now the kingdom of heaven suffereth violence, and the violent take it by force. For all the prophets and the law prophesied until John. And if ye will receive it, this is Elias, which was for to come. He that hath ears to hear, let him hear.

Let him listen to what the heaven-sent messenger has to say; let him especially pay attention to his accents when he says, 'Behold the Lamb of God, which taketh away the sin of the world.'

16-17   But whereunto shall I liken this generation? It is like unto children sitting in the markets, and calling unto their fellows, And saying, We have piped unto you, and ye have not danced; we have mourned unto you, and ye have not lamented.

'You would not join in our game; whichever we chose to do, to imitate a festival or a funeral, you would not take part with us.'

18-19   For John came neither eating nor drinking, and they say, He hath a devil. The Son of man came eating and drinking, and they say, Behold a man gluttonous, and a winebibber, a friend of publicans and sinners. But wisdom is justified of her children.

There was no pleasing them anyhow; they were prepared to find fault with any sort of man, whether he lived an ascetic life or mixed with others as a man among men. 'But wisdom is justified of her children.' She sends the right sort of men to do her work, and God will take care that those who reject them shall not be without guilt: 'Wisdom is justified of her children.'

20   Then began he to upbraid the cities wherein most of his mighty works were done, because they repented not:

That was the point that Christ aimed at — their repentance. He did not seek to dazzle them with wonders and marvels, but to break their hearts away from their sins. This is what his mighty works ought to have done, for they proved him to be the Messiah, and those mighty works also warned those who witnessed them that God had come near to them; and that, therefore, it was time for them to turn from their evil ways.

21-24 Woe unto thee, Chorazin! woe unto thee, Bethsaida! for if the mighty works, which were done in you, had been done in Tyre and Sidon, they would have repented long ago in sackcloth and ashes. But I say unto you, It shall be more tolerable for Tyre and Sidon at the day of judgment, than for you. And thou, Capernaum, which art exalted unto heaven, shalt be brought down to hell: for if the mighty works, which have been done in thee, had been done in Sodom, it would have remained until this day. But I say unto you, That it shall be more tolerable for the land of Sodom in the day of judgment, than for thee.

There is a great depth of mystery here, which we cannot hope to fathom. The gospel was not preached to those who would have repented if they had heard it, and it was preached to those who did not repent when they listened to it even from the lips of Christ himself. Upon this latter class, the sole effect of the gospel preached to them was to plunge them into yet deeper depths of guilt because of their refusal of it. It is not for us to solve the mystery; it will be our wisdom to see that, being ourselves favoured with the plain declaration of the gospel, we do not put it from us, lest we perish even more miserably than those who never heard it.

25 At that time Jesus answered and said, —

So he had been talking with his Father: 'Jesus answered.' Very often, no doubt, the Saviour spoke with God when it is not recorded in the Gospels that he did so; but here a plain hint is given that Christ was in intimate communion and fellowship with God. At such times, great doctrines which, to the shallow minds of those who live at a distance from God, even seem dreadful, become delightful, and are lit up with unusual splendour. At that time, the doctrine of election was specially upon the heart of Christ because he was dwelling near to God himself: 'Jesus answered and said' —

25-30 I thank thee, O Father, Lord of heaven and earth, because thou hast hid these things from the wise and prudent, and hast revealed them unto babes. Even so, Father: for so it seemed good in thy sight. All things are delivered unto me of my Father: and no man knoweth the Son, but the Father; neither knoweth any man the Father, save the Son, and he to whomsoever the Son will reveal him. Come unto me, all ye that labour and are heavy laden, and I will give you rest. Take my yoke upon you, and learn of me; for I am meek and lowly in heart: and ye shall find rest unto your souls. For my yoke is easy, and my burden is light.

MATTHEW 11

Matt. 11:1   And it came to pass, when Jesus had made an end of commanding his twelve disciples, he departed thence to teach and to preach in their cities.

Whatever he commanded, he himself did. He was always the example as well as the legislator of his people. How well it will be for us who are called upon to teach others, if we can teach them as much by what we *do* as by what we *say*! 'When Jesus had made an end of commanding his twelve disciples, he departed thence to teach and to preach in their cities.'

2-3   Now when John had heard in the prison the works of Christ, he sent two of his disciples, And said unto him, Art thou he that should come, or do we look for another?

Poor John! His spirit was brave enough amid the wilds when he was by the riverside; but shut up in prison, it was probably otherwise with him. Those bold spirits, when they lose liberty, are apt to be depressed. Perhaps, too, John sent the disciples as much for their sakes as for his own. At any rate, what a question it was to put to our Lord, 'Art thou he that should come, or do we look for another?' I would call your attention to the quietness of our Saviour's mind — the absence of anything like anger. See how he answers them.

4-6   Jesus answered and said unto them, Go and shew John again those things which ye do hear and see: The blind receive their sight, and the lame walk, the lepers are cleansed, and the deaf hear, the dead are raised up, and the poor have the gospel preached to them. And blessed is he, whosoever shall not be offended in me.

Now if it had been the very least of us who had been attempting to do such service for God, and we had been questioned about what we were doing, should we not have felt hurt and aggrieved? And, maybe, there are some that would not have deigned an answer, especially if they were dignified with the name of an office. But our blessed Lord does not take a huff at it. He is not vexed, but he answers with the utmost gentleness, not by a word of authority commanding John to believe, but by an exposition of those blessed seals of grace which were the best evidence that he was indeed the Messiah. He pointed to the very miracles which prophecy declared the Messiah would perform, and he did this with that suavity of temper which was ever about our Divine Master, in which let us copy him.

7-11 And as they departed, Jesus began to say unto the multitudes concerning John, What went ye out into the wilderness to see? A reed shaken with the wind? But what went ye out for to see? A man clothed in soft raiment? behold, they that wear soft clothing are in kings' houses. But what went ye out for to see? A prophet? yea, I say unto you, and more than a prophet. For this is he, of whom it is written, Behold, I send my messenger before thy face, which shall prepare thy way before thee. Verily I say unto you, Among them that are born of women there hath not risen a greater than John the Baptist: notwithstanding he that is least in the kingdom of heaven is greater than he.

Never did our Saviour bear a more emphatic testimony to John than on this occasion, and it is remarkable that it should have followed upon the heels of John's doubt and John's question. How generously the Master repays his servant — not in his own coin, but in the heavenly coin of love. He seems to say, 'Through the infirmity of thy flesh thou hast been half-inclined to question me; but, through the strength of my grace I turn round and extol thee. Time was when thou couldst say, "He must increase, but I must decrease", and now I turn round and say to those whom thou hast sent, and to those who saw thy messengers, that there is none like to thee.' Not even Moses himself is greater than John the Baptist; though he that has entered into the light and the glory of the kingdom of grace, since the coming of the Master, is greater than he.

12-15 And from the days of John the Baptist until now the kingdom of heaven suffereth violence, and the violent take it by force. For all the prophets and the law prophesied until John. And if ye will receive it, this is Elias, which was for to come. He that hath ears to hear, let him hear.

But how many there are that have ears and do not hear! The external organ is affected, but the internal ear of the soul is not reached at all. Blessed are they who, having ears, do in very truth hear.

16-17 But whereunto shall I liken this generation? It is like unto children sitting in the markets, and calling unto their fellows, And saying, We have piped unto you, and ye have not danced; we have mourned unto you, and ye have not lamented.

The children would not agree, Whatever game was proposed, some of them would not follow it. At one time they imitated the pipers, and then the offsets would not dance. Then they imitated the lamentations of a funeral, and then the others would not join in them.

18-19 For John came neither eating nor drinking, and they say, He hath a devil. The Son of man came eating and drinking, and they say, Behold a man gluttonous, and a winebibber, a friend of publicans and sinners. —

There was no pleasing them. And there is no pleasing people now, whoever it is that God sends. One man is much too homely. In fact, he is vulgar. Another is much too rhetorical. In fact, his rhetoric runs away with him. One man is doctrinal. Oh! He is dogmatical. Another man is practical. He is much too censorious. Another man is full of experience. He is mystical. Oh! Surely God himself cannot please the evil tempers of ungodly men. One thing is that he does not try to do so nor do his servants, if they are truly sent of him. That is a matter about which they have small concern.

19 But wisdom is justified of her children.

Whoever Christ sends, he sends in wisdom, and there is an adaptation about each of his servants, even if men do not perceive it. The day shall come when wisdom shall be justified of her children.

20-24 Then began he to upbraid the cities wherein most of his mighty works were done, because they repented not: Woe unto thee, Chorazin! woe unto thee, Bethsaida! for if the mighty works, which were done in you, had been done in Tyre and Sidon, they would have repented long ago in sackcloth and ashes. But I say unto you, It shall be more tolerable for Tyre and Sidon at the day of judgment, than for you. And thou, Capernaum, which art exalted unto heaven, shalt be brought down to hell: for if the mighty works, which have been done in thee, had been done in Sodom, it would have remained until this day. But I say unto you, That it shall be more tolerable for the land of Sodom in the day of judgment, than for thee.

There was a tenderness about the tone of Christ when he spoke thus. The words are burning, but the eyes were full of tears. He could not contemplate the possibility of the gospel being rejected without a broken heart. He sighed and cried as he bore testimony against those who refused eternal life. With what tenderness must Christ regard some that are present here tonight, whose privileges from their childhood until now have been so great that they could scarcely be greater, and yet they seem determined to reject the admonitions of love, and trample over tenderness in their desperate resolve to perish. God have mercy upon such.

25   At that time Jesus answered —

He seemed to answer himself. He answered to the thoughts that passed through his own mind. 'At that time Jesus answered' —

25-27   and said, I thank thee, O Father, Lord of heaven and earth, because thou hast hid these things from the wise and prudent, and hast revealed them unto babes. Even so, Father: for so it seemed good in thy sight. All things are delivered unto me of my Father: and no man knoweth the Son, but the Father; neither knoweth any man the Father, save the Son, and he to whomsoever the Son will reveal him.

Did the Lord Jesus Christ in his address to Bethsaida and Capernaum awaken in his own mind all those difficulties that hover round about the doctrine of predestination? Did it not seem strange that God should send the gospel to people who rejected it, and did not send the gospel to a people who would have received it? How can these things be? And the dear Saviour answers the question to his own mind by falling back upon that other truth sublime and, to him, full of thanksgiving — the infinite sovereignty of God. I do not know what some of us would do if we did not believe that truth. There are so many things which puzzle us — so many questions, but the Judge of all the earth must do right. He must, he will do as he pleases with his own, and it is not for us to question the prerogatives of the Most High. Now the Saviour at last seems to give vent to his soul in one grand burst of gospel preaching. And whenever you and I get worried about any doctrine, it is always well to come back to the simplicity of the gospel and proclaim it again.

28   Come unto me, all ye that labour and are heavy laden, and I will give you rest.

There is no rest in the difficulties of metaphysics. There is no rest in the labours of human merit. 'Come unto me, and I will give you rest.'

29   Take my yoke upon you, and learn of me; for I am meek and lowly in heart: and ye shall find rest unto your souls.

First, he gives rest to all that come, but afterwards there is a second rest which they find who become obedient and bear his yoke. The rest that comes of *pardoned* sin is sweet, but the rest that comes of *conquered* sin through obedience is sweeter still. The rest he gives is precious, but there is rest upon rest, as there is grace upon grace, and let us go in for the highest form of that rest. 'Ye shall find rest unto your souls.' The very innermost part of your being shall be full of peace.

30   For my yoke is easy, and my burden is light.

Blessed be his name, we have found it so.

MATTHEW 12:38-42

Matt. 12:38-39   Then certain of the scribes and of the Pharisees answered, saying, Master, we would see a sign from thee. But he answered and said unto them, An evil and adulterous generation seeketh after a sign; and there shall no sign be given to it, but the sign of the prophet Jonas:

The Pharisees change their manner, but they are in pursuit of the same object. How hopeless had the religionists of that age become! Nothing would convince them. They manifested their hate of the Lord Jesus, by ignoring all the wonders he had wrought. What further signs could they seek than those he had already given? Pretty inquirers these! They treat all the miracles of our Lord as if they had never occurred. Well might the Lord call them 'evil and adulterous', since they were so given to personal lasciviousness and were spiritually so untrue to God. We have those among us now who are so uncandid as to treat all the achievements of evangelical doctrine as if they were nothing and talk to us as if no result had followed the preaching of the gospel. There is need of great patience to deal wisely with such.

40 For as Jonas was three days and three nights in the whale's belly; so shall the Son of man be three days and three nights in the heart of the earth.

The great sign of our Lord's mission is his resurrection, and his preparing a gospel of salvation for the heathen. His life-story is well symbolized by that of Jonah. They cast our Lord overboard, even as the sailors did the man of God. The sacrifice of Jonah calmed the sea for the mariners, our Lord's death made peace for us. Our Lord was a while in the heart of the earth as Jonah was in the depths of the sea; but, he rose again and his ministry was full of the power of his resurrection. As Jonah's ministry was certified by his restoration from the sea, so is our Lord's ministry attested by his rising from the dead. The man who had come back from death and burial in the sea commanded the attention of all Nineveh, and so does the risen Saviour demand and deserve the obedient faith of all to whom his message comes.

41 The men of Nineveh shall rise in judgment with this generation, and shall condemn it: because they repented at the preaching of Jonas; and, behold, a greater than Jonas is here.

The heathen of Nineveh were convinced by the sign of a prophet restored from burial in the sea, and moved by that convincement, they repented at his preaching. Without cavil or delay they put the whole city in mourning and pleaded with God to turn from his anger. Jesus came with a clearer command of repentance and a brighter promise of deliverance; but, he spoke to obdurate hearts. Our Lord reminds the Pharisees of this, and as they were the most Jewish of Jews, they were touched to the quick by the fact that heathens perceived what Israel did not understand, and that Ninevites repented while Jews were hardened. All men will rise at the judgement: 'The men of Nineveh shall rise.' The lives of penitents will condemn those who did not repent: the Ninevites will condemn the Jews, 'because they repented at the preaching of Jonas', and the Jews did not. Those who heard Jonah and repented will be swift witnesses against those who heard Jesus and refused his testimony. The standing witness to our Lord is his resurrection from the dead. God grant that every one of us, believing that unquestionable fact, may be so assured of his mission, that we may repent and believe the gospel. *Resurrection* is one proof, in fact, it is *the sign*; although, as we shall see, it is supplemented by another. The two will convince us or condemn us.

42   The queen of the south shall rise up in the judgment with this generation, and shall condemn it: for she came from the uttermost parts of the earth to hear the wisdom of Solomon; and, behold, a greater than Solomon is here.

The second sign of our Lord's mission is *his kingly wisdom*. As the fame of Solomon brought the queen of the south from the uttermost parts of the earth, so does the doctrine of our Lord command attention from the utmost isles of the sea. If Israel perceives not his glorious wisdom, Ethiopia and Seba shall hear of it and come bowing before him. The queen of Sheba will rise again and will 'rise up' as a witness against unbelieving Jews, for she journeyed far to hear Solomon, while they would not hear the Son of God himself who came into their midst. The superlative excellence of his wisdom stands for our Lord as a sign which can never be effectually disputed. What other teaching meets all the wants of men? Who else has revealed such grace and truth? He is infinitely greater than Solomon, who from a moral point of view exhibited a sorrowful littleness. Who but the Son of God could have made known the Father as he has done?

MATTHEW 13:1-23

Matt. 13:1-2   The same day went Jesus out of the house, and sat by the sea side. And great multitudes were gathered together unto him, so that he went into a ship, and sat; and the whole multitude stood on the shore.

I think I can see the little ship at a convenient distance from the shore so as to keep off the multitudes of people, in order that the Saviour might speak the more freely; there he sits with a boat for a pulpit. There were no conventionalities about the Lord Jesus when he was upon the earth — he was willing to speak to the people anywhere from any pulpit whatsoever

3 And he spake many things unto them in parables, saying, Behold, a sower went forth to sow;

It was probably at that season of the year when the sowers were going forth to sow their seed, so Jesus pointed to them as to a living text. He was always wide awake to make use of everything that occurred round about him. 'A sower went forth to sow.' For what else should he go forth? Yet some sowers that I know of do not go forth to sow, but to exhibit themselves and to show how well they can do their work. This man aimed at sowing and nothing else. Oh, that all preachers did the same!

4 And when he sowed, some seeds fell by the way side, —

He could not help that; he was not sent to pick the soil, that would be too much responsibility for him. If we had to preach only to certain characters, we should be taking up all our time in picking out those characters, and probably we should make many mistakes while trying to do it. Our business is to scatter the good seed broadcast. We are not to dibble in the Word. We are to throw it as far as we can and to let it fall wherever God pleases. 'Some seeds fell by the way side' — on ground trodden hard by the passers-by.

4 and the fowls came and devoured them up:

Those fowls are always ready to devour the good seed. Wherever there is a congregation met to hear the Word, there are always plenty of devils ready to do their evil work. 'The fowls came', they had not far to fly. The birds know a sower by the very look of him, so they hurry up and come wherever the seed may be cast that they may devour it.

O Lord, keep the fowls away; or, better still, break up the soil so that the seed may enter and not lie upon the surface!

5 Some fell upon stony places, where they had not much earth: —

There was a pan of unbroken limestone an inch or two below the soil, but there was no depth of earth where the seeds could grow.

5 and forthwith they sprung up, because they had no deepness of earth:

They seemed to be converts, but they proved to be worthless. They were enthusiastic, carried away with excitement, but all was soon over with them 'because they had no deepness of earth'. Everything was superficial; there was no depth of character or feeling or emotion.

6 And when the sun was up, they were scorched; and because they had no root, they withered away.

They seemed to be alive at the top, but they were really dead below. How many there are of that sort still; they make a bold profession, but it is only for a while, and then they wither away.

7-8 And some fell among thorns; and the thorns sprung up, and choked them: But other fell into good ground, —

Thank God, we do not lose all our efforts. If one in four succeeds, it is a great deal for which we ought to praise the Lord. So, brother, sister, —

Sow in the morn thy seed,
At eve hold not thine hand;
To doubt and fear give thou no heed,
Broadcast it o'er the land.

8 and brought forth fruit, some an hundredfold, some sixtyfold, some thirtyfold.

There are degrees even in fruitfulness; Christians are not all alike. Oh, that we had a hundredfold return for our sowing everywhere! We do not get it, and can scarcely expect it; let us thank God if are have 'some a hundredfold, some sixtyfold, some thirtyfold'.

9-12 Who hath ears to hear, let him hear. And the disciples came, and said unto him, Why speakest thou unto them in parables? He answered and said unto them, Because it is given unto you to know the mysteries of the kingdom of heaven, but to them it is not given. For whosoever hath, to him shall be given, and he shall have more abundance: but whosoever hath not, from him shall be taken away even that he hath.

It is so even in common things; the man of intelligence, who has a good groundwork of education, picks up something everywhere, but the ignorant man learns nothing anywhere. He only finds out more and more of his own ignorance till there is taken away from him even that which he had. Oh, that the Lord would give us a good groundwork of saving knowledge, so that we might go on learning more and more under the Holy Spirit's teaching!

13-16   Therefore speak I to them in parables: because they seeing see not; and hearing they hear not, neither do they understand. And in them is fulfilled the prophecy of Esaias, which saith, By hearing ye shall hear, and shall not understand; and seeing ye shall see, and shall not perceive: For this people's heart is waxed gross, and their ears are dull of hearing, and their eyes they have closed; lest at any time they should see with their eyes and hear with their ears, and should understand with their heart, and should be converted, and I should heal them. But blessed are your eyes, for they see: and your ears, for they hear.

It is an awful thing when God gives men up to spiritual blindness and dullness and hardness, but it does happen. If you hear the Word and refuse to receive it, you do to that extent harden your heart; and if you continue to do so, you will by degrees lose the capacity for understanding the Word. Take heed what you hear. O my dear hearers, I am afraid that many of you are not aware of the solemn responsibility of hearing the gospel and of the terrible peril of having your ears made dull and your heart made hard! I am responsible for preaching to you faithfully, but you are equally responsible for hearing what is preached. Let us not waste any opportunity that we have of hearing the Word, but use it wisely and well that we may be able to give a good account of it before God in our fruitfulness. Now, if the Saviour's main design in the use of parables had been that men should not understand him, he could have answered that end better by not speaking at all. But see how mercy blends with justice and gives them another opportunity of hearing the Word. They might have come to Jesus even as his disciples did and asked him questions, and he would have explained the truth to them. If any of you today hear anything which you do not understand, go to the Lord about it in private prayer, and he will explain it to you. I tremble lest any of you should hear the Word and not receive it and yet be contented — that is the worst state of all for anyone to be in. May God save you from it! But as for you who know the Lord, 'blessed are your eyes, for they see'. Those are blessed eyes that can really see; eyes that cannot see are a trial, but 'blessed are your eyes, for they see: and your ears, for they hear'. It is nothing but the grace of God that can make our ears spiritually hear. He that made the ear can alone make an open passage from the ear to the heart. If you have received this blessing, be very grateful for it and bless the God of grace for giving it to you.

17   For verily I say unto you, That many prophets and righteous men have desired to see those things which ye see, and have not seen them; and to hear those things which ye hear, and have not heard them.

To you Christian people, there is given a very full revelation of the truth of God. You live in the mid-day glory of the gospel, but the 'prophets and righteous men' of old lived in the morning twilight. Be the more grateful, and bless the Lord with all your hearts

18-19   Hear ye therefore the parable of the sower. When any one heareth the word of the kingdom, and understandeth it not, then cometh the wicked one, and catcheth away that which was sown in his heart. This is he which received seed by the way side.

There are many such hearers. They just hear the Word, and that is all. They are very like the country man who said that he liked Sunday for it was such an easy day — he had nothing to do but go to church, put up his legs and think of nothing. There are far too many hearers of that sort who think of nothing, and therefore they get no good out of what they hear.

20-21 But he that received the seed into stony places, the same is he that heareth the word, and anon with joy receiveth it; Yet hath he not root in himself, but dureth for a while: for when tribulation or persecution ariseth because of the word, by and by he is offended.

He soon ceases even to profess to be a Christian. He jumped into religion, and he jumps out again. Revival always produce a large quantity of such people; and yet, if there is one soul truly saved, the revival is a success so far as that one is concerned.

22-23 He also that received seed among the thorns is he that heareth the word; and the care of this world, and the deceitfulness of riches, choke the word, and he becometh unfruitful. But he that received seed into the good ground is he that heareth the word, and understandeth it; —

Knows what it means, thinks it over, takes it in as the good ground takes in the seed and keeps it.

23 which also beareth fruit, and bringeth forth, some an hundredfold, some sixty, some thirty.

I say again — oh, that we had a hundredfold return for our sowing! Yet let us not forget to give God thanks if we have sixtyfold or even thirtyfold.

MATTHEW 13:24-50

Matt. 13:24 Another parable put he forth unto them, saying, The kingdom of heaven is likened unto a man which sowed good seed in his field:

He knew that it was good. It had been tested: it was unmixed; it was good throughout.

25 But while men slept, his enemy came and sowed tares among the wheat, and went his way.

It was a very malicious action. The thing has been done many times. Bastard wheat was sown in among the true wheat, so as to injure the crop.

26-27 But when the blade was sprung up, and brought forth fruit, then appeared the tares also. So the servants of the householder came and said unto him, Sir, didst not thou sow good seed in thy field? from whence then hath it tares?

We often have to ask that question. How comes this about? It was a true

gospel that was preached, from whence then come these hypocrites —
these that are like the wheat but are not wheat? For it is not the tare
that we call a tare in England that is meant here, but a false wheat —
very like to wheat, but not wheat.

28 He said unto them, An enemy hath done this. —

The enemy could not do a worse thing than to adulterate the church
of God. Pretenders outside do little hurt. Inside the fold they do much
mischief.

28-30 The servants said unto him, Wilt thou then that we go and gather them up? But he said,
Nay; lest while ye gather up the tares, ye root up also the wheat with them. Let both grow
together until the harvest: and in the time of harvest I will say to the reapers, Gather ye together
first the tares, and bind them in bundles to burn them: but gather the wheat into my barn.

The separation will be more in season, more easily and more accurately
done when both shall have been fully developed — when the wheat shall
have come to its fulness and the counterfeit wheat shall have ripened.

31-32 Another parable put he forth unto them, saying, The kingdom of heaven is like to a
grain of mustard seed, which a man took, and sowed in his field: Which indeed is the least
of all seeds: —

Commonly known in that country.

32-35 but when it is grown, it is the greatest among herbs, and becometh a tree, so that the
birds of the air come and lodge in the branches thereof. Another parable spake he unto them;
The kingdom of heaven is like unto leaven, which a woman took, and hid in three measures of
meal, till the whole was leavened. All these things spake Jesus unto the multitude in parables;
and without a parable spake he not unto them: That it might be fulfilled which was spoken by
the prophet, saying, I will open my mouth in parables; I will utter things which have been kept
secret from the foundation of the world.

How thoroughly impregnated our Lord was with the very spirit of
Scripture. And he ever acted as if the Scriptures were uppermost in his
mind. They seemed to be ever in their fulness before his soul.

36 Then Jesus sent the multitude away, and went into the house: and his disciples came
unto him, —

Those house-talks, those explanations of the great public sermons and parables, were sweet privileges which he reserved for those who had given their utter confidence to him.

36-44 saying, Declare unto us the parable of the tares of the field. He answered and said unto them, He that soweth the good seed is the Son of man; The field is the world; the good seed are the children of the kingdom; but the tares are the children of the wicked one; The enemy that sowed them is the devil; the harvest is the end of the world; and the reapers are the angels. As therefore the tares are gathered and burned in the fire; so shall it be in the end of this world. The Son of man shall send forth his angels, and they shall gather out of his kingdom all things that offend, and them which do iniquity; And shall cast them into a furnace of fire: there shall be wailing and gnashing of teeth. Then shall the righteous shine forth as the sun in the kingdom of their Father. Who hath ears to hear, let him hear. Again, the kingdom of heaven is like unto treasure hid in a field; the which when a man hath found, —

Stumbling upon it, perhaps, when he was at the plough — turning up the old crop in which it was concealed.

44 he hideth, and for joy thereof goeth and selleth all that he hath, and buyeth that field.

Some persons do stumble upon the gospel when they are not looking for it. 'I am found of them that sought me not' is a grand free grace text. Some of those who have been most earnest in the kingdom of heaven were at one time most indifferent and careless, but God in infinite sovereignty put the treasure in their way — gave them the heart to value it, and they obtained it to their own joy.

45 Again, the kingdom of heaven is like unto a merchant man, seeking goodly pearls:

He does not stumble at it: he is seeking pearls.

46-47 Who, when he had found one pearl of great price, went and sold all that he had, and bought it. Again, the kingdom of heaven is like unto a net, that was cast into the sea, and gathered of every kind:

Bad fish and good fish, and creeping things and broken shells, and bits of seaweed, and pieces of old wreck. Did you ever see such an odd assortment as they get upon the deck of a fishing vessel when they empty out the contents of a drag net? Such is the effect of the ministry. It drags together all sorts of people. It is quite as well that we have not eyes enough to see one another's hearts tonight, or else I dare say we should make about as queer a medley as I have already attempted to describe as being in the fisherman's vessel.

48 Which, when it was full, they drew to shore, and sat down, and gathered the good into vessels, but cast the bad away.

All a mixture. We cannot sort one from the other now, but when the net comes to shore then will be the picking over the heap. No mistakes will be made. The good will go into vessels, and the bad, and none but the bad, will be cast away.

49-50 So shall it be at the end of the world: the angels shall come forth, and sever the wicked from among the just, And shall cast them into the furnace of fire: there shall be wailing and gnashing of teeth.

Not fire, then, which annihilates, but fire which leaves in pain and causes weeping and gnashing of teeth.

MATTHEW 13:24-58

Matt. 13:24 Another parable put he forth unto them, saying, The kingdom of heaven is likened unto a man which sowed good seed in his field:

Jesus never sowed any other kind of seed. The truth which he taught is pure and unadulterated. It is good seed — good and only good, the very best of seed.

25 But while men slept, his enemy came and sowed tares among the wheat, and went his way.

Wherever Christ is active the enemy is sure to be active too. If you have a sleeping church, you may have a sleeping devil; but as soon as ever Christ is in the congregation sowing the good seed, the devil wakes up, and by night, when men are off their guard, the bad seed — the mock wheat, here translated 'tares' — is sown among the true wheat.

26 But when the blade was sprung up, and brought forth fruit, then appeared the tares also.

The false wheat came up with the true. Perhaps the seed in the one case may have looked like the other, even as there is 'another gospel which is not another' with which comes still trouble us. The only true test is: 'By their fruits ye shall know them'. So, when the seeds had sprung up, there was the blade of true wheat and 'then appeared the tares also'.

27 So the servants of the householder came and said unto him, Sir, didst not thou sow good seed in thy field? from whence then hath it tares?

How often we have asked that question! We have seen children trained by the most godly parents, yet they have developed a sad propensity to sin, and we have said, 'From whence then have these tares come?' We have seen a ministry which has been sound and faithful, and yet in the congregation, there have sprung up divers errors which have done a world of mischief, and we have had sorrowfully to ask, 'From whence then have these tares come?'

28-29 He said unto them, An enemy hath done this. The servants said unto him, Wilt thou then that we go and gather them up? But he said, Nay; lest while ye gather up the tares, ye root up also the wheat with them.

We are so fallible, we make so many mistakes, that we cannot be trusted to do this uprooting, for we might pull up wheat as well as tares. If there had been briars or thorns growing in that field, those servants might have pulled them up without damage to the corn, just as an open evildoer, who breaks the laws of God openly, may be cut off from the church without damage; but these tares must be left for the present.

30 Let both grow together until the harvest: and in the time of harvest I will say to the reapers, Gather ye together first the tares, and bind them in bundles to burn them: but gather the wheat into my barn.

There will be an end of this mixture in due time; the hypocrite shall not always stand in the congregation of the righteous; the wheat and the tares shall be separated 'in the time of harvest'.

31-32 Another parable put he forth unto them, saying, The kingdom of heaven is like to a grain of mustard seed, which a man took, and sowed in his field: Which indeed is the least of all seeds: but when it is grown, it is the greatest among herbs, and becometh a tree, so that the birds of the air come and lodge in the branches thereof.

The kingdom of heaven is just like that in this world; wherever it comes, it comes to grow. And it is just like that in our hearts. Oh, how small is the first sign of grace in the soul! Perhaps it is only a single thought. The life divine may begin with but a wish, or with one painful conviction of error, but if it be the true and living seed of God, it will *grow*. And there is no telling how great will be its growth till, in that soul where all was darkness, many graces, like sweet songbirds, shall come and sing and make joy and gladness there. Oh, that you and I might experimentally know the meaning of the parable of the mustard seed!

33 Another parable spake he unto them; The kingdom of heaven is like unto leaven, which a woman took, and hid in three measures of meal, till the whole was leavened.

And although leaven is usually the symbol of evil, yet it may be here a fair representation of the kingdom of heaven itself, for it operates mysteriously and secretly, yet powerfully, till it permeates the whole of man's nature; and the gospel will keep on winning its way till the whole world shall yet be leavened by it.

More and more it spreads and grows,
Ever mighty to prevail.

34-36 All these things spake Jesus unto the multitude in parables; and without a parable spake he not unto them: That it might be fulfilled which was spoken by the prophet, saying, I will open my mouth in parables; I will utter things which have been kept secret from the foundation of the world. Then Jesus sent the multitude away, and went into the house: and his disciples came unto him, saying, Declare unto us the parable of the tares of the field.

I again remind you that, wherever there is anything that you do not understand, the best way is to consult the Master concerning it. If I read a book in which there is an obscure passage, and I can write to the author and ask him what he means by it, I shall most probably get to understand it. So, the best expositor of the Word of God is the Spirit of God; therefore appeal to him whenever you are puzzled with anything that is taught in the Scriptures, and say to him, 'Blessed Spirit, wilt thou graciously expound to me this parable, this doctrine, this experience?' and he will do it, and so you shall become wise unto salvation.

37-43 He answered and said unto them, He that soweth the good seed is the Son of man; The field is the world; the good seed are the children of the kingdom; but the tares are the children of the wicked one; The enemy that sowed them is the devil; the harvest is the end of the world; and the reapers are the angels. As therefore the tares are gathered and burned in the fire; so shall it be in the end of this world. The Son of man shall send forth his angels, and they shall gather out of his kingdom all things that offend, and them which do iniquity; And shall cast them into a furnace of fire: there shall be wailing and gnashing of teeth. Then shall the righteous shine forth as the sun in the kingdom of their Father. Who hath ears to hear, let him hear.

May God give us such ears as can hear his voice, and may we take to heart the solemn teachings of our Lord!

44-46 Again, the kingdom of heaven is like unto treasure hid in a field; the which when a man hath found, he hideth, and for joy thereof goeth and selleth all that he hath, and buyeth that field. Again, the kingdom of heaven is like unto a merchant man, seeking goodly pearls: Who, when he had found one pearl of great price, went and sold all that he had, and bought it.

It would be a good bargain for anyone to part with all he has in exchange for the kingdom of heaven, yet that great 'treasure' is to be had for *nothing* by everyone who trusts the Lord Jesus Christ.

47-50 Again, the kingdom of heaven is like unto a net, that was cast into the sea, and gathered of every kind: Which, when it was full, they drew to shore, and sat down, and gathered the good into vessels, but cast the bad away. So shall it be at the end of the world: the angels shall come forth, and sever the wicked from among the just, And shall cast them into the furnace of fire: there shall be wailing and gnashing of teeth.

We are to cast the great seine-net of the gospel into the sea of humanity, but we must not expect that all we catch will prove to be good. There is time of separation coming when 'the angels shall come forth, and sever the wicked from among the just'.

51 Jesus saith unto them, Have ye understood all these things? —

This is a question which constantly needs to be put to all hearers and readers of the Word. 'Have ye understood all these things?' To be hearers only, or readers only, will avail nothing. The Word must be understood, accepted, assimilated, and so shall it make us wise unto salvation.

51   They say unto him, Yea, Lord.

They answered very glibly, yet probably not one of them fully understood the seven parables in this chapter. If anyone did so, he would be like the instructed scribe described in the next verse:

52   Then said he unto them, Therefore every scribe which is instructed unto the kingdom of heaven is like unto a man that is an householder, which bringeth forth out of his treasure things new and old.

He who has learned anything concerning the kingdom of heaven should teach it to others, bringing forth the truth in pleasing variety, 'new and old', to edify all his hearers.

53-54   And it came to pass, that when Jesus had finished these parables, he departed thence. And when he was come into his own country, he taught them in their synagogue, insomuch that they were astonished, and said, Whence hath this man this wisdom, and these mighty works?

They were highly privileged in having Jesus back in their midst, yet they failed to appreciate his teaching; they were astonished at his wisdom, but were unable to perceive the divine source from which it sprang.

55-58   Is not this the carpenter's son? is not his mother called Mary? and his brethren, James, and Joses, and Simon, and Judas? And his sisters, are they not all with us? Whence then hath this man all these things? And they were offended in him. But Jesus said unto them, A prophet is not without honour, save in his own country, and in his own house. And he did not many mighty works there because of their unbelief.

This was a notable illustration of John's words concerning Christ: 'He came unto his own, but his own received him not.' Let us beware of unbelief lest it should tie the hands of Christ as it did there in his own country.

MATTHEW 14:13-36

Matt. 14:13   When Jesus heard of it, he departed thence by ship into a desert place apart: —

It is well for us to get alone with God when he takes home the best and most faithful of his servants. Neither the church nor the world could afford to lose such a man as John the Baptist; so it was well for Christ's disciples to retire with him to a desert place that he might teach them the lesson of that proto-martyr's death.

13-14 and when the people had heard thereof, they followed him on foot out of the cities. And Jesus went forth, and saw a great multitude, and was moved with compassion toward them, and he healed their sick.

He needed quiet, but he could not get it; yet he was not moved with indignation against the crowd that had sought him out, but he 'was moved with *compassion* toward them, and he healed their sick'. Out of the fulness of his heart of love, he condescended to do for the people what they most needed.

15 And when it was evening, his disciples came to him, saying, This is a desert place, and the time is now past; send the multitude away, that they may go into the villages, and buy themselves victuals.

Human compassion might have moved the disciples to say something more kind than that heartless request: 'Send the multitude away.' Perhaps they wished to spare themselves the sight of so much distress, but they evidently did not expect the answer that Christ gave them.

16 But Jesus said unto them, They need not depart; give ye them to eat.

Christ seemed to say to his disciples, 'If you only exercise the power that is within your reach, with Me in your midst, you are equal to this emergency: "Give ye them to eat."'

17-18 And they say unto him, We have here but five loaves, and two fishes. He said, Bring them hither to me.

'They are little enough in your hands, but they will be ample when they get into mine.' When everything that we have is in the hands of Christ, it is wonderful how much he can make of it. Bring your talent to the Lord Jesus, be it never so little; sanctify to him every possibility that lies within your reach. You cannot tell how much he can and will do with it.

19   And he commanded the multitude to sit down on the grass, —

It must have been a beautiful sight to see those thousands of men, women and children at once obeying his command. There were five loaves and two fishes — probably five small barley cakes and a couple of sardines. So the people might have said, 'What is the use of such a multitude sitting down on the grass to partake of such scanty fare as that?' But they did not say so; there was a divine power about the very simplest command of Christ which compelled instant obedience: 'He commanded the multitude to sit down on the grass' —

19   and took the five loaves, and the two fishes, and looking up to heaven, he blessed, —

This was that 'blessing of the Lord' of which Solomon says that 'it maketh rich, and he addeth no sorrow with it' [Proverbs 10:22]. If you get this blessing on your five loaves and two fishes, you may feed 5,000 men with them, besides the women and the children.

19-20   and brake, and gave the loaves to his disciples, and the disciples to the multitude. And they did all eat, and were filled: and they took up of the fragments that remained twelve baskets full.

Much more than they began with! For it is a law of the heavenly kingdom that he who gives to God shall be no loser — his five loaves and two fishes shall turn to twelve baskets full after thousands have eaten, and been satisfied. The more there is of complete consecration to Christ and his blessed service, the more reward will there be in the world to come and, possibly, even here.

21-22   And they that had eaten were about five thousand men, beside women and children. And straightway Jesus constrained his disciples to get into a ship, and to go before him unto the other side, while he sent the multitudes away.

He always takes the heavier task upon himself. They may go off by themselves, but he will remain to send the multitudes away. Besides, no one but Christ could have done it. Only he who had made them sit down to the feast could make them go to their homes.

23 And when he had sent the multitudes away, he went up into a mountain apart to pray: —

He had had a long day of preaching, and healing, and distributing the bread and fish, and now he closed the day with prayer to his Father.

23 and when the evening was come, he was there alone.

Dr Watts was right in saying of his Lord,

> *Cold mountains, and the midnight air*
> *Witnessed the fervour of thy prayer.*

He is not now on the bare mountainside, but he is engaged in the same holy exercise up yonder before his Father's throne.

24 But the ship was now in the midst of the sea, tossed with waves: for the wind was contrary.

This is the case with the good ship of the church of Christ today; it is 'tossed with waves' and 'the wind' is 'contrary'. It is very contrary just now. But then, Christ is still pleading for the ship and all on board — and while he pleads it can never sink.

25-29 And in the fourth watch of the night Jesus went unto them, walking on the sea. And when the disciples saw him walking on the sea, they were troubled, saying, It is a spirit; and they cried out for fear. But straightway Jesus spake unto them, saying, Be of good cheer; it is I; be not afraid. And Peter answered him and said, Lord, if it be thou, bid me come unto thee on the water. And he said, Come. And when Peter was come down out of the ship, he walked on the water, to go to Jesus.

You who are wanting to get to Jesus should make a desperate effort to get to him — even walk on the water to get to Jesus. Walking on the water might be an idle and evil exhibition; but to walk on the water to go to Jesus is another matter. Try it, and the Lord enable you to get to him!

30-32 But when he saw the wind boisterous, he was afraid; and beginning to sink, he cried, saying, Lord, save me. And immediately Jesus stretched forth his hand, and caught him, and said unto him, O thou of little faith, wherefore didst thou doubt? And when they were come into the ship, the wind ceased.

The Greek word implies that the wind was tired, weary, 'done up', as we say. It had had its boisterous time and spent its force; and now it knew its Lord's voice and, like a tired child, fell asleep.

33   Then they that were in the ship came and worshipped him, saying, Of a truth thou art the Son of God.

This seems to have been the first time that the disciples arrived at this conclusion so as to state it so positively. Yet, do you not think that after the miraculous multiplication of the loaves and fishes, they might have very fitly said, 'Of a truth thou art the Son of God'? Sometimes, however, one wonder will strike us more than another; and, possibly, it was because they were in danger when this second miracle was wrought, and therefore they the more appreciated the coming of Christ to them at midnight. They were in no danger when the multitude were fed; perhaps they were not themselves hungry. That strikes us most which comes most home to us, as this miracle did.

34-36   And when they were gone over, they came into the land of Gennesaret. And when the men of that place had knowledge of him, they sent out into all that country round about, and brought unto him all that were diseased; And besought him that they might only touch the hem of his garment: and as many as touched were made perfectly whole.

MATTHEW 14:22-33

Matt. 14:22   And straightway Jesus constrained his disciples to get into a ship, and to go before him unto the other side, while he sent the multitudes away.

Straightway is a business word: Jesus loses no time. No sooner is the banquet over than he sends off the guests to their homes. While they are well fed he bids them make the best of their way home. He who made the multitude sit down was able also to send the multitude away, but they needed sending, for they were loath to go. The sea must be crossed again, or Jesus cannot find seclusion. How he must run the gauntlet to get a little rest! Before he starts again across the sea, he performs another act of self-denial, for he cannot leave till he sees the crowd happily dispersed. He attends to that business himself giving the disciples the opportunity to depart in peace. As the captain is the last to leave the ship, so is the Lord the last to leave the scene of labour. The disciples would have chosen to stay in his company, and to enjoy the thanks of the people; but he constrained them to get into a ship. He could not get anyone to go away from him at this time without sending and constraining. This loadstone has great attractions. He evidently promised his disciples that he would follow them for the words are: 'to go before him unto the other side'. How he was to follow he did not say, but he could always find a way of keeping his appointments. How considerate of him to wait amid the throng while the disciples sailed away in peace He always takes the heavy end of the load himself.

23 And when he had sent the multitudes away, he went up into a mountain apart to pray: and when the evening was come, he was there alone.

Now that the crowd is gone, he can take his rest, and he finds it in prayer. He went up into a mountain apart. In a place where he might speak aloud, and not be overheard or disturbed, he communed with the Father alone. This was his refreshment and his delight. He continued therein till the thickest shades of night had gathered, and the day was gone. 'Alone', yet not alone, he drank in new strength as he communed with his Father. He must have revealed this private matter to the recording evangelist, and surely it was with the intent that we should learn from his example. We cannot afford to be always in company, since even our blessed Lord felt that he must be alone.

24 But the ship was now in the midst of the sea, tossed with waves: for the wind was contrary.

While Jesus was alone, they, in the ship, were in the same condition, but not occupied with the same spiritual exercise When they first quitted the shore it was fair sailing in the cool of the evening; but a storm gathered hastily as night covered the sky. On the lake of Galilee the wind rushes down from the gullies between the mountains and causes grievous peril to little boats, sometimes fairly lifting them out of the water and, anon, submerging them beneath the waves. That deep lake was peculiarly dangerous for small craft. They were far from land, for they were 'in the midst of the sea', equally distant from either shore. The sea was furious and their ship was 'tossed with waves'. The hurricane was terrible. 'The wind was contrary' and would not let them go to any place which they sought. It was a whirlwind, and they were whirled about by it, but could not use it for reaching either shore. How much did their case resemble ours when we are in sore distress! We are tossed about and can do nothing; the blast is too furious for us to bear up against it, or even to live while driven before it. One happy fact remains: Jesus is pleading on the shore, though we are struggling on the sea. It is also comfortable to know that we are where he constrained us to go (see verse 22), and he has promised to come to us in due time, and therefore, all must be safe, though the tempest rages terribly.

25   And in the fourth watch of the night Jesus went unto them, walking on the sea.

Jesus is sure to come. The night wears on and the darkness thickens; the fourth watch of the night draws near, but where is he? Faith says, 'He must come.' Though he should stay away till almost break of day, he must come. Unbelief asks, 'How can he come?' Ah, he will answer for himself: he can make his own way. 'Jesus went unto them, walking on the sea.' He comes in the teeth of the wind and on the face of the wave. Never fear that he will fail to reach the storm-tossed barque: his love will find out the way. Whether it be to a single disciple or to the church as a whole, Jesus will appear in his own chosen hour, and his time is sure to be the most timely.

26   And when the disciples saw him walking on the sea, they were troubled, saying, It is a spirit; and they cried out for fear.

Yes, the disciples saw him — saw Jesus their Lord — and derived no comfort from the sight. Poor human nature's sight is a blind thing compared with the vision of a spiritual faith. They saw, but knew not what they saw. What could it be but a phantom? How could a real man walk on those foaming billows? How could he stand in the teeth of such a hurricane? They were already at their wits' end, and the apparition put an end to their courage. We seem to hear their shriek of alarm: 'They cried out for fear.' We read not that 'they were troubled' before: they were old sailors and had no dread of natural forces. But a spirit — ah, that was too much of a terror. They were at their worst now, and yet, if they had known it, they were on the verge of their best. It is noteworthy that the nearer Jesus was to them, the greater was their fear. Want of discernment blinds the soul to its richest consolations. Lord, be near, and let me *know* thee! Let me not have to say with Jacob: 'Surely the LORD is in this place; and I knew it not!' [Genesis 28:16].

27 But straightway Jesus spake unto them, saying, Be of good cheer; it is I; be not afraid.

He did not keep them in suspense: 'Straightway Jesus spake unto them.' How sweetly sounded that loving and majestic voice! Above the roar of waves and howling of winds, they heard the voice of the Lord. This was his old word also: 'Be of good cheer.' The most conclusive reason for courage was his own presence: 'It is I; be not afraid.' If Jesus be near, if the Spirit of the storm be, after all, the Lord of love, all room for fear is gone. Can Jesus come to us through the storm? Then we shall weather it, and come to him. He who rules the tempest is not the devil, not chance, not a malicious enemy, but Jesus. This should end all fear.

28 And Peter answered him and said, Lord, if it be thou, bid me come unto thee on the water.

Peter must be the first to speak. He is impulsive, and besides, he was a sort of foreman in the company. The first speaker is not always the wisest man. Peter's fears have gone, all but one 'if'; but that 'if' was working him no good, for it seemed to challenge his Master: 'Lord, if it be thou'. What a test to suggest: 'Bid me come unto thee on the water'! What did Peter want with walking the waters? His name might have suggested that like a stone he would go to the bottom. It was an imprudent request: it was the swing of the pendulum in Peter from despair to an injudicious venturing. Surely, he wist not what he said. Yet we, too, have put our Lord to tests almost as improper. Have we not said, 'If thou hast ever blessed me, give me this and that'? We, too, have had our water-walking, and have ventured where nothing but special grace could uphold us. Lord, what is man?

29 And he said, Come. And when Peter was come down out of the ship, he walked on the water, to go to Jesus.

When good men are unwise and presumptuous, it may be for their lasting good to learn their folly by experience. 'He said, Come.' Peter's Lord is about to teach him a practical lesson. He asked to be bidden to come. He may come. He does come. He leaves the boat; he treads the wave. He is on the way towards his Lord. We can do anything if we have divine authorization and courage enough to take the Lord at his word. Now there were two on the sea — two wonders! Which was the greater? The reader may not find it easy to reply. Let him consider.

30 But when he saw the wind boisterous, he was afraid; and beginning to sink, he cried, saying, Lord, save me.

'But': a sorrowful 'but' for poor Peter! His eye was off his Lord and on the raging of the wind: 'He saw the wind boisterous.' His heart failed him, and then his foot failed him. Down he began to go — an awful moment is this 'beginning to sink'. Yet it was only a 'beginning'. He had time to cry to his Lord who was not sinking. Peter cried and was safe. His prayer was as full as it was short. He had brought his eye and his faith back to Jesus, for he cried, 'Lord!' He had come into this danger through obedience, and therefore he had an appeal in the word 'Lord'. Whether in danger or not, Jesus was still his Lord. He is a lost man, and he feels it, unless his Lord will save him — save him altogether, save him now. Blessed prayer: 'Lord, save me'. Reader, does it not suit you? Peter was nearer his Lord when he was sinking than when he was walking. In our low estate we are often nearer to Jesus than in our more glorious seasons.

31   And immediately Jesus stretched forth his hand, and caught him, and said unto him, O thou of little faith, wherefore didst thou doubt?

Our Lord delays not when our peril is imminent and our cry is urgent: 'Immediately Jesus stretched forth his hand.' He first 'caught him' and then taught him. Jesus saves first and upbraids afterwards, when he must needs do so. When we are saved is the fit time for us to chasten ourselves for our unbelief. Let us learn from our Lord that we may not reprove others till we have first helped them out of their difficulties. Our doubts are unreasonable: 'Wherefore didst thou doubt?' If there be reason for little faith, there is evidently reason for great confidence. If it be right to trust Jesus at all, why not trust him altogether? Trust was Peter's strength, doubt was his danger. It looked like great faith when Peter walked the water; but a little wind soon proved it to be 'little faith'. Till our faith is tried, we can form no reliable estimate of it. After his Lord had taken him by the hand, Peter sank no further, but resumed the walk of faith. How easy to have faith when we are close to Jesus! Lord, when our faith fails, come thou to us, and we shall walk on the waves.

32   And when they were come into the ship, the wind ceased.

So that Peter's walk and his rescue had happened in the face of the tempest. He could walk the water well enough when his Lord held his hand, and so can we. What a sight! Jesus and Peter, hand in hand, walking upon the sea! The two made for the ship at once: miracles are never spun out to undue length. Was not Peter glad to leave the tumultuous element, and at the same time to perceive that the gale was over? 'When they were come into the ship, the wind ceased.' It is well to be safe in a storm, but more pleasant to find the calm return and the hurricane end. How gladly did the disciples welcome their Lord and their brother Peter, who, though wet to the skin, was a wiser man for his adventure!

33 Then they that were in the ship came and worshipped him, saying, Of a truth thou art the Son of God.

No wonder that Peter 'worshipped him' nor that his comrades did the same. The whole of the disciples, who had been thus rescued by their Lord's coming to them on the stormy sea, were overwhelmingly convinced of his Godhead. Now they were doubly sure of it by unquestionable evidence, and in lowly reverence they expressed to him their adoring faith, saying, 'Of a truth thou art the Son of God.'

MATTHEW 15

Matt. 15:1   Then came to Jesus scribes and Pharisees, which were of Jerusalem, saying,

Our Lord had been busily engaged in healing the sick, and now these pettifoggers (or rascals) came round about him to try and worry him. They were a kind of mosquito swarm to Christ. Had he not been a perfect man, they might have worried him.

2 Why do thy disciples transgress the tradition of the elders? for they wash not their hands when they eat bread.

'Why do thy disciples transgress the traditions of the elders?' Generally a good man is held responsible for the acts of his followers. If they cannot find fault with Christ they will find fault with his disciples, who must have been men of admirable character when even scribes and Pharisees had no worse charge to bring than the following: 'For they wash not their hands when they eat bread.' The Saviour must have been gentle, indeed, to bear with such people as these. It would have given us the fidgets to have such folks round about us. Here is he healing the sick, curing the lepers, feeding the hungry, and these people are talking about washing their hands. Oh! how many religious people there are that are occupying their time about nothing of vital importance at all, questions of washing their hands or something of that kind.

3 But he answered and said unto them, Why do ye also transgress the commandment of God by your tradition?

He did not deign to answer their question but posed them another.

4-6 For God commanded, saying, Honour thy father and mother: and, He that curseth father or mother, let him die the death. But ye say, Whosoever shall say to his father or his mother, It is a gift, by whatsoever thou mightest be profited by me; And honour not his father or his mother, he shall be free. Thus have ye made the commandment of God of none effect by your tradition.

They actually taught that a man might escape the happy duty of succouring his father and mother, the first duty surely of a son, by saying: 'I have dedicated so much of my goods to the temple and the worship of God that I cannot afford it.' There are not many in these days that talk that way; they generally cannot afford to dedicate *anything* to the temple because they are keeping their father and mother. They go the other way, but one way or another, men will if possible escape from moral or religious duty. Now God loves not that we should bring one duty to him smeared with the blood of another, and for a man to give his money to the temple which he ought to have given to his father and mother was a violation of the strict law of God and could not possibly be acceptable to him. Thus they made void the law of God by their traditions.

7-10 Ye hypocrites, well did Esaias prophesy of you, saying, This people draweth nigh unto me with their mouth, and honoureth me with their lips; but their heart is far from me. But in vain they do worship me, teaching for doctrines the commandments of men. And he called the multitude, —

Christ spoke very plainly to them. There is no dealing with hypocrites with kid gloves. These nettles must be boldly grasped, and the Saviour did so. Brethren, stick to the Scriptures in doctrine and in precept. What have you to do with modern thought, the imaginations of men, the vain thoughts of crazy brains? Hold you to God's thoughts, which are as high above men's thoughts as the heavens are above the earth. One word of God is worth a whole world full of the thoughts of men, and time shall show us yet that it is so. We have but to wait, and we shall see that the thoughts of man are vanity, but the Word of God abideth for ever. 'And he called the multitude' — one of the finest ways of rebuking the Pharisees and scribes; he seemed to turn his back on these gentlemen who knew so much.

10-11 and said unto them, Hear, and understand: Not that which goeth into the mouth defileth a man; but that which cometh out of the mouth, this defileth a man.

Religion stands not in meats and drinks and divers washings or anything external: it lies in the *heart*. It is that which comes out of the heart that is the true index of the character not that which is done externally.

12-13 Then came his disciples, and said unto him, Knowest thou that the Pharisees were offended, after they heard this saying? But he answered and said, Every plant, which my heavenly Father hath not planted, shall be rooted up.

They stand like a grove of trees — men take shelter under their great knowledge, but God never planted them, and therefore they shall be plucked up. And he did pluck them up without ceremony.

14 Let them alone: they be blind leaders of the blind. And if the blind lead the blind, both shall fall into the ditch.

So you need not trouble to shove them in. You let them alone; it will come to an end. There are some forms of error which Christ may denounce, but which his disciples had better let alone. There is a ditch ready and waiting for them somewhere or other.

15-20 Then answered Peter and said unto him, Declare unto us this parable. And Jesus said, Are ye also yet without understanding? Do not ye yet understand, that whatsoever entereth in at the mouth goeth into the belly, and is cast out into the draught? But those things which proceed out of the mouth come forth from the heart; and they defile the man. For out of the heart proceed evil thoughts, murders, adulteries, fornications, thefts, false witness, blasphemies: These are the things which defile a man: but to eat with unwashen hands defileth not a man.

By and by in this chapter we shall see thousands of people eating with unwashen hands, who could not have eaten at all, if it had been requisite first for them to wash their hands, for they were in a desert place. Not but what it is well even to wash the hands and every other part of the flesh. It should be true of every Christian: 'Having your bodies washed with pure water.' Cleanliness should always go with godliness. But this was a mere ceremonial rite, a washing of the hands whether they wanted it or not for form's sake, and the Saviour pours contempt upon it.

21-22 Then Jesus went thence, and departed into the coasts of Tyre and Sidon. And, behold, a woman of Canaan came out of the same coasts, and cried unto him, saying, Have mercy on me, O Lord, thou son of David; my daughter is grievously vexed with a devil.

He made a long journey to go and meet one woman. An instance of how far you and I ought to be willing to go to save a soul. 'And, behold, a woman of Canaan came out of the same coasts.' She came a little way but he had come a long way. Perhaps some sinner has come here today as Christ has come too. The woman 'cried unto him'. Sinners and the Saviour will meet; for the sinners are seeking him, and they will perhaps meet sooner than they expect. Perhaps she meant to have gone a long journey, but he met her, and she cried unto him saying, 'Have mercy on me, O Lord, thou son of David.' She knew his deity: 'O Lord'. She knew his humanity: 'thou son of David'. She knew his royalty: 'thou son of David'. She had but one prayer: 'Have mercy on me.' That prayer suits me very well too, today. Is it too humble for you? I pity you then. 'Have mercy on me, O Lord, thou son of David.'

And yet her prayer was not for herself. 'Have mercy on me, for my daughter is grievously vexed with a devil.' Many a mother feels that the greatest mercy to herself would be salvation for her child. How we are wrapped up in these who are the offspring of our body. How we desire their salvation. How careful we should be if they are saved; how should we pray for the children of others, that God would have mercy on mothers by healing daughters.

23   But he answered her not a word. —

You may pray, and pray acceptably, and yet not get an immediate answer.

23   And his disciples came and besought him, saying, Send her away; for she crieth after us.

She makes too much noise. Oh! The poor disciples! 'She crieth after *us*.' That she did not; she cried after the Master, not after them. Oh! The big disciples! How large they are, and how easily troubled. 'She crieth after us.'

24   But he answered and said, I am not sent but unto the lost sheep of the house of Israel.

My mission as a prophet is to Israel, not to the Gentiles just now.

25-27   Then came she and worshipped him, saying, Lord, help me. But he answered and said, It is not meet to take the children's bread, and to cast it to dogs. And she said, Truth, Lord: yet the dogs eat of the crumbs which fall from their masters' table.

Splendid faith! To make it out that to heal her daughter would be, after all, to Christ nothing but to give her a lot of crumbs! She thought so much of him; he was so great in her estimate that much as she valued the healing of her daughter she reckoned it to be to his royal majesty only as a bit of dog's food. Oh! Splendid faith!

28   Then Jesus answered and said unto her, O woman, great is thy faith: be it unto thee even as thou wilt. And her daughter was made whole from that very hour.

Write, sir, out a blank cheque, she may fill it in just as she likes. There is no limit to what God will give an unlimited faith. If we limit our faith, then we limit the Holy One of Israel.

29   And Jesus departed from thence, —

He had done his business. He is always on the move but loiters never.

29-30   and came nigh unto the sea of Galilee; and went up into a mountain, and sat down there. And great multitudes came unto him, having with them those that were lame, blind, dumb, maimed, and many others, and cast them down at Jesus' feet; and he healed them:

What an assemblage and in the middle of a great hospital! What a sight for him to see all these sick people carried like so many burdens and then laid down at his feet! Cannot we today each one bring somebody? Think of somebody, some friend of yours, that is yet unsaved. Take him on your back, nay, carry him in your bosom, and bring him by faith and lay him down at Jesus' feet just now. Who shall it be? Think about it!

31-34 Insomuch that the multitude wondered, when they saw the dumb to speak, the maimed to be whole, the lame to walk, and the blind to see: and they glorified the God of Israel. Then Jesus called his disciples unto him, and said, I have compassion on the multitude, because they continue with me now three days, and have nothing to eat: and I will not send them away fasting, lest they faint in the way. And his disciples say unto him, Whence should we have so much bread in the wilderness, as to fill so great a multitude? And Jesus saith unto them, How many loaves have ye? And they said, Seven, and a few little fishes.

And I daresay they thought: 'We shall want all these ourselves.' It was noble on their part that they were willing to give away all they had: every bit of it, little fish and loaves and all — none too much for the company, and yet they parted with all at the Master's bidding.

35 And he commanded the multitude to sit down on the ground.

I think I see him rising from the place where he sat, and saying, 'Now you have been standing up and you are all hungry, sit down all of you.' What a sight to see them all dropping into their places. According to Mark they fell into order by rank, by hundreds and by fifties. What a Commander-in-Chief Christ is! When he makes a banquet it is not a scramble; it is always orderly, and when there is anything very disorderly it is generally because Christ is not there; if he is there, everything seems to fit into its place.

36-37 And he took the seven loaves and the fishes, and gave thanks, and brake them, and gave to his disciples, and the disciples to the multitude. And they did all eat, and were filled: —

'They did all eat and were filled.' I remember a country brother putting it, 'And they did all eat a lot', which I think is very likely. They were very hungry; they did all eat and were filled; they were ravenous, but they were not stinted.

37-39   and they took up of the broken meat that was left seven baskets full. And they that did eat were four thousand men, beside women and children. And he sent away the multitude, and took ship, and came into the coasts of Magdala.

And if the women and children bore any proportion to most congregations they would make a larger number than the men. And then comes the finish: 'And he sent away the multitude.' You and I, if we had done this, would have let them stop for an hour while somebody proposed and somebody else seconded a vote of thanks for this good dinner that they had had, but he fed them and then 'He sent away the multitude, and took ship, and came into the coasts of Magdala.' May we learn our Lord's blessed absence of self-seeking!

MATTHEW 15:21-39

Jesus had been in conflict with the scribes and Pharisees. He never liked such discussions, and though he was always victorious in every controversy, it grieved his spirit.

Matt. 15:21   Then Jesus went thence, and departed into the coasts of Tyre and Sidon.

He was glad to get away and made a journey over the hills to get at as great a distance as possible from these cavillers.

22   And, behold, a woman of Canaan came —

A Syrophenician woman, one of the old, condensed race living in Tyre and Sidon.

22-23   out of the same coasts, and cried unto him, saying, Have mercy on me, O Lord, thou son of David; my daughter is grievously vexed with a devil. But he answered her not a word. —

Answers to prayers may be delayed, but delays are not always denials. Christ's silence must have been a great trial to the poor woman, but our Lord knew with whom he was dealing.

23 And his disciples came and besought him, saying, Send her away; for she crieth after us.

Ah! These disciples made a grand mistake. She did not cry after *them*; she cried after *him*. So they understood it; therefore, they said, 'Get rid of her; she disturbs us; when we are in the street, we can hear her cry. Send her away; for she crieth after us.' Ah! Poor disciples. She was not so foolish as to cry after you; she was crying after your Master. If any here have come only to hear the preacher, they have made a great mistake; but, if you have come for a word from the Master, I pray that you may be gratified.

24 But he answered and said, I am not sent but unto the lost sheep of the house of Israel.

Christ did what he was sent to do; he was the Messiah, the sent One. He would not go beyond his mission, so he says, 'I am sent.' He was sent as a Preacher and a Teacher, not to the Gentiles, but to Israel. He had a larger commission in reserve and was yet to be a Saviour to the Gentiles as well as to the Jews; but for the present, he was to be a Shepherd to 'the lost sheep of the house of Israel'.

25 Then came she and worshipped him, saying, Lord, help me.

A very short prayer, but how much there was in it!

26-27 But he answered and said, It is not meet to take the children's bread, and to cast it to dogs. And she said, Truth, Lord: yet the dogs eat of the crumbs which fall from their masters' table.

It is the faculty of faith to see in the dark. This woman spied out light in what seemed to be a very dark saying. Did Christ call her a dog? Well, dogs have their privileges when they lie under the table. Even if their master does not throw them a crumb, yet they may take that which falls from his hand. If Jesus would but allow any mercy to drop, as it were, accidentally, this woman would be content.

28-29 Then Jesus answered and said unto her, O woman, great is thy faith: be it unto thee even as thou wilt. And her daughter was made whole from that very hour. And Jesus departed from thence, —

When he had done his business, he was off. Our Lord was a great itinerant; he was always on the move. He had come all the way to the parts of Tyre and Sidon to help one woman; and when that one woman had been attended to, he went back again immediately to his old post by the sea of Galilee.

29-30 and came nigh unto the sea of Galilee; and went up into a mountain, and sat down there. And great multitudes came unto him, having with them those that were lame, blind, dumb, maimed, and many others, and cast them down at Jesus' feet; and he healed them:

In the prayer-meeting, held by the deacons and elders this morning, before I came in here, one of our friends observed in prayer that there might be many lame, blind and maimed in the congregation, and he prayed that they might be brought to Jesus. Let us, by faith, bring them to him and lay them at his feet. Oh, that this word, 'He healed them', might be true again today!

31 Insomuch that the multitude wondered, when they saw the dumb to speak, the maimed to be whole, the lame to walk, and the blind to see: and they glorified the God of Israel.

Oh, for glory to God! There is no glory to God which equals that which comes from blind eyes which have been made to see and from dumb lips which have been made to speak. The glories of nature and providence are eclipsed by the glories of grace. May we see such things today.

32 Then Jesus called his disciples unto him, and said, I have compassion on the multitude, because they continue with me now three days, and have nothing to eat: and I will not send them away fasting, lest they faint in the way.

Ah, dear friends. They were willing to put up with inconvenience to hear the gospel in those days! Three days of sermon-hearing! People want sermons wonderfully short now, and the sermons must be marvelously interesting, too, or else the people grow dreadfully tired. If dinner time came around, the dinner bell, at any time, in these days, would drown all the attraction of the pulpit. But here were people that attended Christ's ministry for three days, and they had nothing to eat. He had compassion upon them and said to his disciples, 'I will not send them away fasting, lest they faint in the way.'

33-34 And his disciples say unto him, Whence should we have so much bread in the wilderness, as to fill so great a multitude? And Jesus saith unto them, How many loaves have ye? —

That is the point. It is idle to enquire about how much you want. 'How many loaves have ye?'

34-35 And they said, Seven, and a few little fishes. And he commanded the multitude to sit down on the ground.

It was a token of Christ's presence and power that they were willing to sit down on the ground. Think of thousands of people taking their places in an orderly way to feed upon seven cakes and a few little fishes! Without any demur, the crowd arranged itself into banquet order at the command of Jesus.

36-37 And he took the seven loaves and the fishes, and gave thanks, and brake them, and gave to his disciples, and the disciples to the multitude. And they did all eat, and were filled: and they took up of the broken meat that was left seven baskets full.

They were large baskets, too; not like the small food baskets mentioned when the 5,000 were fed. The word used here is the same that is employed to describe the basket in which Saul was let down by the wall of Damascus.

38 And they that did eat were four thousand men, beside women and children.

Now, if the women and children bore the same proportion to the men as they generally do in our congregation, there must have been a very large crowd indeed. Why is the number of the women and children not mentioned? Was it because there were so many? Or was it because their appetites being smaller than the appetites of men, the men are put down as the great eaters, and the women and children, as it were, thrown into the count? What a mercy it is that the Lord adds to the church daily a vast number of men, women, and children! The Lord send us many more, until we cannot count them!

39 And he sent away the multitude, and took ship, and came into the coasts of Magdala.

He had taught the people, and fed them; so, now he goes elsewhere to carry similar blessings to others also.

MATTHEW 16:24 – 17:13

Matt. 16:24-25   Then said Jesus unto his disciples, If any man will come after me, let him deny himself, and take up his cross, and follow me. For whosoever will save his life shall lose it: and whosoever will lose his life for my sake shall find it.

This is the law of self-sacrifice, based on the sacrifice of Christ, and leading up to the complete sacrifice of the redeemed. We are not our own; we are bought with a price. To try to keep ourselves to ourselves would be acting contrary to the whole spirit of the redemption which Christ has wrought for us; and that is the last thing that any Christian should think of doing.

26-28   For what is a man profited, if he shall gain the whole world, and lose his own soul? or what shall a man give in exchange for his soul? For the Son of man shall come in the glory of his Father with his angels; and then he shall reward every man according to his works. Verily I say unto you, There be some standing here, which shall not taste of death, till they see the Son of man coming in his kingdom.

By which, I suppose he meant that they should see him in his majesty — that, notwithstanding the cross, they should see something of his crown of glory, as they did when they beheld him after his resurrection; and as they did, even better, when he ascended on high; and as they did, some of them, in vision, when they saw him standing at the right hand of God, even the Father.

Matt. 17:1   And after six days —

Luke says, 'about an eight days after these sayings', but I suppose he counted the day before and the day after. 'After six days' — and the first day was probably the first day of the week, so he was now coming to another Lord's day. One of the high Christian festivals of the life of Christ was about to be celebrated. Jesus was not yet dead, therefore it was not the resurrection that was celebrated on that day, but the transfiguration. 'After six days' — six days' teaching concerning the cross before he revealed his glory. Dear brethren, there are many in these days who delight to speak almost exclusively about the glory of the second advent. Now, God forbid that we should be silent concerning that great theme! But I think our teaching concerning it must be given after six days' consideration of the sufferings of Christ. Let those who will say, 'We preach Christ glorified' mean still to say, with Paul, 'But we preach Christ crucified.' When I have had my six days for that topic, then am I right glad to have another day to speak concerning Christ's glory. We must never forget his death; all our immortal hopes are centred in the death of our great Substitute. 'After six days' —

1-2 Jesus taketh Peter, James, and John his brother, and bringeth them up into an high mountain apart, And was transfigured before them: and his face did shine as the sun, and his raiment was white as the light.

'White and glistering', says Luke. 'Exceeding white as snow; so as no fuller on earth can white them', says Mark.

3 And, behold, —

As if this was a great wonder: the transfiguration of Christ could scarcely be called miraculous, for it is according to the nature of Christ that his face should shine, and his very raiment become glorious.

3 there appeared unto them Moses and Elias talking with him.

Moses, the great representative of the law, and Elias, the chief of the prophets — one who had died, and one who had entered heaven without dying — thus representing both the quick and the dead.

4 Then answered Peter, and said unto Jesus, Lord, it is good for us to be here: if thou wilt, let us make here three tabernacles; one for thee, and one for Moses, and one for Elias.

If Peter had known that hymn by Dr Watts —

> *My willing soul would stay*
> *In such a frame as this,*
> *And sit and sing herself away*
> *To everlasting bliss.*

— he would have thought it appropriate to sing at that moment; and whenever we get up on the mount, we have no desire to go down again. Our one thought is, 'Oh, that this happy experience would last! Oh, that we might keep in this blessed company for ever!' Yet our highest religious excitements cannot continue, even as the sea is not always at flood tide. The talk between those three — Jesus and Moses and Elias — must have been well worth hearing. I would like to have been one of the three untransfigured, unglorified apostles, to listen to the conversation of the three glorified ones. We know what they talked about, for Luke tells us that they 'spake of his decease which he should accomplish at Jerusalem' [Luke 9:31], and it is very singular that the Greek word which he used to describe Christ's decease is the word 'exodus'. They 'spake of his exodus which he should accomplish at Jerusalem'. Moses knew all about the exodus out of Egypt. And what a type that was of Christ's departure out of this world — the death of the lamb, the sprinkling of the blood, the slaying of the firstborn among the Egyptians, even as Christ smote sin, death and hell; the triumphant coming out of Israel, with silver and gold, setting forth Christ's ascension to his Father with all his precious treasures captured from the hand of the enemy.

How changed must the feelings of Elias have been since the day when he said, 'I, even I only, am left; and they seek my life, to take it away' [1 Kings 19:10,14]; for now he was seeing the King in his glory and talking with him about his approaching departure. How did Peter and James and John know that these two men were Moses and Elias? They had never seen them in the flesh, yet they evidently recognized them; so, as they knew people whom they had not known on earth, I am sure that I shall know in heaven those whom I did know here; I shall have the advantage of them in that respect. I suppose they said to one another, as soon as they saw these men, 'That is Moses, and that is Elijah'; yet they had never seen them. And shall not we, when we meet our dear kindred and friends, say at once, 'That is So-and-so, with whom I took sweet counsel on earth when we walked to the house of God in company'? Surely, the mutual recognition of the saints hardly needs a better support than this passage supplies.

5 While he yet spake, behold, a bright cloud overshadowed them: —

The Shekinah cloud, which was the type of the divine presence in the wilderness — bright, yet a cloud, softening the excessive glory of the face of Jesus with its overshadowing, yet casting no dimness upon it: 'A bright cloud overshadowed them.'

5-6 and behold a voice out of the cloud, which said, This is my beloved Son, in whom I am well pleased; hear ye him. And when the disciples heard it, they fell on their face, and were sore afraid.

We cannot bear for God to come too near us; for we are such frail earthen vessels that if he reveals his glory too much within us we are ready to break.

7 And Jesus came and touched them, and said, Arise, and be not afraid.

Aye, it was Jesus only who could give them comfort; and I have to say:

Till God in human flesh I see,
　My thoughts no comfort find;
The holy, just, and sacred Three
　Are terrors to my mind.

But if Immanuel's face appear,
　My hope, my joy, begins;
His name forbids my slavish fear,
　His grace removes my sins.

The hand of a man touched the apostles, and the voice of a man said to them, 'Arise, and be not afraid.'

8 And when they had lifted up their eyes, they saw no man, save Jesus only.

And they did not want any other man 'save Jesus only'. Let Moses and Elijah and all others go, so long as Christ remains. There will be the most blessed company for us so long as he abides with us.

9-10 And as they came down from the mountain, Jesus charged them, saying, Tell the vision to no man, until the Son of man be risen again from the dead. And his disciples asked him, saying, Why then say the scribes that Elias must first come?

'May we not tell the story of what has happened on this mountain? Elias has come. If we publish this news, it may convince even the scribes that thou art the Messiah.'

11-12 And Jesus answered and said unto them, Elias truly shall first come, and restore all things. But I say unto you, That Elias is come already, and they knew him not, but have done unto him whatsoever they listed. Likewise shall also the Son of man suffer of them.

How he comes back to that point! Evidently the chief thought in our Saviour's mind was concerning his suffering. On another occasion, he said, 'I have a baptism to be baptized with; and how am I straitened till it be accomplished!' [Luke 12:50]. As the magnetic needle ever points to the pole, so did the heart of Jesus ever point to the cross.

13 Then the disciples understood that he spake unto them of John the Baptist.

John had indeed come 'in the spirit and power of Elias', yet Herod had put him to death, as other wicked men would deal with his Lord and Master whose way he so gloriously prepared.

MATTHEW 17:1-5

Matt. 17:1-2 And after six days Jesus taketh Peter, James, and John his brother, and bringeth them up into an high mountain apart, And was transfigured before them: and his face did shine as the sun, and his raiment was white as the light.

Were these 'six days' a week's quiet interval, in which our Lord prepared himself for the singular transaction upon the 'mountain apart'? Did the little company of three know from one Sabbath to another that such an amazing joy awaited them? The three were elect out of the elect and favoured to see what none else in all the world might behold. Doubtless our Lord had reasons for his choice, as he has for every choice he makes; but he does not unveil them to us. The same three beheld the agony in the garden; perhaps the first sight was necessary to sustain their faith under the second. The name of the 'high mountain' can never be known; for those who knew the locality have left no information. Tabor, if you please; Hermon, if you prefer it. No one can decide. It was a lone and lofty hill.

While in prayer, the splendour of the Lord shone out. His face, lit up with its own inner glory, became a sun; and all his dress, like clouds irradiated by that sun, became white as the light itself. 'He was transfigured before them.' He alone was the centre of what they saw. It was a marvellous unveiling of the hidden nature of the Lord Jesus. Then was, in one way, fulfilled the word of John: 'The Word was made flesh, and dwelt among us, and we beheld his glory.'

The transfiguration occurred but once: special views of the glory of Christ are not enjoyed every day. Our highest joy on earth is to see Jesus. There can be no greater bliss in heaven, but we shall be better able to endure the exceeding bliss when we have laid aside the burden of this flesh.

3 And, behold, there appeared unto them Moses and Elias talking with him.

Thus the Law and the Prophets, 'Moses and Elias', communed with our Lord, 'talking with him', and entering into familiar conversation with their Lord. Saints long departed still live — live in their personality, are known by their names and enjoy near access to Christ. It is a great joy to holy ones to be with Jesus: they find it heaven to be where they can talk with him. The heads of former dispensations conversed with the Lord as to his decease, by which a new economy would be ushered in. After condescending so long to his ignorant followers, it must have been a great relief to the human soul of Jesus to talk with two master minds like those of Moses and Elijah. What a sight for the apostles, this glorious trio! They 'appeared unto them', but they 'talked with him'; the object of the two holy ones was not to converse with apostles, but with their Master. Although saints are seen of men, their fellowship is with Jesus

4 Then answered Peter, and said unto Jesus, Lord, it is good for us to be here: if thou wilt, let us make here three tabernacles; one for thee, and one for Moses, and one for Elias.

The sight spoke to the three beholders, and they felt bound to answer to it. Peter must speak: 'Then answered Peter.' That which is uppermost comes out: 'Lord, it is good for us to be here.' Everybody was of his opinion. Who would not have been? Because it was so good, he would fain stay in this beatific state, and get still more good from it. But he has not lost his reverence, and therefore he would have the great ones sheltered suitably. He submits the proposal to Jesus: 'If thou wilt.' He offers that, with his brethren, he will plan and build shrines for the three holy ones: 'Let us make here three tabernacles.' He does not propose to build for himself and James and John, but he says, 'one for thee, and one for Moses, and one for Elias'. His talk sounds rather like that of a bewildered child. He wanders a little; yet his expression is a most natural one. Who would not wish to abide in such society as this? Moses, and Elias, and Jesus — what company! But yet how unpractical is Peter! How selfish the one thought: 'It is good for us'! What was to be done for the rest of the twelve and for the other disciples and for the wide, wide world? A sip of such bliss might be good for the three, but to continue to drink thereof might not have been really good even for them. Peter knew not what he said. The like might be said of many another excited utterance of enthusiastic saints.

5 While he yet spake, behold, a bright cloud overshadowed them: and behold a voice out of the cloud, which said, This is my beloved Son, in whom I am well pleased; hear ye him.

'While he yet spake' — such wild talk might well be interrupted. What a blessed interruption! We may often thank the Lord for stopping our babbling. 'A bright cloud overshadowed them.' It was bright and cast a shadow. They felt that they were entering it and feared as they did so. It was a singular experience; yet we have had it repeated in our own cases. Do we not know what it is to get shadow out of brightness, and 'a voice out of the cloud'? This is after the frequent manner of the Lord in dealing with his favoured ones. The voice was clear and distinct. First came the divine attestation of the Sonship of our Lord: 'This is my beloved Son'; and then the Father's declaration of delight in him: 'in whom I am well pleased'. What happiness for us that Jehovah is well pleased in Christ and with all who are in him! Then followed the consequent divine requirement: 'Hear ye him.' It is better to hear the Son of God than to see saints or to build tabernacles. This will please the Father more than all else that love can suggest. The good pleasure of the Father in the Lord Jesus is a conspicuous part of his glory. The voice conveyed to the ear a greater glory than the lustre of light could communicate through the eye. The audible part of the transfiguration was as wonderful as the visible.

MATTHEW 18:1-22

Matt. 18:1   At the same time came the disciples unto Jesus, saying, Who is the greatest in the kingdom of heaven?

The question we have sometimes heard asked in other forms: 'Which is the highest office; which form of service shall have the greatest honour?' — as if we were courtiers and were to take our positions according to precedent.

2   And Jesus called a little child unto him, and set him in the midst of them,

They all wondered what he was going to do. The little child was no doubt pleased to find itself in such happy company.

3   And said, Verily I say unto you, —

To you, men or women, who think no small things of yourselves, and are wanting to know which is greatest, implying that you, each one, think yourself pretty good as it is.

3 Except ye be converted, and become as little children, ye shall not enter into the kingdom of heaven.

Someone said to me this morning, 'This is a growing day.' 'Ah!' I said, 'I hope we shall all grow spiritually.' 'Which way?' said he, 'Smaller or larger?' Let it be smaller, brethren, that will be the surest way of growth certainly. If we can become much less today, we shall be growing. We have grown up, as we call it; let us grow down today and become as little children, or else we shall not enter into the kingdom of heaven.

4 Whosoever therefore shall humble himself as this little child, the same is greatest in the kingdom of heaven.

The lower down, the higher up. In a certain sense, the way to heaven is downward, in our own esteem certainly. 'He must increase; I must decrease.' And when that straight-backed letter 'I', which often becomes so prominent, vanishes altogether — till there is not an iota of it left — then we shall become like our Lord.

5 And whoso shall receive one such little child in my name receiveth me.

The humblest and the least in the family of divine love, if received, brings with that reception the same blessing as the reception of Christ.

6 But whoso shall offend one of these little ones which believe in me, —

It does not mean, put him out of temper by his taking his silly offence, but, shall cause him to sin, shall make him stumble, shall scandalize him — whosoever shall do that.

6 it were better for him that a millstone were hanged about his neck, and that he were drowned in the depth of the sea.

If you have the Revised Version, you will see in the margin that it is an ass millstone — not a common millstone, which women used to turn, but a bigger stone, which was turned by an ass, in a mill which thus was of a larger kind altogether. The very heaviest conceivable doom was better than to be a stumbling block in the way of the very least of God's people. Yet I have known some say, 'Well, the thing is lawful, and if a weak brother does not like it, I cannot help it, he should not be weak.' No, my dear brother, but that is not the way Christ would have you talk. You must consider the weakness of your brother; all things may be lawful to you, but all things are not expedient, and if meat make your brother to offend, eat no meat while the world standeth. Remember, we must, after all, measure the pace which the flock can travel by the weakest in the flock, or else we shall have to leave behind us many of the sheep of Christ. The pace at which a company must go, must depend upon how fast the weak and the sick can travel — Is it not so? — unless we are willing to part company with them, which I trust we are not willing to do. So let us take care that we cause not even the weakest to stumble by anything that we can do without harm to ourselves but which would bring harm to them. Then I am not sure if it would harm the weakest, whether it would not harm us also, because we are not as strong as we think we are; and, perhaps, if we took a better measure, we might put ourselves among the weakest, too.

7-8 Woe unto the world because of offences! for it must needs be that offences come; but woe to that man by whom the offence cometh! Wherefore if thy hand or thy foot offend thee, cut them off, and cast them from thee: —

Get rid of that which is most useful to you, most necessary to you, rather than be led astray by it and made to sin, for:

8 it is better for thee to enter into life halt or maimed, rather than having two hands or two feet to be cast into everlasting fire.

Remember that is the word of Jesus — 'everlasting fire' — not the word of some of those coarse, cruel theologians that you hear a great deal about nowadays, but the word of Jesus Christ, the Master himself. You cannot be more tender than he; to pretend to be so, will only prove us to be very foolish.

9 And if thine eye offend thee, —

So needful to thy pleasure and to thy knowledge and to thy guidance yet if it make thee sin —

9 pluck it out, and cast it from thee: it is better for thee to enter into life with one eye, rather than having two eyes to be cast into hell fire.

Better to be but a maimed believer than to be an accomplished unbeliever; better to be an uncultured saint than a cultured modern thinker; better that thou lose an eye or lose a hand than lose thy faith in God and his Word — and so lose thy soul and be cast into hell fire.

10 Take heed that ye despise not one of these little ones; —

So apt to do so, when a man appears to have no perfect knowledge, no large pretensions, we are so apt to think: 'Oh! he is a nobody.'

10 for I say unto you, That in heaven their angels do always behold the face of my Father which is in heaven.

There is an angel to watch over each child of God; the heirs of heaven have those holy spirits to keep watch and ward over them. These sacred intelligences, who watch over the people of God, do at the same time behold God's face. They do his commandments, hearkening unto the voice of his word and beholding his face all the while. And if these little ones are thus honourably attended by the angels of God, never despise them. They may be dressed in fustian (or thick cotton), they may wear the very poorest of print, but they are attended like princes; therefore, treat them as such.

11-12 For the Son of man is come to save that which was lost. How think ye?

Another reason why you must not despise them. 'How think ye?' Put on your considering cap, and think a minute.

12-14 if a man have an hundred sheep, and one of them be gone astray, doth he not leave the ninety and nine, and goeth into the mountains, and seeketh that which is gone astray? And if so be that he find it, verily I say unto you, he rejoiceth more of that sheep, than of the ninety and nine which went not astray. Even so it is not the will of your Father which is in heaven, that one of these little ones should perish.

Nor shall they. Christ has come on purpose that he may find them out, and find them out he will; and having an hundred, whom his Father gave him, he will not be satisfied with ninety-and-nine, but the whole hundred shall be there. Now, as if to show us that we are not to despise the very least in the family, nor even the most erring, he brings it personally home to us.

15 Moreover if thy brother shall trespass against thee, go and tell him his fault between thee and him alone: if he shall hear thee, thou hast gained thy brother.

Do not say, 'You must come to me.' Go to him! He has trespassed against you — it is a personal affair. Go and seek him out. It is useless to expect the person who does the injury to try and make peace. It is the injured one who always has to forgive, though he has nothing to be forgiven; it always comes to that, and it is the injured one who should, if he be of the mind of Christ, be the one to commence the reconciliation.

16-17 But if he will not hear thee, then take with thee one or two more, that in the mouth of two or three witnesses every word may be established. And if he shall neglect to hear them, tell it unto the church: but if he neglect to hear the church, let him be unto thee as an heathen man and a publican.

Quit his company. He has despised the last tribunal. Now you must leave him. Be not angry with him. Freely forgive him, but quit him.

18 Verily I say unto you, Whatsoever ye shall bind on earth shall be bound in heaven: and whatsoever ye shall loose on earth shall be loosed in heaven.

Where the church acts rightly, it has the solemn sanction of God; this lesser tribunal on earth shall have its decrees sanctioned by the great tribunal above. Hence it becomes a very serious matter, this binding and loosing which Christ has given to his church.

19-20 Again I say unto you, That if two of you shall agree on earth as touching any thing that they shall ask, it shall be done for them of my Father which is in heaven. For where two or three are gathered together in my name, there am I in the midst of them.

It is not a large church, therefore, that is girded with the wonderful power of prayer, but even two or three. Christ will not have us despise one; he will not have us despise two or three. Who hath despised the day of small things? On the contrary, measure by quality, rather than by quantity. And even if the quality fail, measure by love, rather than by some rule of justice that you have set up.

21   Then came Peter to him, and said, Lord, how oft shall my brother sin against me, and I forgive him? till seven times?

He thought he had opened his mouth very wide when he said that.

22   Jesus saith unto him, I say not unto thee, Until seven times: but, Until seventy times seven.

I do not wonder that we read in another place that the disciples said, 'Lord, increase our faith.' For it needs much faith to have so much patience and to continue still to forgive.

MATTHEW 19:13 – 20:16

All sorts of persons are invited to come to Christ, whatever their age may be. We begin here with the children.

Matt. 19:13-15   Then were there brought unto him little children, that he should put his hands on them, and pray: and the disciples rebuked them. But Jesus said, Suffer little children, and forbid them not, to come unto me: for of such is the kingdom of heaven. And he laid his hands on them, and departed thence.

The principal difficulty of children in coming to Christ frequently lies in their friends. Their parents or their other relatives think they are too young and discourage them. Oh, that we all had a right idea of the possibility of the conversion of little children; nay, not only of the possibility, but that we looked for it, watched for it and encouraged young children to come to Christ! You know that, in the parable I am going to read presently, we are told that the householder 'went out early in the morning to hire labourers into his vineyard'. What a privilege it is to be brought to Christ early in the morning — that is, while we are yet children.

16   And, behold, one came and said unto him, Good Master, what good thing shall I do, that I may have eternal life?

This was not a child, but a young man, who had come to riper years.

17-20   And he said unto him, Why callest thou me good? there is none good but one, that is, God: but if thou wilt enter into life, keep the commandments. He saith unto him, Which? Jesus said, Thou shalt do no murder, Thou shalt not commit adultery, Thou shalt not steal, Thou shalt not bear false witness, Honour thy father and thy mother: and, Thou shalt love thy neighbour as thyself. The young man saith unto him, All these things have I kept from my youth up: what lack I yet?

Externally, in the letter, very likely this young man had kept these commandments, and so far he was to be commended; yet internally, in their spirit, he had not kept one of them. Our Saviour did not tell him that he had failed, but he took him on his own ground: 'You say that you love your neighbour as yourself; I will give you a test to prove whether you do.'

21-22   Jesus said unto him, If thou wilt be perfect, go and sell that thou hast, and give to the poor, and thou shalt have treasure in heaven: and come and follow me. But when the young man heard that saying, he went away sorrowful: for he had great possessions.

See, then, that often with men — with young men — the great hindrance in coming to Christ may be the world. They may have riches, or they may have a great craving for riches; and this may stand in the way of their coming to the Saviour. If any man loves riches better than he loves Christ, he cannot be saved.

23-24   Then said Jesus unto his disciples, Verily I say unto you, That a rich man shall hardly enter into the kingdom of heaven. And again I say unto you, It is easier for a camel to go through the eye of a needle, than for a rich man to enter into the kingdom of God.

Somehow or other,

> *Gold and the gospel seldom do agree;*
> *Religion always sides with poverty.*

because a man's possessions are so liable to get into his heart. He is apt to turn them into idols, and to make devotion to them the great object of his life; as long as he does so, he cannot be saved.

25-27 When his disciples heard it, they were exceedingly amazed, saying, Who then can be saved? But Jesus beheld them, and said unto them, With men this is impossible; but with God all things are possible. Then answered Peter and said unto him, Behold, we have forsaken all, and followed thee; what shall we have therefore?

Always too fast is this impetuous Peter; ever ready to put in a good word for himself if he can.

28-29 And Jesus said unto them, Verily I say unto you, That ye which have followed me, in the regeneration when the Son of man shall sit in the throne of his glory, ye also shall sit upon twelve thrones, judging the twelve tribes of Israel. And every one that hath forsaken houses, or brethren, or sisters, or father, or mother, or wife, or children, or lands, for my name's sake, shall receive an hundredfold, and shall inherit everlasting life.

He shall find himself a gainer by his losses for Christ's sake. If he has lost friends, he shall find better and truer friends in the church of God. If he has lost possessions, he shall get a spiritual wealth that shall be better to him than houses and lands.

30 But many that are first shall be last; and the last shall be first.

Matt. 20:1-2 For the kingdom of heaven is like unto a man that is an householder, which went out early in the morning to hire labourers into his vineyard. And when he had agreed with the labourers for a penny a day, he sent them into his vineyard.

That was the usual wage of the time, the daily pay of a Roman soldier.

3-4 And he went out about the third hour, and saw others standing idle in the marketplace, And said unto them; Go ye also into the vineyard, and whatsoever is right I will give you. And they went their way.

You notice that the first labourers made a bargain with the householder: he agreed with them for a penny a day, and then sent them into his vineyard. So our Lord seemed to say to Peter, 'If you are going to make a bargain concerning your service, you will not find it pays. You are saying, "We have forsaken all, and followed thee; what shall we have therefore?" That spirit will not do.' Christ is not to be served by hirelings. The moment the idea comes in that we deserve to have anything at his hands, we spoil all our service; and those who might be first come to be last if they once get that notion into their heads. This parable shows that it is so.

5-9 Again he went out about the sixth and ninth hour, and did likewise. And about the eleventh hour he went out, and found others standing idle, and saith unto them, Why stand ye here all the day idle? They say unto him, Because no man hath hired us. He saith unto them, Go ye also into the vineyard; and whatsoever is right, that shall ye receive. So when even was come, the lord of the vineyard saith unto his steward, Call the labourers, and give them their hire, beginning from the last unto the first. And when they came that were hired about the eleventh hour, they received every man a penny.

This was the gift of grace, through the generosity of the employer.

10-12 But when the first came, they supposed that they should have received more; and they likewise received every man a penny. And when they had received it, they murmured against the goodman of the house, Saying, These last have wrought but one hour, and thou hast made them equal unto us, which have borne the burden and heat of the day.

See. They put forth their claim on the ground of deserving, so they had what they had bargained for, but they had no more. They were engaged first, but because they had the hireling spirit they were put last.

13-15 But he answered one of them, and said, Friend, I do thee no wrong: didst not thou agree with me for a penny? Take that thine is, and go thy way: I will give unto this last, even as unto thee. Is it not lawful for me to do what I will with mine own? Is thine eye evil, because I am good?

God will have us know that, in dealing with us when we are his servants, he is under no obligation to us. If he chooses to give a reward, the reward is not of debt, but of his sovereign grace. We are bound to serve him by the fact that he is our Creator, altogether apart from any reward, and we must not talk of dealing with him on terms of reward; it is too high a style for us, poor worms, to assume in the presence of almighty God. If we do talk so, he will soon put us down into our right place.

16 So the last shall be first, and the first last: for many be called, but few chosen.

MATTHEW 20:1-7

Matt. 20:1-2 For the kingdom of heaven is like unto a man that is an householder, which went out early in the morning to hire labourers into his vineyard. And when he had agreed with the labourers for a penny a day, he sent them into his vineyard.

The kingdom of heaven is all of grace, and so is the service connected with it. Let this be remembered in the exposition of this parable. The call to work, the ability and the reward are all on the principle of grace, and not upon that of merit. This was no common man that is an householder, and his going out to hire labourers into his vineyard was not after the usual manner of men, for they will have a full day's work for a full day's wage. This householder considered the labourers rather than himself. He was up before the dew was gone from the grass and found labourers and sent them into the vineyard. It was a choice privilege to be allowed to begin holy service so early in the morning. They agreed with the householder and went to work on his terms. They might well be content, since they were promised a full day's hire and were sure to get it: a penny a day represented the usual and accepted wage. The householder and the labourers agreed upon the amount, and this is the point which has to be noted further on. Young believers have a blessed prospect: they may well be happy to do good work, in a good place, for a good Master and on good terms.

3-4 And he went out about the third hour, and saw others standing idle in the marketplace, And said unto them; Go ye also into the vineyard, and whatsoever is right I will give you. And they went their way.

Hating indolence and grieving that he saw others standing idle in the marketplace, he hired more workers about the third hour. They would make only three-quarters of a day, but it was for their good to cease from loafing at the street corner. These are like persons whose childhood is past, but who are not yet old. They are favoured to have a good part of their day of life available for hallowed service. To these the good householder said, 'Go ye also into the vineyard, and whatsoever is right I will give you.' He pointed to those already in the field and said, 'Go ye also'; he promised them not a definite sum, as he did those whom he first hired, but he said, 'Whatsoever is right I will give you.' They went their way to their labour, for they did not wish to remain idlers.

And as right-minded men, they could not quarrel with the householder's agreement to give them whatsoever was right. Oh, that those around us, who are in their rising manhood, would at once take up their tools and begin to serve the great Lord!

5 Again he went out about the sixth and ninth hour, and did likewise.

Had it been altogether and alone a business transaction, the householder would have waited to begin a new day and would not have given a whole day's wage for a fraction of a day's work. The entire matter was alone of grace; therefore, when half the day was gone, about the sixth hour, he called in labourers. Men of forty and fifty are bidden to enter the vineyard. Yes, and about the ninth hour, men were engaged. At sixty, the Lord calls a number by his grace! It is wrong to assert that men are not saved after forty; we know to the contrary and could mention instances. God in the greatness of his love calls into his service men from whom the exuberance of useful vigour has departed; he accepts the waning hours of their day. He has work for the weak as well as for the strong. He allows none to labour for him without the reward of grace, even though they have spent their best days in sin. This is no encouragement to procrastination; but, it should induce old sinners to seek the Lord at once.

6-7 And about the eleventh hour he went out, and found others standing idle, and saith unto them, Why stand ye here all the day idle? They say unto him, Because no man hath hired us. He saith unto them, Go ye also into the vineyard; and whatsoever is right, that shall ye receive.

The day was nearly over: only a single hour remained; yet about the eleventh hour, he went out. The generous householder was willing to take on more workmen and give them hire, though the sun was going down. He found a group lingering at the loafers' corner — standing idle. He wished to clear the whole town of sluggards, so he said to them, 'Why stand ye here all the day idle?' His question to them may be read by making each word in its turn emphatic, and then it yields a fulness of meaning. *Why* are ye idle? What is the good of it? Why *stand ye here* idle where all are busy? Why *all the day* idle? Will not a shorter space suffice? Why are ye *idle*? You have need to work; you are able to do it, and you should set about it at once. Why is any one of us remaining idle towards God? Has nothing yet had power to engage us in sacred service? Can we dare to say, 'No man hath hired us'? Nearly seventy years of age and yet unsaved! Let us bestir ourselves. It is time that we went, without delay, to pull the weeds and prune the vines and do something for our Lord in his vineyard. What but rich grace could lead him to take on the eleven-o'clock lingerers? Yet he invites them as earnestly as those who came in the morning, and he will as surely give them their reward.

MATTHEW 20:1-28

Matt. 20:1-2 For the kingdom of heaven is like unto a man that is an householder, which went out early in the morning to hire labourers into his vineyard. And when he had agreed with the labourers for a penny a day, he sent them into his vineyard.

It was a fair wage. It was for fair and healthful work which they were to do in the vineyard. They were happy men to be hired so early in the morning. Never do those that serve Christ reject him; and, though in this parable some are represented as finding fault with their wages, yet Christ's true servants do not so. Their only request is, 'Dismiss me not from thy service, Lord.' They feel it to be reward enough to be permitted to go on working. Indeed, this is one way in which we get our wages during the day. If we keep one precept, God gives us grace to keep another. If we perform one duty, God gives us the privilege to perform another. So we are paid well. We work *in* the work. We say not 'for the work', for we are unprofitable servants. Yet is there the penny a day.

3 And he went out about the third hour, and saw others standing idle in the marketplace,

It was bad for them to be standing there. No good is learned by idlers in idle company. Idle men together kindle a fire that burns like the flames of hell.

4-5 And said unto them; Go ye also into the vineyard, and whatsoever is right I will give you. And they went their way. Again he went out about the sixth and ninth hour, and did likewise.

Much more out of charity than out of any good that he could get from them. Especially was this manifest when it got towards the latter end of the day. So late, so very late, it was but little they could do. Yet for their good he bade them come in.

6 And about the eleventh hour —

Why, then, surely the day was over. They were ready to put away their tools and go home. But —

6 he went out, and found others standing idle, and saith unto them, Why stand ye here all the day idle?

'Why?' Can you give a reason for it? Why stand ye here in the market-place, where men come together on purpose to be hired? Why stand ye here, ye able-bodied ones that still might work? Why stand ye here all the day? That ye should be idle a little while is bad enough. Why stand ye here all the day, and why stand ye here all the day idle, when there is so much work to be done and such a wage to receive for it?

7 They say unto him, Because no man hath hired us. He saith unto them, Go ye also into the vineyard; and whatsoever is right, that shall ye receive.

And so the great householder was glad when he had emptied the marketplace of the idlers and brought in, from early morning even till set of sun, so many that should be at work — happily at work there. I wonder whether there are any here early in the morning of life who have not yet come into the vineyard. If so, the Master calls you. Are you in middle life? Have you reached the sixth hour, and are you not enlisted in his service? Again the Master calls you. And if you have reached the eleventh hour, where are you? Decrepit — leaning on your staff — leaning downwards to your grave; yet, if you are not called now, now he calleth you and bids you, even at this late hour, come into the vineyard.

8-9 So when even was come, the lord of the vineyard saith unto his steward, Call the labourers, and give them their hire, beginning from the last unto the first. And when they came that were hired about the eleventh hour, they received every man a penny.

And when souls come to Christ, however late it is, they have the same joy, the same matchless, perfect peace, the same salvation even, as those who have come while yet they are young. True, they have lost many days, many hours of happy service. They have permitted the sun to decline and have wasted much time; but yet, the Master gives them the same life within them, the same adoption into the family of God, the same blessing.

10 But when the first came, they supposed that they should have received more; and they likewise received every man a penny.

Why, there are some of us that have now been in Christ's vineyard ever since we were boys, but we must not think that we shall receive, or can have, more than those who have just come in. I have heard people say, 'Why, here are these people just lately converted, and they are singing and rejoicing; and there some of the old people that have been following the Lord for years and do not seem to have half the joy.' No, no; that is true. It is the old story of the elder brother and the prodigal, over again. But do not — do not — let us repeat that for ever and ever. Do not let us get off of the lines of free, rich, sovereign grace and begin to think that there is some desert in us, some merit in us. Oh! my brothers, I will be glad enough to sit at the feet of the meanest child of God, if I am but to be humoured in the family — glad enough to have the same salvation which the dying thief obtained, though at the last moment only he looked to Christ. Yet there is this spirit that will grow up, that some who have been longer in the work ought certainly to have more joy — more of everything — than those that have just come in. See the answer to it.

11-16 And when they had received it, they murmured against the goodman of the house, Saying, These last have wrought but one hour, and thou hast made them equal unto us, which have borne the burden and heat of the day. But he answered one of them, and said, Friend, I do thee no wrong: didst not thou agree with me for a penny? Take that thine is, and go thy way: I will give unto this last, even as unto thee. Is it not lawful for me to do what I will with mine own? Is thine eye evil, because I am good? So the last shall be first, and the first last: for many be called, but few chosen.

The great principle of election in divine sovereignty will crop up, not in one place, but in many. God will have us know that he is Master, and that in the kingdom of grace he will have mercy on whom he will have mercy, and in the distribution of that grace he will give according to his own good pleasure. And the moment we begin to murmur or set up claims, he answers us at once with: 'Is it not lawful for me to do what I will with my own?' Yet that unevangelical spirit, that ungospel spirit of fancying that we have some sort of claim or right will creep in, and it must be sternly repressed. It is of grace — of grace *alone* — of grace to begin with, of grace to go on with, of grace to close with, and human merit must not be allowed to put a single finger anywhere. 'Where is boasting, then?' says the apostle. 'It is excluded.' It is shut out — the door shut in its face. It must not come in. If you and I serve God throughout a long life, we shall certainly have much greater happiness in life than those can have who come to Christ only at the last. But, as far as the gospel blessing is concerned, which Christ gives, it is the same salvation which the newly born Christian enjoys as that which the most advanced believer is now enjoying. It is to every man the penny, hearing the King's own impress.

17-20 And Jesus going up to Jerusalem took the twelve disciples apart in the way, and said unto them, Behold, we go up to Jerusalem; and the Son of man shall be betrayed unto the chief priests and unto the scribes, and they shall condemn him to death, And shall deliver him to the

Gentiles to mock, and to scourge, and to crucify him: and the third day he shall rise again. Then came to him the mother of Zebedee's children with her sons, worshipping him, and desiring a certain thing of him.

Then, at the most inopportune time in all the world, when Jesus was talking of being mocked and crucified, and put to death, here comes Mistress Zebedee with an ambitious request about her sons.

21   And he said unto her, What wilt thou? She saith unto him, Grant that these my two sons may sit, the one on thy right hand, and the other on the left, in thy kingdom.

He is thinking of a cross, and they are dreaming of a crown. He is speaking of being mocked and put to death, and they have ideas of royalty, that they want to have the chief place in the coming kingdom. Oh! how like ourselves. Our Master thinks of how he can condescend, and we are thinking of how people ought to respect us, and treat us better than they do. Oh! the selfishness that there is in us. May our Master's example help to stay it.

22-24   But Jesus answered and said, Ye know not what ye ask. Are ye able to drink of the cup that I shall drink of, and to be baptized with the baptism that I am baptized with? They say unto him, We are able. And he saith unto them, Ye shall drink indeed of my cup, and be baptized with the baptism that I am baptized with: but to sit on my right hand, and on my left, is not mine to give, but it shall be given to them for whom it is prepared of my Father. And when the ten heard it, they were moved with indignation against the two brethren.

Thus showing that they were exactly like them, 'For', said they, 'look at these two — these James and John — they want to have the preference over us. We will not have it.' It was exactly the same spirit in each one — ambition in them all for priority of honour. Ah! dear friends, it often happens that when we are so intense in our condemnation of others, it is only because we fall into the same sin. Some, I have no doubt whatever, hate the pope because they have the essence of popery in themselves. Two of a trade will never agree; and one man is very angry with another because he is so angry; and one is quite indignant that another should be so proud. Is he not proud? He is proud to say he is humble. He is therein proving how proud he is. Oh! that those beams in our eyes could be got out. Then the motes in our brothers' eyes would probably no more be seen.

25-28 But Jesus called them unto him, and said, Ye know that the princes of the Gentiles exercise dominion over them, and they that are great exercise authority upon them. But it shall not be so among you: but whosoever will be great among you, let him be your minister; And whosoever will be chief among you, let him be your servant: Even as the Son of man came not to be ministered unto, but to minister, and to give his life a ransom for many.

MATTHEW 21:1-5

Matt. 21:1-3 And when they drew nigh unto Jerusalem, and were come to Bethphage, unto the mount of Olives, then sent Jesus two disciples, Saying unto them, Go into the village over against you, and straightway ye shall find an ass tied, and a colt with her: loose them, and bring them unto me. And if any man say aught unto you, ye shall say, The Lord hath need of them; and straightway he will send them.

The time was for our Lord to finish his great work on earth, and his going up to Jerusalem was with this intent. He now determines to enter his capital city openly and there to reveal himself as King. To this end, when he came near to the city, Jesus sent two disciples to bring him the foal of an ass whereon he would ride. His orders to the two disciples whom he commissioned, when they were come to Bethphage, are worthy of our serious attention. He directed them as to the place where they should find the animal: 'Go into the village over against you.' The Lord knows where that which he requires is to be found. Perhaps it is nearer to us than we dream: 'over against you'. He told them that they would not have to search: 'straightway ye shall find'. When the Lord sends us on an errand, he will speed us on our way. He described the condition of the creatures: 'an ass tied, and a colt with her'. Our Lord knows the position of every animal in the world, and he counts no circumstances to be beneath his notice. Nor did he leave the disciples without orders how they were to proceed: 'loose them, and bring them'. Demur and debate there would be none; they might act at once. To stand questioning is not for the messengers of our King: it is their duty to obey their Lord's orders and to fear nothing. The two animals would be willingly yielded up by their owner when the disciples said, 'The Lord hath need of them'; nay, he would not only give them up, but 'straightway he will send them'. Either the owner was himself a secret disciple or some awe of the Lord Jesus was on his mind, but he would right joyfully consent to lend the ass and its foal for the purpose for which they were required. What a singular conjunction of words is here, 'the Lord' and 'hath need'! Jesus, without laying aside his sovereignty, had taken a nature full of needs; yet, being in need, he was still the Lord and could command his subjects, and requisition their property. Whenever we have anything of which the Lord's cause has need, how cheerfully should we hand it over to him! The owner of the ass and her colt regarded it as an honour to furnish Jesus with a creature to ride upon. How great is the power of Jesus over human minds, as that by a word he quietly moves them to do his bidding!

We have here the record of two disciples being sent to fetch an ass: those who do little things for Jesus are honoured thereby. Their errand appeared strange, for what they did might seem like robbery; but, he who sent them took care to protect them from the least shade of suspicion. The messengers raised no question, offered no objection and met with no difficulty. It is ours to do *what* Jesus bids us, *just as* he bids us, and *because* he bids us, for his command is our authority.

4-5 All this was done, that it might be fulfilled which was spoken by the prophet, saying, Tell ye the daughter of Sion, Behold, thy King cometh unto thee, meek, and sitting upon an ass, and a colt the foal of an ass.

Matthew is always reminding us of the Old Testament, as well, indeed, he may, for our Lord is always fulfilling it. Every point of detail is according to the prophetic model: 'All this was done that it might be fulfilled which was spoken by the prophet.' The Old and New

Testaments dovetail into each other. Men have written harmonies of the Gospels, but God has given us a harmony of the Old and New Testament.

The passage referred to is in Zechariah 9:9. It represents Zion's King as meek and lowly even in the hour of his triumphant entrance to his metropolis, riding, not upon a war horse, but upon a young ass, whereon no man had sat. He had before said of himself, 'I am meek and lowly in heart', and now he gives one more proof of the truth of his own words; and, at the same time of the fulfilment of prophecy: 'Tell ye the daughter of Sion, Behold, thy king cometh unto thee, meek and sitting upon an ass.' He did not, like Solomon, fetch horses out of Egypt to minister to his pride, but he who was greater than Solomon was content with a colt, the foal of an ass, and even that humble creature was borrowed for he had none of his own. The tenderness of Jesus comes out in the fact of his having the ass brought with her foal that they might not be parted. He was, as a King, all gentleness and mercy: his grandeur involved no pain, even for the meanest living thing. How blessed is it for us to be ruled by such a King!

MATTHEW 21:23-46

Matt. 21:23   And when he was come into the temple, the chief priests and the elders of the people came unto him as he was teaching, and said, By what authority doest thou these things? and who gave thee this authority?

Jesus knew that these men came to him for no good purpose and that they were only trying to trip him up in his speech. He was always willing to teach when men were willing to learn, but he did not care to cast his pearls before swine. Therefore, mark the holy caution, the sacred ingenuity, with which our Lord replied to these men.

24-27   And Jesus answered and said unto them, I also will ask you one thing, which if ye tell me, I in like wise will tell you by what authority I do these things. The baptism of John, whence was it? from heaven, or of men? And they reasoned with themselves, saying, If we shall say, From heaven; he will say unto us, Why did ye not then believe him? But if we shall say, Of men; we fear the people; for all hold John as a prophet. And they answered Jesus, and said, We cannot tell. And he said unto them, Neither tell I you by what authority I do these things.

He carried the war into the enemy's camp. He answered his accusers by asking them a question which they could not answer in either way without condemning themselves.

28-32 But what think ye? A certain man had two sons; and he came to the first, and said, Son, go work to day in my vineyard. He answered and said, I will not: but afterward he repented, and went. And he came to the second, and said likewise. And he answered and said, I go, sir: and went not. Whether of them twain did the will of his father? They say unto him, The first. Jesus saith unto them, Verily I say unto you, That the publicans and the harlots go into the kingdom of God before you. For John came unto you in the way of righteousness, and ye believed him not: but the publicans and the harlots believed him: and ye, when ye had seen it, repented not afterward, that ye might believe him.

Those poor fallen women and degraded tax-gatherers practically said, by their conduct: 'We will not serve the Lord.' Their past evil life had been a deliberate rejection of the authority of God; and yet, when John the Baptist came, they repented and they believed. Each of them had said, like the elder son, 'I will not', yet they did it. But as for these chief priests and elders, who all their lives had been outwardly serving the Lord and saying, 'We will go and work in God's vineyard', when John came and pointed them to God's own Son, they would not accept him. They had, just now, by refusing to tell whether the Lord's messenger was from heaven or of men, again rejected him and proved that they had not repented. They did not believe John. They had themselves confessed that it was so; and therefore, out of their own mouths they were condemned. I wonder whether there is any lesson in this parable to some who are here; I should not be surprised if there is. I hope that there are some among you, who hitherto have said, 'I will not go', who will repent and go and serve your God. On the other hand, it is to be feared that there may be some here, who have always been saying, 'I go, sir', who nevertheless have not gone and, perhaps, never will go, but will remain, to the last, disobedient to the command of God. The Lord grant that it may not be so!

33-41 Hear another parable: There was a certain householder, which planted a vineyard, and hedged it round about, and digged a winepress in it, and built a tower, and let it out to husband-men, and went into a far country: And when the time of the fruit drew near, he sent his servants to the husbandmen, that they might receive the fruits of it. And the husbandmen took his ser-vants, and beat one, and killed another, and stoned another. Again, he sent other servants more than the first: and they did unto them likewise. But last of all he sent unto them his son, saying, They will reverence my son. But when the husbandmen saw the son, they said among them-selves, This is the heir; come, let us kill him, and let us seize on his inheritance. And they caught him, and cast him out of the vineyard, and slew him. When the lord therefore of the vineyard cometh, what will he do unto those husbandmen? They say unto him, He will miserably destroy those wicked men, and will let out his vineyard unto other husbandmen, which shall render him the fruits in their seasons.

You see at once how this parable related to the leaders of the Jewish people. From generation to generation, they scorned the prophets of God, persecuted them, and put them to death; and when our Lord himself appeared, though his glory might easily have been seen by them, yet they cast him out from among them and put him to death. Yet, beloved friends, we must never regard the Scriptures as referring only to strangers and people of past ages; we must also look to see what bearing they have upon ourselves. The rejection of God's prophets is the sin of our common humanity, and the murder of the Son of God was the crime, not of the Jews only, 'but of the whole human race'. We, too, have a share in it, for we have rejected the Son of the Highest. 'But we were not there', say you. No; and yet we may have repeated that terrible tragedy in our own lives. God has sent you many messengers, and if you remain, at this moment, unconverted, you have not treated them well, else you would have yielded your heart to God. Some of them you have rejected by your neglect, and others have been the subject of your ridicule and contempt. Against some you have striven violently, for your own conscience has been touched, and you have had to do violence to conscience in order to reject their message. Last of all, the Son of God himself has come to you in the preaching of the gospel. You have heard of his death and of his atoning sacrifice, but you have rejected them; and in acting thus, you have done, as far as you could, the same as they did who crucified the Saviour. You still refuse to have him for your Saviour; you disown him as your King; you strive against his righteous sway. You tell me that you do not? Well, then you have yielded to him, and you are saved. But if that be not the case, you still remain such an adversary of God that you reject his Son. Take care lest of you also that prophecy should become true: 'He will miserably destroy those wicked men, and will let out his vineyard unto other husbandmen, which shall render him the fruits in their seasons.'

42 Jesus saith unto them, Did ye never read in the scriptures, —

What a question this was for our Lord to put to men who professed to have the whole of the Scriptures at their fingers ends and to be the only qualified interpreters of them: 'Did ye never read in the Scriptures' —

42-43 The stone which the builders rejected, the same is become the head of the corner: this is the Lord's doing, and it is marvellous in our eyes? Therefore say I unto you, The kingdom of God shall be taken from you, and given to a nation bringing forth the fruits thereof.

And, at this day, we Gentiles enjoy the privileges of the gospel, while poor Israel is scattered to the four winds of heaven. But he, that spared not the natural olive, will not spare the engrafted branches if we are found unfruitful. God takes the gospel away from one nation and gives it to another; but if it is not accepted by the other one, and if he has not all the glory of it ascribed to him, he will take it away from that nation, too. He may deal there with us; if England becomes and remains a drunken nation, a cruel nation, a proud nation, an unbelieving nation, a superstitious nation, and brings forth the evil fruits of the vine of Sodom, we may not expect that God will always continue his kingdom among us. He will say to us, as Christ said to these chief priests and elders: 'The kingdom of God shall be taken from you, and given to a nation bringing forth the fruits thereof.'

44 And whosoever shall fall on this stone shall be broken: —

If you stumble over Christ, the chief Cornerstone of God's building, you will be broken in pieces. If you reject him, you shall suffer serious loss.

44 but on whomsoever it shall fall, it will grind him to powder.

If you arouse the wrath of Christ, and the Rock of ages falls on you — a huge cliff comes toppling from its lofty height upon the traveller and crushes him past all recognition — you will be ground to powder.

45-46 And when the chief priests and Pharisees had heard his parables, they perceived that he spake of them. But when they sought to lay hands on him, they feared the multitude, because they took him for a prophet.

Unhappy people — to reject him who alone could bless them, and yet to stand in fear of him whom they tried to despise! Let it not be so with any of us, but may Jesus become our Teacher and our Friend and our Saviour for ever, by his abounding grace! Amen.

MATTHEW 22:1-14

Matt. 22:1-3 And Jesus answered and spake unto them again by parables, and said, The kingdom of heaven is like unto a certain king, which made a marriage for his son, And sent forth his servants to call them that were bidden to the wedding: and they would not come.

Observe, that it was a king who made this wedding feast; therefore, to refuse to come to it when the command implied great honour to those who were bidden, was as distinct an insult as could very well be perpetrated against both the king and his son. 'They would not come.' Had the one who invited them been only an ordinary person, it might not have been their duty to come, and they might even have been justified in their refusal. But this was a king, who sent his servants to summon the guests to the marriage of his son. And I bid you to take notice that the gospel marriage feast, to which you are invited, is the feast not only of a king, but of the King of kings, your Creator, and your God; and in refusing to come in obedience to his command, you commit an overt act of rebellion against his divine majesty. The king 'sent forth his servants to call them that were bidden to the wedding: and they would not come'. They were bidden, yet they would not come; from whence I gather that those who think the invitations of the gospel are to be restricted to certain characters, because they say it is useless to invite others, 'do err, not knowing the Scriptures'. What have we to do with the apparent uselessness of what we are commanded to do? It is our duty to give the invitation according as our King directs us, but it is not our business to decide whether that invitation will be accepted or rejected. In this case, we know what happened: 'They would not come.'

4 Again, he sent forth other servants, —

Perhaps, in the kindness of his heart, he thought that the first servants whom he sent were somewhat offensive in their manner and that, therefore, the guests would not come. Just as it may be that some of you will never receive the gospel from one minister, for you have a prejudice against his way of putting it, so the Lord may, in the greatness of his mercy, send you his Word by the mouth of another. I am quite sure that any of us, who are the King's servants, would be very glad for somebody else to take our place if he could succeed better with you than we can. This king, in his wisdom and kindness, 'sent forth other servants' —

4-6 saying, Tell them which are bidden, Behold, I have prepared my dinner: my oxen and my fatlings are killed, and all things are ready: come unto the marriage. But they made light of it, and went their ways, one to his farm, another to his merchandise: And the remnant took his servants, and entreated them spitefully, and slew them.

The great majority of those who heard the invitation, 'made light of it', and still is this the habit of the bulk of mankind, and even of many whom I am now addressing. Any day will do for you to think about Christ, so you seem to fancy. He may have your leavings; when it shall come to the last, you think that you can send for a minister to come and pray with you, and that then all will be well. You make light of it — you make light of present mercy, of immediate reconciliation to God. You make light of the love and grace of God and of the precious blood of Jesus. Take heed what ye are doing, for the great King in heaven regards this as high treason against himself; he looks upon it as a presumptuous attempt to lower his infinite majesty in the eyes of men. When a king has killed his oxen and fatlings for his son's wedding feast, and there is nobody to eat the provision, then is it a dishonour to him; and if it were possible for the gospel provisions to be universally rejected, God would be dishonoured. There are some, however, who go further than merely making light of the invitation: 'the remnant' who would, if they could, maltreat and slay the messengers of mercy; and as they cannot, nowadays, kill their bodies, they try to slay their reputations. Any slander which they have heard or any lie which they have invented will do to tell in order to make the minister of Christ of less repute than he deserves to be.

7-10 But when the king heard thereof, he was wroth: and he sent forth his armies, and destroyed those murderers, and burned up their city. Then saith he to his servants, The wedding is ready, but they which were bidden were not worthy. Go ye therefore into the highways, and as many as ye shall find, bid to the marriage. So those servants went out into the highways, and gathered together all as many as they found, both bad and good: and the wedding was furnished with guests.

This is the glorious rule of the gospel still. Those who were first bidden to the great wedding feast were the Jews; they would not come, and therefore, Jerusalem was destroyed. Now the gospel is preached to all nations and all sorts of people in all nations; yet the same sinful rejection of the invitation is constantly being repeated. You, who hear the gospel from Sunday to Sunday, are bidden by it to come to the great supper; and, as some of you will not come, God, in his infinite mercy, is sending his gospel to the poorest and the vilest of mankind. Many of them do come, and thus the Lord provokes you to jealousy by a people who were not a people and astonishes you as you find that many come from the east and from the west and from the north and from the south and sit down in the kingdom of God, while you, who reckoned yourselves to be the children of the kingdom, because you have long been privileged to hear the gospel, shall be cast out. The king's servants 'gathered together all as many as they found, both bad and good'. The best gathering into the visible church is sure to be a mixture; there will be some coming into it who should not be there.

11 And when the king came in to see the guests, —

For whom he had provided sumptuous garments suitable for the wedding — for, as we provide what is supposed to be appropriate array for mourners at a funeral, so, in the east, they provide, on a much larger scale, suitable apparel for wedding guests.

11 he saw there a man which had not on a wedding garment:

He might have had one, for it was provided. The fact that he had not one was as great an insult to the king as a refusal of his invitation would have been. He was not bound to provide himself with a wedding garment; he could not have done it, for he was probably one of those swept up out of the highways. But there it hung, and he was requested to put it on; but he refused, and he had the impertinence to sit there without the indispensable wedding garment. If he could not show his contempt for the king in one way, he would do so in another; and he dared, in the midst of the wedding feasters, to defy the authority of the king and to refuse to do honour to the newly married prince.

12 And he saith unto him, Friend, how camest thou in hither not having a wedding garment? And he was speechless.

He could give no reply; the king's presence awed him into silence.

13 Then said the king to the servants, Bind him hand and foot, and take him away, and cast him into outer darkness, there shall be weeping and gnashing of teeth.

You may manage to get into the church even though you are not converted, but if you are not trusting in Christ, you are not saved, and your false profession will only make your destruction the more terrible. Woe unto us unless we are found wearing the righteousness of Christ — unless our lives are made holy by the gracious influence of his blessed Spirit! These are the wedding garments which we are to wear. If we have them not, our presence at the festival will not avail us in the great testing time that is coming.

14 For many are called, but few are chosen.

All who hear the gospel are called, but the call does not come with equal power to every heart. And with some, the power with which it comes is not that which saves; it only convinces the intellect, so that an outward homage is paid to the Word, and the inward obedience of the soul is not rendered to the Lord. God grant that each of us may have on the wedding garment when the King comes in to see the guests!

MATTHEW 23:29 – 24:21

Matt. 23:29-31 Woe unto you, scribes and Pharisees, hypocrites! because ye build the tombs of the prophets, and garnish the sepulchres of the righteous, And say, If we had been in the days of our fathers, we would not have been partakers with them in the blood of the prophets. Wherefore ye be witnesses unto yourselves, that ye are the children of them which killed the prophets.

They talk in the same conceited manner, and they claim self-righteousness as their fathers did; and if their ancestors killed the prophets, these men garnish their sepulchres and so are sharers in their forefathers' deeds. How often it happens that men say they would not have done such crimes as others have committed, whereas they do not know the vileness of their own hearts. If they were under the same conditions as others, they would act in the same way. It would have been a better sign if the scribes and Pharisees had lamented before God that they themselves were not treating his prophets as they ought to be treated. How very faithful was our Master! He was very tender in spirit; but still, he spoke very severely. The old proverb says that 'a good surgeon often cuts deeply', and so it was with the Lord Jesus Christ. He did not film the evil matter over, he lanced the wound. He is not the most loving who speaks the smoothest words; true love often compels an honest man to say that which pains him far more than it affects his callous hearers.

32-33 Fill ye up then the measure of your fathers. Ye serpents, ye generation of vipers, how can ye escape the damnation of hell?

This is Christ's utterance, let me remind you. Our modern preachers would not talk like this, even to scribes and Pharisees who were crucifying Christ afresh and putting him to an open flame. They would search the dictionary through to find very smooth and pretty words to say to Christ's enemies. We are not of their way of thinking and speaking, nor shall we be while we desire to follow in the footsteps of our Lord.

34 Wherefore, behold, I send unto you prophets, and wise men, and scribes: and some of them ye shall kill and crucify; and some of them shall ye scourge in your synagogues, and persecute them from city to city:

Which they did; the servants of Christ were thus worried and harried all over the land.

35-36 That upon you may come all the righteous blood shed upon the earth, from the blood of righteous Abel unto the blood of Zacharias son of Barachias, whom ye slew between the temple and the altar. Verily I say unto you, All these things shall come upon this generation.

So they did. The destruction of Jerusalem was more terrible than anything that the world has ever witnessed, either before or since. There must have been nearly 1,250,000 people killed during that terrible siege, and even Titus, when he saw the awful carnage, said, 'What must be the folly of this people that they drive me to such work as this? Surely, the hand of an avenging God must be in it.' Truly, the blood of the martyrs slain in Jerusalem was amply avenged when the whole city became a veritable *Aceldama*, or field of blood.

37-38 O Jerusalem, Jerusalem, thou that killest the prophets, and stonest them which are sent unto thee, how often would I have gathered thy children together, even as a hen gathereth her chickens under her wings, and ye would not! Behold, your house is left unto you desolate.

What a picture of pity and disappointed love the King's face must have presented when, with flowing tears, he spoke these words! It was the utterance of the righteous Judge, choked with emotion. Jerusalem was too far gone to be rescued from its self-sought doom, and its guilt was about to culminate in the death of the Son of God.

39 – Matt. 24:1 For I say unto you, Ye shall not see me henceforth, till ye shall say, Blessed is he that cometh in the name of the Lord. And Jesus went out, and departed from the temple: and his disciples came to him for to shew him the buildings of the temple.

Ah, me! The rejected King took but slight interest in the temple of which his disciples thought so much. To them the appearance was glorious; but to their Lord it was a sad sight. His Father's house, which ought to have been a house of prayer for all nations, had become a den of thieves and soon would be utterly destroyed.

2 And Jesus said unto them, See ye not all these things? verily I say unto you, There shall not be left here one stone upon another, that shall not be thrown down.

And it was so. Josephus tells us that Titus at first tried to save the temple, even after it was set on fire, but his efforts were of no avail; and at last he gave orders that the whole city and temple should be levelled, except a small portion reserved for the garrison. Yet the stones of the temple were such as men very seldom see, so exceedingly great; they looked as if, once in their place, they would stand there throughout eternity. But, all are gone, according to our Lord's prophecy.

3 And as he sat upon the mount of Olives, —

The little procession continued ascending the Mount of Olives, until Jesus reached a resting place from which he could see the temple.

3 the disciples came unto him privately, saying, Tell us, when shall these things be? and what shall be the sign of thy coming, and of the end of the world?

There are here two distinct questions, perhaps three. The disciples inquired first about the time of the destruction of the temple, and then about the sign of Christ's coming and of 'the consummation of the age', as it is in the margin of the Revised Version. The answers of Jesus contained much that was mysterious and that could only be fully understood as that which he foretold actually occurred. He told his disciples some things which related to the siege of Jerusalem, some which concerned his Second Advent and some which would immediately precede 'the end of the world'. When we have clearer light, we may possibly perceive that all our Saviour's predictions on this memorable occasion had some connection with all three of these great events.

4 And Jesus answered and said unto them, Take heed that no man deceive you.

Jesus was always practical. The most important thing for his disciples was not that they might know when 'these things' would be, but that they might be preserved from the peculiar evils of the time.

5 For many shall come in my name, saying, I am Christ; and shall deceive many.

And they did. A large number of impostors came forward before the destruction of Jerusalem, giving out that they were Messiahs.

6 And ye shall hear of wars and rumours of wars: —

And they did. The armies of Rome were soon after this on their way to the doomed city.

6-8 see that ye be not troubled: for all these things must come to pass, but the end is not yet. For nation shall rise against nation, and kingdom against kingdom: and there shall be famines, and pestilences, and earthquakes, in divers places. All these are the beginning of sorrows.

One would think that there was sorrow enough in 'famines, and pestilences, and earthquakes, in divers places', but our Lord said that all these were only 'the beginning of sorrows', the first birth pangs of the travail that must precede his coming, either to Jerusalem or to the whole world.

9-14 Then shall they deliver you up to be afflicted, and shall kill you: and ye shall be hated of all nations for my name's sake. And then shall many be offended, and shall betray one another, and shall hate one another. And many false prophets shall rise, and shall deceive many. And because iniquity shall abound, the love of many shall wax cold. But he that shall endure unto the end, the same shall be saved. And this gospel of the kingdom shall be preached in all the world for a witness unto all nations; and then shall the end come.

But as for this destruction of Jerusalem, the Saviour gave them clear warning.

15-16 When ye therefore shall see the abomination of desolation, spoken of by Daniel the prophet, stand in the holy place, (whoso readeth, let him understand:) Then let them which be in Judaea flee into the mountains:

As soon as Christ's disciples saw 'the abomination of desolation', that is the Roman ensigns, with their idolatrous emblems, stand in the holy place, they knew that the time for them to escape had arrived, and they did 'flee into the mountains'. You will say to me, perhaps, 'but there were Romans there before'. Yes, the Romans were in possession, but the eagles and other idolatrous symbols were never exhibited in Jerusalem. The Romans were often very lenient to the different people whom they subdued, and these symbols were kept out of sight until the last war came. Then wherever the Jews and Christians looked, they could see those various images of Caesar and of the Roman state which were worshipped by the soldiery, and then were the faithful to flee to the mountains. It is a remarkable fact that no Christians perished in the siege of Jerusalem; the followers of Christ fled away to the mountain city of Pella, in Perea, where they were preserved from the general destruction which overthrew the unbelieving Jews.

17-18 Let him which is on the housetop not come down to take any thing out of his house: Neither let him which is in the field return back to take his clothes.

They were to flee in all haste the moment they saw the Roman standards.

19-21 And woe unto them that are with child, and to them that give suck in those days! But pray ye that your flight be not in the winter, neither on the sabbath day: For then shall be great tribulation, such as was not since the beginning of the world to this time, no, nor ever shall be.

You and I would have believed that all this came true without any confirmation from outside history, but it was very remarkable that God should raise up the Jew Josephus and put it into his mind to write a record of the siege of Jerusalem, which curdles the blood of everyone who reads it and exactly bears out the statement of the Master that there was to be 'great tribulation, such as was not since the beginning of the world, no, nor ever shall be'.

MATTHEW 24:1-28

Matt. 24:1-2 And Jesus went out, and departed from the temple: and his disciples came to him for to shew him the buildings of the temple. And Jesus said unto them, See ye not all these things? verily I say unto you, There shall not be left here one stone upon another, that shall not be thrown down.

The King, having finished his first discourse in the temple, left it, never to return: 'Jesus went out, and departed from the temple.' His ministry there was ended. As his disciples moved away with him towards the Mount of Olives, they called his attention to the great stones of which the temple was constructed and the costly adornments of the beautiful building. To them the appearance was glorious; but to their Lord it was a sad sight. His Father's house, which ought to have been a house of prayer for all nations, had become a den of thieves and soon would be utterly destroyed: Jesus said unto them, 'See ye not all these things? verily I say unto you, There shall not be left here one stone upon another, that shall not be thrown down.' Josephus tells us that Titus at first tried to save the temple, even after it was set on fire, but his efforts were of no avail; and at last he gave orders that the whole city and temple should be levelled, except a small portion reserved for the garrison. This was so thoroughly done that the historian says that there was but nothing to make those that came thither believe it had ever been inhabited. We sometimes delight in the temporal prosperity of the church as if it were something that must certainly endure, but all that is external will pass away or be destroyed. Let us only reckon that to be substantial which comes from God and is God's work. The things which are seen are temporal.

3 And as he sat upon the mount of Olives, the disciples came unto him privately, saying, Tell us, when shall these things be? and what shall be the sign of thy coming, and of the end of the world?

The little procession continued ascending the Mount of Olives until Jesus reached a resting place from which he could see the temple (Mark 13:3). There he sat down, and the disciples came unto him privately, saying, 'Tell us, when shall these things be? and what shall be the sign of thy coming, and of the end of the world?' These are the questions that have been asked in every age since our Saviour's day. There are here two distinct questions, perhaps three. The disciples inquired first about the time of the destruction of the temple, and then about the sign of Christ's coming and of 'the consummation of the age' (Revised Version margin). The answers of Jesus contained much that was mysterious and that could only be fully understood as that which he foretold actually occurred. He told his disciples some things which related to the siege of Jerusalem, some which concerned his Second Advent and some which would immediately precede 'the end of the world'. When we have clearer light, we may possibly perceive that all our Saviour's predictions on this memorable occasion had some connection with all three of these great events.

4-6 And Jesus answered and said unto them, Take heed that no man deceive you. For many shall come in my name, saying, I am Christ; and shall deceive many. And ye shall hear of wars and rumours of wars: see that ye be not troubled: for all these things must come to pass, but the end is not yet.

Jesus was always practical. The most important thing for his disciples was not that they might know when 'these things' would be, but that they might be preserved from the peculiar evils of the time. Therefore, Jesus answered and said unto them, 'Take heed that no man deceive you. For many shall come in my name, saying, I am Christ; and shall deceive many.' They were to beware lest any of the pretended Messiahs should lead them astray, as they would pervert many others. A large number of impostors, came forward before the destruction of Jerusalem, giving out that they were the annointed of God. Almost every page of history is blotted with the names of such deceivers; and in our own day we have seen some come in Christ's name, saying that they are Christ's. Such men seduce many, but they who heed their Lord's warning will not be deluded by them. Our Saviour's words, 'Ye shall hear of wars, and rumours of wars', might be applied to almost any period of the world's history. Earth has seldom had a long spell of quiet. There have almost always been both the realities of war and the rumours of war. There were many such ere Jerusalem was overthrown; there have been many such ever since, and there will be many such until that glorious period when 'nation shall not lift up sword against nation, neither shall they learn war any more' [Micah 4:3]. 'See that ye be not troubled' is a timely message for the disciples of Christ in every age. 'For all these things must come to pass', therefore let us not be surprised or alarmed at them, 'but the end is not yet'. The destruction of Jerusalem was the beginning of the end, the great type and antici-pation of all that will take place when Christ shall stand at the latter day upon the earth. It was an end; but not *the* end: 'the end is not yet'.

7-8 For nation shall rise against nation, and kingdom against kingdom: and there shall be famines, and pestilences, and earthquakes, in divers places. All these are the beginning of sorrows.

One would think that there was sorrow enough in 'famines, and pestilences, and earthquakes, in divers places', but our Lord said that 'all these' were only 'the beginning of sorrows', the first birth pangs of the travail that must precede his coming, either to Jerusalem or to the whole world. If famines, pestilences and earthquakes are only 'the beginning of sorrows', what may we not expect the end to be? This prophecy ought both to warn the disciples of Christ what they may expect and wean them from the world where all these and greater sorrows are to be experienced.

9 Then shall they deliver you up to be afflicted, and shall kill you: and ye shall be hated of all nations for my name's sake.

Our Lord not only foretold the general trial that would come upon the Jews, and upon the world; but also the special persecution which would be the portion of his chosen followers: 'Then shall they deliver you up to be afflicted, and shall kill you: and ye shall be hated of all nations for my name's sake.' The New Testament gives abundant proof of the fulfilment of these words. Even in Paul's day, 'this sect' was 'everywhere spoken against'. Since then, has there been any land unstained by the blood of the martyrs? Wherever Christ's gospel has been preached, men have risen up in arms against the messengers of mercy and afflicted and killed them wherever they could.

10 And then shall many be offended, and shall betray one another, and shall hate one another.

This would be a bitter trial for the followers of Christ, yet this they have always had to endure. Persecution would reveal the traitors within the church as well as the enemies without. In the midst of the chosen ones there would be found successors of Judas, who would be willing to betray the disciples as he betrayed his Lord. Saddest of all is the betrayal of good men by their own relatives, but even this they have, many of them, had to bear for Christ's sake.

11-12 And many false prophets shall rise, and shall deceive many. And because iniquity shall abound, the love of many shall wax cold.

What could not be accomplished by persecutors outside the church, and traitors inside, would be attempted by teachers of heresy: 'Many false prophets shall rise, and shall deceive many.' They have risen in all ages. In these modern times they have risen in clouds, till the air is thick with them, as with an army of devouring locusts. These are the men who invent new doctrines, and who seem to think that the religion of Jesus Christ is something that a man may twist into any form and shape that he pleases. Alas, that such teachers should have any disciples! It is doubly sad that they should be able to lead astray 'many'. Yet, when it so happens, let us remember that the King said that it would be so. Is it any wonder that, where such 'iniquity abounds' and such lawlessness is multiplied, 'the love of many shall wax cold'? If the teachers deceive the people and give them 'another gospel which is not another', it is no marvel that there is a lack of love and zeal. The wonder is that there is any love and zeal left after they have been subjected to such a chilling and killing process as that adopted by the advocates of the modern 'destructive criticism'. Verily, it is rightly named 'destructive', for it destroys almost everything that is worth preserving.

13   But he that shall endure unto the end, the same shall be saved.

Again our Saviour reminded his disciples of the personal responsibility of each one of them in such a time of trial and testing as they were about to pass through. He would have them remember that it is not the man who *starts* in the race, but the one who runs to the goal, who wins the prize: 'He that shall endure unto the end, the same shall be saved.' If this doctrine were not supplemented by another, there would be but little good tidings for poor, tempted, tried and struggling saints in such words as these. Who among us would persevere in running the heavenly race if God did not preserve us from falling and give us persevering grace? But, blessed be his name, 'the righteous shall hold on his way'. 'He which hath begun a good work in you will perform it until the day of Jesus Christ' [Philippians 1:6].

14 And this gospel of the kingdom shall be preached in all the world for a witness unto all nations; and then shall the end come.

The world is to the church like a scaffold to a building. When the church is built, the scaffold will be taken down; the world must remain until the last elect one is saved: 'then shall the end come'. Before Jerusalem was destroyed, 'this gospel of the kingdom' was probably 'preached in all the world' so far as it was then known, but there is to be a fuller proclamation of it 'for a witness unto all nations' before the great consummation of all things: 'then shall the end come', and the King shall sit upon the throne of his glory, and decide the eternal destiny of the whole human race.

15-18 When ye therefore shall see the abomination of desolation, spoken of by Daniel the prophet, stand in the holy place, (whoso readeth, let him understand:) Then let them which be in Judaea flee into the mountains: Let him which is on the housetop not come down to take any thing out of his house: Neither let him which is in the field return back to take his clothes.

This portion of our Saviour's words appears to relate solely to the destruction of Jerusalem. As soon as Christ's disciples saw 'the abomination of desolation', that is, the Roman ensigns, with their idolatrous emblems, 'stand in the holy place', they knew that the time for them to escape had arrived, and they did 'flee into the mountains'. The Christians in Jerusalem and the surrounding towns and villages, 'in Judaea', availed themselves of the first opportunity for eluding the Roman armies, and fled to the mountain city of Pella, in Perea, where they were preserved from the general destruction which overthrew the Jews. There was no time to spare before the final investment of the guilty city, the man 'on the house-top' could 'not come down to take anything out of his house', and the man 'in the field' could not 'return back to take his clothes'. They must flee to the mountains in the greatest haste the moment that they saw 'Jerusalem compassed with armies' (Luke 21:20).

19-21 And woe unto them that are with child, and to them that give suck in those days! But pray ye that your flight be not in the winter, neither on the sabbath day: For then shall be great tribulation, such as was not since the beginning of the world to this time, no, nor ever shall be.

It must have been a peculiarly trying time for the women who had to flee from their homes just when they needed quiet and rest. How thoughtful and tender was our pitiful Saviour in thus sympathizing with suffering mothers in their hour of need! 'Flight…in the winter' or 'on the sabbath day' would have been attended with special difficulties; so the disciples were exhorted to 'pray' that some other time might be available. The Lord knew exactly when they would be able to escape, yet he bade them pray that their flight might not be in the winter nor on the Sabbath day. The wise men of the present day would have said that prayer was useless under such conditions, not so the great Teacher and Example of his praying people; he taught that such a season was the very time for special supplication. The reason for this injunction was thus stated by the Saviour: 'For then shall be great tribulation, such as was not since the beginning of the world to this time, no, nor ever shall be.'

Read the record written by Josephus of the destruction of Jerusalem, and see how truly our Lord's words were fulfilled. The Jews impiously said, concerning the death of Christ: 'His blood be on us, and on our children.' Never did any other people invoke such an awful curse upon themselves, and upon no other nation did such a judgement ever fall. We read of Jews crucified till there was no more wood for making crosses; of thousands of the people slaying one another in their fierce faction fights within the city; of so many of them being sold for slaves that they became a drug in the market, and all but valueless; and of the fearful carnage when the Romans at length entered the doomed capital and the blood-curdling story exactly bears out the Saviour's statement uttered nearly forty years before the terrible events occurred.

22 And except those days should be shortened, there should no flesh be saved: but for the elect's sake those days shall be shortened.

These were the words of the King as well as of the Prophet, and as such, they were both authentic and authoritative. Jesus spoke of what 'should be', not only as the Seer who was able to gaze into the future, but as the sovereign Disposer of all events. He knew what a fiery trial awaited the unbelieving nation, and that 'except those days should be shortened, there should no flesh be saved'. If the horrors of the siege were to continue long, the whole race of the Jews would be destroyed. The King had the power to cut short the evil days, and he explained his reason for using that power: 'For the elect's sake those days shall be shortened.' Those who had been hated and persecuted by their own countrymen became the means of preserving them from absolute annihilation. Thus has it often been since those days, and for the sake of his elect the Lord has withheld many judgements and shortened others. The ungodly owe to the godly more than they know, or would care to own.

23-26 Then if any man shall say unto you, Lo, here is Christ, or there; believe it not. For there shall arise false Christs, and false prophets, and shall shew great signs and wonders; insomuch that, if it were possible, they shall deceive the very elect. Behold, I have told you before. Wherefore if they shall say unto you, Behold, he is in the desert; go not forth: behold, he is in the secret chambers; believe it not.

It is a grand thing to have such faith in Christ that you have none to spare for imposters. It is important not to distribute your faith too widely. Those who believe in a little of everything will, in the end, believe nothing of anything. If you exercise full faith in that which is sure and steadfast, 'false Christs and false prophets' will not be able to make you their dupes. In one respect, the modern teachers of heresy are more successful than their Judaean prototypes, for they do actually 'deceive the very elect', even though they cannot 'shew great signs and wonders'. One of the saddest signs of the times in which we live is the ease with which 'the very elect' are deceived by the smooth-tongued 'false Christs and false prophets' who abound in our midst. Yet our Saviour expressly forewarned his followers against them: 'Behold, I have told you before.' Forewarned is forearmed. Let it be so in our time. Our Saviour's expressive command may be fitly applied to the whole system of 'modern thought', which is contrary to the inspired Word of God: 'Believe it not.'

27 For as the lightning cometh out of the east, and shineth even unto the west; so shall also the coming of the Son of man be.

When *he* comes, we shall know who he is and why he has come. There will be no longer any mystery or secret about 'the coming of the Son of man'. There will be no need to ask any questions then; no one will make a mistake about his appearing when it actually takes place. 'Every eye shall see him.' Christ's coming will be sudden, startling, universally visible, and terrifying to the ungodly: 'as the lightning cometh out of the east, and shineth even unto the west'. His first coming in judgement at the destruction of Jerusalem had terrors about it that, till then, had never been realized on the earth; his last coming will be more dreadful still.

28 For wheresoever the carcase is, there will the eagles be gathered together.

Judaism had become a 'carcass', dead and corrupt — fit prey for the vultures or carrion kites of Rome. By and by, there will arrive another day, when there will be a dead church in a dead world, and 'the eagles' of divine judgement 'will be gathered together' to tear in pieces those whom there shall be none to deliver. The birds of prey gather wherever dead bodies are to be found; and the judgements of Christ will be poured out when the body politic of religion becomes unbearably corrupt.

MATTHEW 24:42 – 25:13

Matt. 24:42 Watch therefore: for ye know not what hour your Lord doth come.

That he will come, is certain. That his coming may be at any moment, is equally sure; and therefore, we ought to be always ready for his appearing. The Lord make us to be so!

43-44 But know this, that if the goodman of the house had known in what watch the thief would come, he would have watched, and would not have suffered his house to be broken up. Therefore be ye also ready: for in such an hour as ye think not the Son of man cometh.

Perhaps you can imagine how eagerly the householder watches when he expects thieves. Every little sound alarms him. He thinks he hears someone at the door; then he fancies it is someone at the window; but he is on the alert, with eye and ear and his whole being wide awake. So ought we to be, with regard to the coming of the Lord, as watchful as if we knew that Christ would come tonight; we do not know that he will come so soon, yet it may be so, 'for in such an hour as ye think not the Son of man cometh'.

45-46 Who then is a faithful and wise servant, whom his lord hath made ruler over his household, to give them meat in due season? Blessed is that servant, whom his lord when he cometh shall find so doing.

Doing whatever the Master has appointed him to do: if he be a minister, preaching the truth with all his heart; if he be a teacher, endeavouring to feed the minds of the young with sound doctrine; whatever may be his calling, endeavouring to fulfill it to the great Taskmaster's satisfaction, as if he should suddenly break in upon the work, and look at it there and then, and judge his servant by it. This is the way to live.

47 Verily I say unto you, That he shall make him ruler over all his goods.

There are rewards for faithful service — not of debt, but of grace — not according to the law, but according to the discipline of the house of God. Oh, that we may be such faithful servants that our Lord may make us rulers over all that he has!

48-51 But and if that evil servant shall say in his heart, My lord delayeth his coming; And shall begin to smite his fellowservants, and to eat and drink with the drunken; The lord of that servant shall come in a day when he looketh not for him, and in an hour that he is not aware of, And shall cut him asunder, and appoint him his portion with the hypocrites: there shall be weeping and gnashing of teeth.

He was a servant, you see; so this is a warning, not to the outside world, but to you who are inside the nominal church, and who profess to be servants of God; and it is especially a warning to those of us who are ministers of the gospel. Oh, that we may never begin to smite our fellow-servants! Of course, we shall not do it with the fist, but we may do it with the tongue; and may we never be numbered with those who are living for the delights of the flesh! If so, see what must come to us. Our Lord still continued to speak upon the same subject of watchfulness by delivering the very stirring parable of the wise and foolish virgins.

Matt. 25:1-4 Then shall the kingdom of heaven be likened unto ten virgins, which took their lamps, and went forth to meet the bridegroom. And five of them were wise, and five were foolish. They that were foolish took their lamps, and took no oil with them: But the wise took oil in their vessels with their lamps.

There did not seem to be much difference between them. They were all virgins, they all carried lamps, their lamps were all lit; sad, peradventure, the lamps of the foolish were quite as bright as those of the wise. The difference was unobservable to most onlookers, but it was an essential and fatal difference. Ah! dear friends, it is the lack of oil that is the ruin of many a professor's lamp. Men have a name to live, but they have not the true life which is the evidence of the effectual working of the grace of God within their souls. They make a profession of religion, but they have not the secret grace to keep it up. There is a glitter and flash, but there is no permanency; and there cannot be any, unless the Spirit of God be in us indeed and of a truth. We may make a fair show in the flesh for a while, but what will be the end of it? This is the all-important question: Can we hold on and hold out? Certainly, not without that heavenly oil which only the Spirit of God can supply.

5 While the bridegroom tarried, they all slumbered and slept.

Oh, how sadly true it is that, sometimes, true saints as well as mere professors slumber and sleep! Even those who have the oil of grace are not always wide awake to serve their Master and to proclaim the gospel as they should. There are, alas, sleeping believers and sleeping hypocrites side by side.

6-7 And at midnight there was a cry made, Behold, the bridegroom cometh; go ye out to meet him. Then all those virgins arose, and trimmed their lamps.

They were suddenly awakened, and they leaped to their feet:

> *Upstarting at the midnight cry,*
> *'Behold the heavenly Bridegroom nigh!'*

They all trimmed their lamps. That was the first thing for them to do, to look to their torches, and have them ready. They could not meet the Bridegroom in the dark; they must each have a light; so they began their lamp-trimming. It is a pity to have to trim your lamp at the last. O dear friends, it is hard work, upon a dying bed, to have to be tending to one's lamp! You want your evidences to be bright there — your faith to be firm and all your graces brilliant. There must be no doubts and questions there, else they make a dying bed feel hard as granite to the head. May we none of us have at last to trim our lamps! Those virgins who had oil in their vessels were able to trim their lamps; and, though the work was done hurriedly, it was done, and they were able to take their places in the bridal procession.

8 And the foolish said unto the wise, Give us of your oil; for our lamps are gone out.

The modern rendering of this request is, 'Send for the minister, and ask him to pray for us, for our lamps are gone out.' Take heed, I pray you, you who are bold professors now, lest you should have to say at the last, 'Our lamps are gone out.' It was too late for trimming and lighting then.

9-10 But the wise answered, saying, Not so; lest there be not enough for us and you: but go ye rather to them that sell, and buy for yourselves. And while they went to buy, the bridegroom came; —

There are death-bed repentances, undoubtedly; but I fear that, in the great majority of cases, people who wake up so late will find that, while they go to buy, the Bridegroom will come, and there will not be, after all, the time in which to find the Saviour. The mental capacity with which to think of him may fail. The poor head may be so distracted with pain that it may not be able to catch the meaning of what faith in Christ is, or how it can be exercised; and so, the lamp will have gone out, and it will be too late to buy the oil which alone can make it burn. 'While they went to buy, the bridegroom came' —

10-11 and they that were ready went in with him to the marriage: and the door was shut. Afterward came also the other virgins, saying, Lord, Lord, open to us.

'Open the door at least to us, for we came to meet thee, and we carried lamps, and we were with the other virgins: "Lord, Lord, open to us."' You know, perhaps, those striking lines which describe the foolish virgins request, and the Bridegroom's response to it:

> *Late, late, so late; and dark the night and chill!*
> *Late, late, so late; but we may enter still.*
> *'Too late! Too late! Ye cannot enter now.'*

12 But he answered and said, Verily I say unto you, I know you not.

When that door is once shut, it will never again be opened; all Scripture goes to prove that. There are some who foolishly dream about an opening of that door, after death, for men who have died impenitent; but there is nothing in Scripture to warrant us in having any such expectation. The final answer of the Bridegroom to these foolish virgins is: 'Verily I say unto you, I know you not.'

13 Watch therefore, for ye know neither the day nor the hour wherein the Son of man cometh.

That is, we do not know when it will be. Some have foolishly said,

'We do not know the day, or the hour, of Christ's coming, but we may find out the year.' We shall not do anything of the kind; the time is hidden altogether, it is not revealed to us, and it shall not be known till, suddenly, the Lord himself shall come in the clouds with his bright heavenly retinue, to be glorified in his saints and to be admired in all them that believe. Wherefore, be always on the watch, beloved, 'for ye know neither the day nor the hour wherein the Son of man cometh'. God help us to be ready for his appearing at any moment, for his dear name's sake! Amen.

MATTHEW 25:1-13

Matt. 25:1-2 Then shall the kingdom of heaven be likened unto ten virgins, which took their lamps, and went forth to meet the bridegroom. And five of them were wise, and five were foolish.

What a division this makes in the visible church of God! Let us hope that we are not to gather from this that as many as half the professors of Christianity at any time are like these foolish virgins; yet our Lord would not have mentioned so high a proportion if there were not a very large mixture of foolish with the wise: 'Five of them were wise, and five were foolish.'

3 They that were foolish took their lamps, and took no oil with them:

They thought that, if they had the external, it would be quite enough. The secret store of oil, they judged to be unnecessary, because it would be unseen. They would employ one hand in carrying the lamp, but to occupy the other hand by holding the oil-flask seemed to them to be doing too much — giving themselves up too thoroughly to the work. So, they 'took their lamps, and took no oil with them'. They might just as well have had no lamps at all.

4 But the wise took oil in their vessels with their lamps.

Oil in their lamps, and oil *with* their lamps. Lamps are of no use without oil; yet, the oil needs the lamp or else it cannot be rightly used. The light of profession cannot be truly sustained without the oil of grace. Grace, wherever it exists, ought to show itself, as the oil is made to burn by means of the lamp. But it is no use to attempt to make a show unless there is that secret store somewhere by which the external part of religion may be maintained.

5 While the bridegroom tarried, they all slumbered and slept.

Both the wise and the foolish fell into a state which seemed alike in them both. In the case of good men, Christ's delaying his coming often causes disappointment, weariness, and then lethargy, and even the true church falls into a deep slumber. In the foolish, the mere professors, this condition goes much further. There being in them no true life, the very name to live becomes abandoned, and before long, they give up even the profession of religion when there is no secret oil of grace to sustain it.

6 And at midnight —

When things had come to the worst — 'at midnight' — the coldest and darkest hour, when everybody was asleep.

6 there was a cry made, Behold, the bridegroom cometh; go ye out to meet him.

That was a cry which startled everybody; none of the virgins could sleep when once it was announced that the bridegroom was coming. I wish, dear friends, that we thought more of the great truth of the Second Advent. The oftener it is preached, in due proportion with other truths, the better. We need still to hear that midnight cry, 'Go ye out to meet him.'

7 Then all those virgins arose, and trimmed their lamps.

They could not sleep any longer; they were fairly startled and aroused.

8 And the foolish said unto the wise, Give us of your oil; —

Ah, me! Now they began to value what they had aforetime despised.

They were foolish enough to think that oil was unnecessary; but now they saw that it was the one essential thing, so they cried to the wise virgins: 'Give us of your oil.' And hear the dreadful reason:

8 for our lamps are gone out.

I do not know any more terrible words than those: 'Our lamps are gone out.' It is worse to have a lamp that has gone out than never to have had a lamp at all. 'Our lamps are gone out.' We once rejoiced in them. We promised ourselves a bright future. We said, 'All is well for the marriage supper.' But 'our lamps are gone out', and we have no oil with which to replenish them. O sirs, may none of us ever have to lift up that mournful cry! On a dying bed, in the extremity of pain, in the depth of human weakness, it is an awful thing to find one's profession burning low, one's hope of heaven going out, like the snuff of a candle.

9 But the wise answered, saying, Not so; lest there be not enough for us and you: but go ye rather to them that sell, and buy for yourselves.

It is no easy matter to go and rouse up the seller of oil when the midnight hour has struck. O you who are putting off repentance to a dying bed, you are foolish virgins indeed! Your folly has reached the utmost height. You will have more than enough to do, when you lie there with the death-sweat cold upon your brow, without then having to seek the grace which you are neglecting to obtain today, but which you will value then.

10 And while they went to buy, the bridegroom came; —

While they were going.

10-11 and they that were ready went in with him to the marriage: and the door was shut. Afterward came also the other virgins, saying, Lord, Lord, open to us.

Too late, so that they could not enter.

12 But he answered and said, Verily I say unto you, I know you not.

'I never knew you', says Christ in another place; and this knowledge of his is always bound up with affection. He loves no heart that he knows not in this sense. Those whom he knows, he loves. Will he ever say to me or to you, dear friend, 'I know you not'? God grant that he never may have cause to do so.

13   Watch therefore, for ye know neither the day nor the hour wherein the Son of man cometh.

MATTHEW 26:14-35

Matt. 26:14-16 Then one of the twelve, called Judas Iscariot, went unto the chief priests, And said unto them, What will ye give me, and I will deliver him unto you? And they covenanted with him for thirty pieces of silver. And from that time he sought opportunity to betray him.

It was one of the twelve who went unto the chief priests to bargain for the price of his Lord's betrayal. He did not even mention Christ's name in his infamous question, 'What will ye give me, and I will deliver him unto you?' The amount agreed upon, thirty pieces of silver, was the price of a slave and showed how little value the chief priests set upon Jesus, and also revealed the greed of Judas in selling his Master for so small a sum. Yet many have sold Jesus for a less price than Judas received; a smile or a sneer has been sufficient to induce them to betray their Lord. Let us, who have been redeemed with Christ's precious blood, set high store by him, think much of him and praise him much. As we remember with shame and sorrow, these thirty pieces of silver, let us never undervalue him or forget the priceless preciousness of him who was reckoned as worth no more than a slave.

17-18 Now the first day of the feast of unleavened bread the disciples came to Jesus, saying unto him, Where wilt thou that we prepare for thee to eat the passover? And he said, Go into the city to such a man, and say unto him, The Master saith, My time is at hand; I will keep the passover at thy house with my disciples.

How truly royal was Jesus of Nazareth even in his humiliation! He had no home of his own therein he could 'keep the Passover' with his disciples. He was soon to be put to a public and shameful death. Yet he had only to send two of his disciples 'into the city to such a man' and the guest-chamber, furnished and prepared, was at once placed at his disposal. He did not take the room by arbitrary force, as an earthly monarch might have done, but he obtained it by the diviner compulsion of almighty love. Even in his lowest estate, our Lord Jesus had the hearts of all men beneath his control. What power he has now that he reigns in glory!

19 And the disciples did as Jesus had appointed them; and they made ready the passover.

If Christ's disciples always loyally did as Jesus appointed them, they would always speed well on his errands. There are many more people in the world ready to yield to Christ than some of us think. If we would only go to them as Peter and John went to this man in Jerusalem, and say to them what 'the Master saith', we should find that their hearts would be opened to receive Christ even as this man's house was willingly yielded up at our Lord's request.

20-21 Now when the even was come, he sat down with the twelve. And as they did eat, he said, Verily I say unto you, that one of you shall betray me.

Our Lord remained in seclusion until the evening and then went to the appointed place and sat down, or rather, reclined at the paschal table, with the twelve. And as they did eat, he said, 'Verily I say unto you, that one of you shall betray me.' This was a most unpleasant thought to bring to a feast, yet it was most appropriate to the Passover, for God's commandment to Moses concerning the first paschal lamb was, 'With bitter herbs they shalt eat it.' This was a painful reflection for our Lord, and also for his twelve chosen companions: 'One of you', and his eyes would glance round the table as he said it, ' One of you shall betray me.'

22 And they were exceeding sorrowful, and began every one of them to say unto him, Lord, is it I?

That short sentence fell like a bombshell among the Saviour's body-guard. It startled them; they had all made great professions of affection for him and, for the most part, those professions were true. And they were exceeding sorrowful: and well they might be. Such a revelation was enough to produce the deepest emotions of sorrow and sadness. It is a beautiful trait in the character of the disciples that they did not suspect one another, but every one of them inquired, almost incredulously, as the form of the question implies, 'Lord, is it I?' No one said, 'Lord, is it Judas?' Perhaps no one of the eleven thought that Judas was base enough to betray the Lord who had given him an honourable place among his apostles. We cannot do any good by suspecting our brethren; but we may do great services by suspecting ourselves. Self-suspicion is near akin to humility.

23-24 And he answered and said, He that dippeth his hand with me in the dish, the same shall betray me. The Son of man goeth as it is written of him: but woe unto that man by whom the Son of man is betrayed! it had been good for that man if he had not been born.

A man may get very near to Christ, aye, may dip his hand in the same dish with the Saviour, and yet betray him. We may be high in office, and may apparently be very useful, as Judas was; yet we may betray Christ. We learn from our Lord's words that divine decrees do not deprive a sinful action of its guilt: 'The Son of man goeth as it is written of him: but woe unto that man by whom the Son of man is betrayed.' His criminality is just as great as though there had been no 'determinate counsel and foreknowledge of God' [Acts 2:23]. 'It had been good for that man if he had not been born.' The doom of Judas is worse than non-existence. To have consorted with Christ as he had done and then to deliver him into the hands of his enemies, sealed the traitor's eternal destiny.

25 Then Judas, which betrayed him, answered and said, Master, is it I? He said unto him, Thou hast said.

Judas appears to have been the last of the twelve to ask the question, 'Is it I?' Those who are the last to suspect themselves are usually those who ought to be the first to exercise self-suspicion. Judas did not address Christ as 'Lord', as the other disciples had done; but called him Rabbi, 'Master'. Otherwise his question was like that of his eleven companions; but he received from Christ an answer that was given to no one else: he said unto him, 'Thou hast said.' Probably the reply reached his ear alone, and if he had not been a hopeless reprobate, this unmasking of his traitorous design might have driven him to repentance, but there was nothing in his heart to respond to Christ's voice. He had sold himself to Satan before he sold his Lord.

26-28 And as they were eating, Jesus took bread, and blessed it, and brake it, and gave it to the disciples, and said, Take, eat; this is my body. And he took the cup, and gave thanks, and gave it to them, saying, Drink ye all of it; For this is my blood of the new testament, which is shed for many for the remission of sins.

The Jewish Passover was made to melt into the Lord's supper, as the stars of the morning dissolve into the light of the sun. As they were eating, while the paschal supper was proceeding, Jesus instituted the new memorial which is to be observed until he comes again. How simple was the whole ceremony! Jesus took bread and blessed it and brake it and gave it to his disciples and said, 'Take, eat; this is my body.' Christ could not have meant that the bread was his body, for his body was reclining by the table, but he intended that broken bread to *represent* his body which was about to be broken on the cross. Then followed the second memorial, the cup, filled with 'the fruit of the vine', of which Christ said, 'Drink ye all of it.' There is no trace here of any altar or priest; there is nothing about the elevation or adoration of the host; there is no resemblance between the Lord's supper and the Romish mass. Let us keep strictly to the letter and spirit of God's Word in everything; for, if one adds a little, another will add more, and if one alters one point and another alters another point, there is no telling how far we shall get from the truth. The disciples had been reminded of their own liability to sin; now their Saviour gives them a personal pledge of the pardon of sin, according to Luke's record of his words, 'This cup is the new testament in my blood, which is shed for you' [Luke 22:20].

29 But I say unto you, I will not drink henceforth of this fruit of the vine, until that day when I drink it new with you in my Father's kingdom.

Thus Jesus took the great Nazarite vow never to drink of the fruit of the vine till he should drink it new with his disciples in his Father's kingdom. He will keep his tryst with all his followers, and they with him shall hold high festival for ever.

30 And when they had sung an hymn, they went out into the mount of Olives.

Was it not truly brave of our dear Lord to sing under such circumstances? He was going forth to his last dread conflict, to Gethsemane, and Gabbatha and Golgotha; yet he went with a song on his lips. He must have led the singing, for the disciples were too sad to start the *hallel* with which the paschal feast closed: 'And when they had sung an hymn, they went out into the mount of Olives.' Then came that desperate struggle in which the great Captain of our salvation wrestled even to a bloody sweat, and prevailed.

31-32 Then saith Jesus unto them, All ye shall be offended because of me this night: for it is written, I will smite the shepherd, and the sheep of the flock shall be scattered abroad. But after I am risen again, I will go before you into Galilee.

Observe our Lord's habit of quoting Scripture. He was able to speak words of infallible truth, yet he fell back upon the inspired record in the Old Testament. His quotation from Zechariah does not seem to have been really necessary, but it was most appropriate to his prophecy to his disciples: 'All ye shall be offended because of me this night: for it is written, I will smite the shepherd, and the sheep of the flock shall be scattered abroad.' Jesus was the Shepherd who was about to be smitten, but he foretold the scattering of the sheep. Even those leaders of the flock that had been first chosen by Christ and had been most with him, would stumble and fall away from him on that dread night, but the Shepherd would not lose them; there would be a reunion between him and his sheep: 'After I am risen again, I will go before you into Galilee.' Once again he would resume, for a little while, the character of their Shepherd-King, and with them he would revisit some of their old haunts in Galilee, ere he ascended to his heavenly home. 'I will go before you' suggests the idea of the Good Shepherd leading his flock after the eastern manner. Happy are his sheep in having such a Leader, and blessed are they in following him whithersoever he goeth.

33 Peter answered and said unto him, Though all men shall be offended because of thee, yet will I never be offended.

This was a very presumptuous speech, not only because of the self-confidence it betrayed but also because it was a flat contradiction of the Master's declaration. Jesus said, 'All ye shall be offended because of me this night', but Peter thought he knew better than Christ, so he answered, 'Though all men shall be offended because of thee, yet will I never be offended.' No doubt these words were spoken from his heart; but 'the heart is deceitful above all things, and desperately wicked' [Jeremiah 17:9]. Peter must have been amazed the next morning, as he discovered the deceitfulness and wickedness of his own heart, as manifested in his triple denial of his Lord. He who thinks himself so much stronger than his brethren is the very man who will prove to be weaker than many of them, as did Peter not many hours after his boast was uttered.

34 Jesus said unto him, Verily I say unto thee, That this night, before the cock crow, thou shalt deny me thrice.

Jesus now tells his boastful disciple that, before the next morning's cock-crowing, he will thrice deny his Lord. Not only would he stumble and fall with his fellow disciples, but he would go beyond them all in his repeated denials of that dear Master whom he professed to love with more intense affection than even John possessed. Peter declared that he would remain true to Christ even if he were the only faithful friend left. Jesus foretold that, of all the twelve, only Judas would exceed the boaster in wickedness.

35 Peter said unto him, Though I should die with thee, yet will I not deny thee. Likewise also said all the disciples.

Here again Peter contradicts his Master straight to his face. It was a pity that he should have boasted once after his Lord's plain prophecy that all the disciples would that night be offended, but it was shameful that Peter should repeat his self-confident declaration in the teeth of Christ's express prediction concerning him. He was not alone in his utterance, for likewise also said *all* the disciples. They all felt that under no circumstances could they deny their Lord. We have no record of the denial of Christ by the other ten apostles, although they all forsook him and fled, and thus practically disowned him. Remembering all that they had seen and heard of him, and especially bearing in mind his most recent discourse, the communion in the upper room and his wondrous intercessory prayer on their behalf, we are not surprised that they felt themselves bound to him for ever. But, alas, notwithstanding their protests, the King's prophesy was completely fulfilled, for that night they were all 'offended'.

MATTHEW 26:14-45

Matt. 26:14-15 Then one of the twelve, called Judas Iscariot, went unto the chief priests, And said unto them, What will ye give me, and I will deliver him unto you? And they covenanted with him for thirty pieces of silver.

At what a price did the traitor sell our blessed Master! O ye who have been redeemed with his precious blood, set a high value upon him, think much of him, say much in praise of him! Remember these thirty pieces of silver, and never be guilty of despising the Lord of glory, as these chief priests did when they paid for him the price of a slave.

16-19   And from that time he sought opportunity to betray him. Now the first day of the feast of unleavened bread the disciples came to Jesus, saying unto him, Where wilt thou that we prepare for thee to eat the passover? And he said, Go into the city to such a man, and say unto him, The Master saith, My time is at hand; I will keep the passover at thy house with my disciples. And the disciples did as Jesus had appointed them; and they made ready the passover.

See the absolute control which Jesus has over the minds of men. He can have any man's house that he wants, and he knows who will be glad to welcome him. Yet this same Jesus was about to die, and this shows how perfectly voluntary was his sacrifice. He was not forced to stand in our stead, nor was he compelled to suffer except by the constraint of his own great love. All was free, as became the freedom of his grace. Then, shall not our heart's love flow out freely to him? Shall we need to be scourged to obedience? Oh, no, beloved! So let us think what we can *voluntarily* do in honour of our divine Lord, who gave his all for us.

20-22   Now when the even was come, he sat down with the twelve. And as they did eat, he said, Verily I say unto you, that one of you shall betray me. And they were exceeding sorrowful, —

And well might they be sad.

22   and began every one of them to say unto him, Lord, is it I?

What anguish does that question always stir within the heart and mind of every true believer! 'Shall I ever betray my Lord and Master? Shall I every deny or forsake him?' God grant that none of us may ever do as Judas did!

23   And he answered and said, He that dippeth his hand with me in the dish, the same shall betray me.

He who had been entrusted with the charge of the finances of the little band of Christ's immediate disciples, he who carried the bag, was the one who was about to betray his Lord. Since then, Christ has often been betrayed by those who have been in positions of trust, those who have led the way among the disciples of Christ, those who have, as it were, been so familiar with Christ as to dip their hand with him in the dish.

24-25 The Son of man goeth as it is written of him: but woe unto that man by whom the Son of man is betrayed! it had been good for that man if he had not been born. Then Judas, which betrayed him, answered and said, Master, is it I? He said unto him, Thou hast said.

Judas seems to have been the last to ask the question, 'Master, is it I?' yet he was the guilty one — the one who had already covenanted with the chief priests to sell his Lord.

26-31 And as they were eating, Jesus took bread, and blessed it, and brake it, and gave it to the disciples, and said, Take, eat; this is my body. And he took the cup, and gave thanks, and gave it to them, saying, Drink ye all of it; For this is my blood of the new testament, which is shed for many for the remission of sins. But I say unto you, I will not drink henceforth of this fruit of the vine, until that day when I drink it new with you in my Father's kingdom. And when they had sung an hymn, they went out into the mount of Olives. Then saith Jesus unto them, All ye shall be offended because of me this night: for it is written, I will smite the shepherd, and the sheep of the flock shall be scattered abroad.

Observe our blessed Lord's habit of quoting Scripture. He was able to utter words of infallible truth which had never before been used, ye he constantly quoted from the inspired Scriptures. Those who nowadays cavil at the Word of God, and yet profess to be followers of Christ, find no excuse for their conduct in the example that he has left us, for he even quoted Scripture sometimes when it might not have seemed to be necessary to do so. Brethren and sisters in Christ, have your Bible first in you hearts, then at your tongue's end. I was going to say at your fingers' end, so that you may always be able to give a good reason, a solid and divinely authoritative reason, for any statement that you may make.

32-33 But after I am risen again, I will go before you into Galilee. Peter answered and said unto him, Though all men shall be offended because of thee, yet will I never be offended.

No doubt Peter said this from his heart, but 'the heart is deceitful above all things' [Jeremiah 17:9]. Peter may have thought that he was stronger than his brethren, yet he was the very one who proved to be the weakest of the whole apostolic band: 'Though all men shall be offended because of thee, yet will I never be offended.'

34 Jesus said unto him, Verily I say unto thee, That this night, before the cock crow, —

That is to say, before that period of time which was called the cock-crowing —

34 thou shalt deny me thrice.

According to Mark's record, the cock was to crow once before Peter had denied his Lord thrice, and this it did; and when he had given his third denial, it crowed a second time, and then his slumbering conscience was awakened, and 'he went out, and wept bitterly' [Matthew 26:75]. Some persons, who are well acquainted with the religious ceremonies of the Jews, say that the period called the cock-crowing was the time for the sacrifice of the morning lamb, and that it was about that time that Peter denied his Lord.

35 Peter said unto him, Though I should die with thee, yet will I not deny thee. —

It is a great pity that Peter said this after he had received so plain a warning from his Master; yet he was not alone in his boasting.

35 Likewise also said all the disciples.

They all felt quite sure that, under no circumstances, could they be so base as to forsake their Lord; and if you think of the washing of their feet by their Lord and Master, the wonderful words of Christ to which they had listened and that solemn communion service in the large upper room, you may not be surprised that they felt themselves bound to Christ forever — felt that they could never leave him nor forsake him; yet they all did so.

36-39 Then cometh Jesus with them unto a place called Gethsemane, and saith unto the disciples, Sit ye here, while I go and pray yonder. And he took with him Peter and the two sons of Zebedee, and began to be sorrowful and very heavy. Then saith he unto them, My soul is exceeding sorrowful, even unto death: tarry ye here, and watch with me. And he went a little farther, and fell on his face, and prayed, saying, O my Father, if it be possible, let this cup pass from me: nevertheless not as I will, but as thou wilt.

Christ had to tread the winepress alone, yet he showed how complete was his humanity by wishing to have a few choice friends near at hand.

Yet even the chosen three failed him in his hour of greatest need.

40 And he cometh unto the disciples, and findeth them asleep, and saith unto Peter, What, could ye not watch with me one hour?

Peter had constituted himself the spokesman of the apostolic company, so the Master addressed the question to him, though it also applied to his companions: 'What, could ye not watch with me one hour?' They had all declared their devotion to him, yet they had fallen asleep while he had bidden them watch.

41-45 Watch and pray, that ye enter not into temptation: the spirit indeed is willing, but the flesh is weak. He went away again the second time, and prayed, saying, O my Father, if this cup may not pass away from me, except I drink it, thy will be done. And he came and found them asleep again: for their eyes were heavy. And he left them, and went away again, and prayed the third time, saying the same words. Then cometh he to his disciples, and saith unto them, Sleep on now, and take your rest: behold, the hour is at hand, and the Son of man is betrayed into the hands of sinners.

MATTHEW 26:17-30; 1 CORINTHIANS 11:18-34

Matt. 26:17-26 Now the first day of the feast of unleavened bread the disciples came to Jesus, saying unto him, Where wilt thou that we prepare for thee to eat the passover? And he said, Go into the city to such a man, and say unto him, The Master saith, My time is at hand; I will keep the passover at thy house with my disciples. And the disciples did as Jesus had appointed them; and they made ready the passover. Now when the even was come, he sat down with the twelve. And as they did eat, he said, Verily I say unto you, that one of you shall betray me. And they were exceeding sorrowful, and began every one of them to say unto him, Lord, is it I? And he answered and said, He that dippeth his hand with me in the dish, the same shall betray me. The Son of man goeth as it is written of him: but woe unto that man by whom the Son of man is betrayed! it had been good for that man if he had not been born. Then Judas, which betrayed him, answered and said, Master, is it I? He said unto him, Thou hast said. And as they were eating, Jesus took bread, and blessed it, —

So the Jewish Passover melted away into the Lord's Supper. Indeed, so gently did the one dissolve into the other that we scarcely know whether this incident, relating to Judas Iscariot, occurred during the passover or the supper. According to one account, it would seem to be one; and according to another account, the other, but, indeed, the one ordinance was almost imperceptibly merged into the other. I want you carefully to notice, as we read this narrative through, whether you can see here any trace of an altar. Look with both your eyes, and see whether you can find any trace of a priest offering a sacrifice. Watch diligently to see whether you can perceive anything about kneeling down, or about the elevation or the adoration of 'the host'. Why, even the Romish church knows better than to believe in what it practices! Most of you have seen copies of the famous painting by Leonardo da Vinci, himself a Catholic of the old school. How does he picture those who were at the institution of the Lord's Supper? Why, they are all sitting around a table, with the Lord Jesus in their midst. I wonder that they exhibit, and still allow to be in their churches, a picture like that, which, painted by one of their own artists, most effectually condemns their base idolatry, in which a wafer-god is lifted up, to be adored by men, who must be besotted indeed before they can prostitute their intellects so grossly as to commit such an act of sin. What a rebuke to that idolatry is conveyed by this simple statement: 'As they were eating, Jesus took bread, and blessed it' —

26   and brake it, and gave it to the disciples, and said, Take, eat; this is my body.

The Romanists do not even break the bread. They have a wafer so as to avoid anything like an imitation of the example set by our blessed Lord and Master. He took a piece of the bread which was provided for the paschal feast — the ordinary unleavened bread — and he broke it, and gave it to his disciples and said to them, 'Take, eat, this is my body.' Not, of course, the literal body, which was there at the table; but this was the emblem of his body about to be broken on the cross on behalf of all his people.

27   And he took the cup, and gave thanks, and gave it to them, saying, Drink ye all of it;

'Every one of you, take your own personal share.' This also the papists have perverted by denying the cup to the laity.

28-30 For this is my blood of the new testament, which is shed for many for the remission of sins. But I say unto you, I will not drink henceforth of this fruit of the vine, until that day when I drink it new with you in my Father's kingdom. And when they had sung an hymn, they went out into the mount of Olives.

It was a social feast, somewhat funereal, and tinctured with sadness, for Jesus was about to go from them, to die. Still, it was a joyous celebration, closing with a hymn. At the paschal feast the Jews always sang Psalms 113 to 118. Probably our Lord sang all these through. At any rate, Christ and his apostles sang a hymn; and I always like to think of him as leading the little company — going to his death with a song upon his lips, his voice full of melody, and made more sweet than ever by the near approach of Gethsemane and Calvary. I would like always to sing, whenever we come to the communion table, after the fashion in which they sang that night: 'When they had sung an hymn, they went out into the mount of Olives.' Now let us read what the apostle Paul writes concerning the Lord's Supper.

1 Cor. 11:18-22 For first of all, when ye come together in the church, I hear that there be divisions among you; and I partly believe it. For there must be also heresies among you, that they which are approved may be made manifest among you. When ye come together therefore into one place, this is not to eat the Lord's supper. For in eating every one taketh before other his own supper: and one is hungry, and another is drunken. What? have ye not houses to eat and to drink in? or despise ye the church of God, and shame them that have not? What shall I say to you? shall I praise you in this? I praise you not.

These Corinthians fell into a great many errors. Everybody was a speaker and said whatever he pleased; and they had no proper order or rule. Among other evils, when they met together to observe the Lord's Supper, they brought their own food with them, thinking that eating thus together was keeping the sacred feast. So the richer ones feasted to the full, and the poor went almost without anything. 'One is hungry, and another is drunken', says the apostle, and he tells them that this was not the right way of observing the Lord's Supper. Yet it is evident that the idea which was in their mind was that of feasting together. They had exaggerated it and carried it to a grievous excess, but that was the idea they had concerning it. Certainly, there was no altar or priest or anything of the sort. Now the apostle tells them how the ordinance *should* be observed.

23-25 For I have received of the Lord that which also I delivered unto you, that the Lord Jesus the same night in which he was betrayed took bread: And when he had given thanks, he brake it, and said, Take, eat: this is my body, which is broken for you: this do in remembrance of me. After the same manner also he took the cup, when he had supped, saying, this cup is the new testament in my blood: this do ye, as oft as ye drink it, in remembrance of me.

How wonderfully simple it all is! There is nothing here of the paraphernalia of a 'sacrament'. It is a simple memorial festival, that is all.

26-27 For as often as ye eat this bread, and drink this cup, ye do shew the Lord's death till he come. Wherefore whosoever shall eat this bread, and drink this cup of the Lord, unworthily, shall be guilty of the body and blood of the Lord.

He shall be guilty with respect to that body, not with respect to that bread, against which he cannot sin, but with respect to that body which is represented by the bread, and with respect to that blood which is represented by the cup. See with what holy solemnity this humble feast is fenced and invested. There is a divinity which doth hedge the simple ordinance of Christ lest men should trifle with it to their eternal ruin.

28-29 But let a man examine himself, and so let him eat of that bread, and drink of that cup. For he that eateth and drinketh unworthily, eateth and drinketh damnation to himself, not discerning the Lord's body.

'Judgement' or 'condemnation' is the word in the original, not 'damnation'. That is not a fair translation neither does it express the truth. He that eateth and drinketh unworthily condemns himself in so doing; he comes under judgement for that act. This is the kind of judgement that falls upon Christians if they come unworthily to the Lord's table:

30-32 For this cause many are weak and sickly among you, and many sleep. For if we would judge ourselves, we should not be judged. But when we are judged, we are chastened of the Lord, that we should not be condemned with the world.

Believers, who are rendered sick, or who even die, because of their offence against the Lord's ordinance, are not therefore condemned to hell. Far from it; it is that they may not be so condemned that God visits them. 'When we' — the people of God — 'are judged, we are chastened of the Lord, that we should not be condemned with the world.'

33-34 Wherefore, my brethren, when ye come together to eat, tarry one for another. And if any man hunger, let him eat at home; that ye come not together unto condemnation. And the rest will I set in order when I come.

By due attention to the apostle's injunctions, they would be able rightly to observe the ordinance; and we also may learn, from what Paul wrote, how we may worthily come to the table of our Lord.

MATTHEW 26:20-30; 1 CORINTHIANS 11:20-26

Matt. 26:20   Now when the even was come, he sat down with the twelve.

Why so many people celebrate the Lord's Supper in the morning, I cannot imagine, unless it be that they desire to do everything contrary to their Lord's command and example: 'When the even was come, he sat down with the twelve.' I do not think there is any binding ordinance making the evening the only time for the observance of this ordinance; but to make the morning the only time is certainly not according to the Word of God.

21-22   And as they did eat, he said, Verily I say unto you, that one of you shall betray me. And they were exceeding sorrowful, —

There was enough to make them sorrowful in the fact that their Lord had just told them that one of the twelve who were his bodyguard, his closest companions, his nearest and dearest friends, would betray him. 'They were exceeding sorrowful' —

22   and began every one of them to say unto him, Lord, is it I?

It shows a beautiful trait in their character that they did not suspect one another, and least of all, I suppose, did they suspect Judas; but each one asked, 'Lord, is it I?' It is an admirable way of hearing a sermon to take it home to yourself, especially if there be a rebuke or a caution in it.

23-24 And he answered and said, He that dippeth his hand with me in the dish, the same shall betray me. The Son of man goeth as it is written of him: but woe unto that man by whom the Son of man is betrayed! it had been good for that man if he had not been born.

The doom of the wicked is something far worse than non-existence, or Christ would not have said, concerning Judas Iscariot: 'It had been good for that man if he had never been born.' This is especially true of all those who, having for a while consorted with Christ, afterwards deny it and betray him. O brothers and sisters, may all of us be kept from this terrible sin! May none of us ever betray our Master after all the fellowship we have had with him! It would be better to die for him than to deny him, and it would be better never to have been born than to have been in intimate association with him and then to have betrayed him.

25 Then Judas, which betrayed him, answered and said, Master, is it I? He said unto him, Thou hast said.

'It is even so.' With a sorrowful gesture, he made it plain to his sad little circle of friends and followers that he knew all that was going to happen, and that Judas was the man who was going to turn traitor.

26 And as they were eating, —

As they were eating the Passover. The one ordinance gradually melted into the other: 'As they were eating' —

26-27 Jesus took bread, and blessed it, and brake it, and gave it to the disciples, and said, Take, eat; this is my body. And he took the cup, and gave thanks, and gave it to them, saying, Drink ye all of it;

'Each one of you, my disciples, take a draught of this cup.'

28 For this is my blood of the new testament, which is shed for many for the remission of sins.

They had had gross sin brought prominently to their minds; they had had a personal reminder of their own liability to sin; now, they were to have a personal pledge concerning the pardon of sin: 'For this is my blood of the new testament, which is shed for many for the remission of sins.'

29 But I say unto you, I will not drink henceforth of this fruit of the vine, until that day when I drink it new with you in my Father's kingdom.

Taking, as it were, the great Nazarite vow never to taste of the fruit of the vine 'until that day'. He will keep his tryst with us, my brethren; and we shall drink the new wine of his Father's kingdom with him by and by; but, until then, he waits.

30 And when they had sung an hymn, they went out into the mount of Olives.
1 Cor. 11:20 When ye come together therefore into one place, this is not to eat the Lord's supper.

Merely meeting together, each person bringing his or her own portion of bread and wine, and each one eating the provided portion, was not celebrating the Lord's Supper.

21 For in eating every one taketh before other his own supper: and one is hungry, and another is drunken.

Bad as some professing Christians are even now, they are not so bad as these Corinthians were. One was hungry, and another was drunken, because they had turned the holy feast into a kind of banquet of a most disorderly sort. There was nothing in their conduct to indicate true Christian fellowship. The very meaning of the ordinance was lost in the fact that each one was feasting himself without fear.

22 What? have ye not houses to eat and to drink in? or despise ye the church of God, and shame them that have not? What shall I say to you? shall I praise you in this? I praise you not.

The Lord's Supper is not to be made an opportunity for eating and drinking in disorderly self-enjoyment. It is a hallowed and holy institution, setting forth the fellowship of true believers with one another and with the Lord Jesus Christ. Paul was an apostle, yet he had not been present at the institution of the Lord's Supper, so he had a special revelation given to him concerning the way in which this ordinance is to be observed.

23   For I have received of the Lord that which also I delivered unto you, —

That is the right kind of teaching which a man first receives from God, and then delivers to the people. Nothing is of authority in the Christian ministry unless we can say of it, 'I have received of the Lord that which also I delivered unto you.'

23   that the Lord Jesus the same night in which he was betrayed took bread:

What a pathetic interest is given to the Lord's Supper by the fact that it was instituted 'the same night in which he was betrayed'. Never forget that; God grant that none of us may betray our Lord this night, or any other night! It would be the darkest night in our life should it ever be so: 'The Lord Jesus the same night in which he was betrayed took bread' —

24-25   And when he had given thanks, he brake it, and said, Take, eat: this is my body, which is broken for you: this do in remembrance of me. After the same manner also he took the cup, when he had supped, saying, this cup is the new testament —

'The new covenant' —

25-26   in my blood: this do ye, as oft as ye drink it, in remembrance of me. For as often as ye eat this bread, and drink this cup, ye do shew the Lord's death till he come.

MATTHEW 26:59-68; LUKE 23:1-26

Matt. 26:59-60   Now the chief priests, and elders, and all the council, sought false witness against Jesus, to put him to death; But found none: —

Neither for love nor money.

60   yea, though many false witnesses came, yet found they none. —

That is, none that agree; the lie that one man spoke was refuted by the next.

60-61 At the last came two false witnesses, And said, This fellow said —

They did not say any other word, as if they did not know any word in any language vile enough for him — 'This'. Our translators have very properly put in the word 'fellow'.

61 I am able to destroy the temple of God, and to build it in three days.

He never said anything of the kind; it was a most wicked misrepresentation of what he had said. If men wish to find an accusation against us, they can do it without any materials.

62-64 And the high priest arose, and said unto him, Answerest thou nothing? what is it which these witness against thee? But Jesus held his peace, And the high priest answered and said unto him, I adjure thee by the living God, that thou tell us whether thou be the Christ, the Son of God. Jesus saith unto him, Thou hast said: nevertheless I say unto you, Hereafter shall ye see the Son of man sitting on the right hand of power, and coming in the clouds of heaven.

He binds them over to make their appearance before him when he becomes the Judge, and they shall take the place of the criminal.

65-66 Then the high priest rent his clothes, saying, He hath spoken blasphemy; what further need have we of witnesses? behold, now ye have heard his blasphemy. What think ye? —

He looks round upon the seventy elders of the people who were sitting there in the great council, and 'They answered and said, He is guilty of death.' Probably Joseph of Arimathea and Nicodemus were not there. They were the only two friends the Lord had in the Sanhedrim.

66-68 They answered and said, He is guilty of death. Then did they spit in his face, and buffeted him; and others smote him with the palms of their hands, Saying, Prophesy unto us, thou Christ, Who is he that smote thee?

This ended the regular ecclesiastical trial of Christ. A little time was spent, before Pilate, the judicial ruler, was ready to see Christ. But soon, as the dawn was come, they dragged him before another tribunal. We shall now turn to Luke 23.

Luke 23:1-2 And the whole multitude of them arose, and led him unto Pilate. And they began to accuse him, saying, We found this fellow —

Put in what word you like — villain, scoundrel — our translators could not find a better word than that inexpressive word 'fellow'.

2   perverting the nation, and forbidding to give tribute to Caesar, saying that he himself is Christ a King.

Now they shift the charge, you see. Before it was blasphemy, now it is sedition.

3   And Pilate asked him, saying, Art thou the King of the Jews? And he answered him and said, Thou sayest it.

Another of the evangelists tells us that he first asked Pilate what he meant by the question, explaining that he only claimed the kingdom in a spiritual sense.

4-5   Then said Pilate to the chief priests and to the people, I find no fault in this man. And they were the more fierce, saying, He stirreth up the people, teaching throughout all Jewry, beginning from Galilee to this place.

When Pilate heard them say 'Galilee', he caught at that; he did not wish to displease the multitude.

6-7   When Pilate heard of Galilee, he asked whether the man were a Galilaean. And as soon as he knew that he belonged unto Herod's jurisdiction, he sent him to Herod, who himself also was at Jerusalem at that time.

So away the Master goes; he must be dragged through the streets again to a third tribunal. Oh! thou blessed Lamb of God! Never were sheep driven to the shambles as thou wert driven to death!

8   And when Herod saw Jesus, he was exceeding glad: for he was desirous to see him of a long season, because he had heard many things of him; and he hoped to have seen some miracle done by him.

But the Lord never worked miracles to gratify idle curiosity. He who would have worked a miracle to heal the poorest beggar in the street would not work a wonder to please the king in whose power he was.

9   Then he questioned with him in many words; but he answered him nothing.

'No', says good Christopher Ness, 'John Baptist was Christ's voice, and Herod had stopped him. There Christ would not speak. It was as if he would say, 'No, no. Thou didst cut off John Baptist's head, who was my messenger, and since thou hast ill-treated my emir, I, the King of kings, will have nothing to say to thee.'

10-11 And the chief priests and scribes stood and vehemently accused him. And Herod with his men of war set him at nought, —

The original word is 'made nought of him' — made him as nothing.

11-12 and mocked him, and arrayed him in a gorgeous robe, and sent him again to Pilate. And the same day Pilate and Herod were made friends together: for before they were at enmity between themselves.

Two dogs could well agree to hunt the same prey, and sinners who quarrel on other things will often be quite agreed to persecute the gospel.

13-16 And Pilate, when he had called together the chief priests and the rulers and the people, Said unto them, Ye have brought this man unto me, as one that perverteth the people: and, behold, I, having examined him before you, have found no fault in this man touching those things whereof ye accuse him: No, nor yet Herod: for I sent you to him; and, lo, nothing worthy of death is done unto him. I will therefore chastise him, and release him.

Ah! That word 'chastise' slips so glibly over the tongue, but you know what it meant, when the Roman lectors laid bare the back and used the terrific scourge? 'I will scourge him', said Pilate. Perhaps he thought that if he scourged him, his suffering would induce the Jews to spare his life.

17-20 (For of necessity he must release one unto them at the feast.) And they cried out all at once, saying, Away with this man, and release unto us Barabbas: (Who for a certain sedition made in the city, and for murder, was cast into prison.) Pilate therefore, willing to release Jesus, spake again to them.

He seems to have gone backward and forward many times, desiring to save the life of Christ, but not having the moral courage to do it.

21-26 But they cried, saying, Crucify him, crucify him. And he said unto them the third time, Why, what evil hath he done? I have found no cause of death in him: I will therefore chastise him, and let him go. And they were instant with loud voices, requiring that he might be crucified. And the voices of them and of the chief priests prevailed. And Pilate gave sentence that it should be as they required. And he released unto them him that for sedition and murder was cast into prison, whom they had desired; but he delivered Jesus to their will. And as they led him away, they laid hold upon one Simon, a Cyrenian, coming out of the country, and on him they laid the cross, that he might bear it after Jesus.

MATTHEW 27:22-50

Our Lord was brought before the Roman governor Pilate. He was anxious to let Jesus go but he was a weak-minded man, easily swayed by the noisy cry of the people, prompted by the chief priests and elders.

Matt. 27:22-23   Pilate saith unto them, What shall I do then with Jesus which is called Christ? They all say unto him, Let him be crucified. And the governor said, Why, what evil hath he done? But they cried out the more, saying, Let him be crucified.

A blind, unreasoning hate had taken possession of the people. They gave no answer to Pilate's wondering inquiry, 'Why, what evil hath he done?' for he had done nothing amiss. They only repeated the brutal demand: 'Let him be crucified! Let him be crucified!' The world's hatred of Christ is shown in similar fashion today. He has done no evil, no one has suffered harm at his hands, all unite to pronounce him innocent; and yet they practically say, 'Away with him! Crucify him!'

24   When Pilate saw that he could prevail nothing, but that rather a tumult was made, he took water, and washed his hands before the multitude, saying, I am innocent of the blood of this just person: see ye to it.

Ah, Pilate. You cannot rid yourself of responsibility by that farce! He who has power to prevent a wrong is guilty of the act if he permits others to do it, even though be does not actually commit it himself. If you are placed in positions of power and responsibility, do not dream that you can escape from guilt by merely allowing other people to do what you would not do yourself.

25   Then answered all the people, and said, His blood be on us, and on our children.

All the people willingly took upon themselves the guilt of the murder of our dear Lord: 'His blood be on us, and on our children.' This fearful imprecation must have been remembered by many when the soldiers of Titus spared neither age nor sex, and the Jewish capital became the veritable *Aceldama*, the field of blood.

26   Then released he Barabbas unto them: and when he had scourged Jesus, he delivered him to be crucified.

Why scourge him before delivering him up to be crucified? Surely this was a superfluity of cruelty. The Roman scourging was something which I scarcely care to describe, one of the most terrible punishments to which anyone could be subjected. Yet Pilate first scourged Jesus, and then gave him up to die by crucifixion.

27-28   Then the soldiers of the governor took Jesus into the common hall, and gathered unto him the whole band of soldiers. And they stripped him, and put on him a scarlet robe.

Some old soldier's coat that they found lying about they cast upon Christ in imitation of the royal robes of Caesar or Herod.

29-31   And when they had platted a crown of thorns, they put it upon his head, and a reed in his right hand: and they bowed the knee before him, and mocked him, saying, Hail, King of the Jews! And they spit upon him, and took the reed, and smote him on the head. And after that they had mocked him, they took the robe off from him, and put his own raiment on him, and led him away to crucify him.

By that fact, though they did not intend it, our Lord was recognized in the street as the same person who had been taken into the Praetorium by the soldiers. Had Jesus been brought forth in the scarlet robe, persons looking at him might not have known him to be the same man who wore the garment woven from the top throughout; but in his own seamless raiment, they readily recognized the Nazarene.

32   And as they came out, they found a man of Cyrene, Simon by name: him they compelled to bear his cross.

I wonder if he was a black man. There was a Simon in the early church; and it certainly was the lot of the Ethiopian to bear the cross for many and many an age. This Simon was a stranger, anyhow, and a foreigner; truly honoured was he to be compelled to bear the cross after Christ.

33   And when they were come unto a place called Golgotha, that is to say, a place of a skull,

From its shape. There appears to be to this day a hill still in the form of a human skull outside the gate of Jerusalem. When they came to that common place of execution — the Tyburn or Old Bailey of the city —

34 They gave him vinegar to drink mingled with gall: and when he had tasted thereof, he would not drink.

A stupefying draught was given to the condemned — that is the only mercy that there was about the whole thing. The Romans did give to the crucified a draught of myrrh to take away something of the agony of crucifixion; but our Lord came not to be stupefied, he came to suffer, therefore he would not take anything that would at all impair his faculties. He drank even to the dregs the bitter cup of grief and woe.

35 And they crucified him, —

Horrible scene, to see those blessed hands and feet pierced with nails, and fastened to the cross!

35 and parted his garments, casting lots: —

Rattling the dice-box at the foot of the cross! Gambling is the most hardening of all vices. I believe that crimes have been committed by persons under the influence of gambling, which never could have been committed by them in any other condition of mind: 'They parted his garments, casting lots.' See here, ye gamblers! With Christ's blood bespattering them, these soldiers dared still to raffle for his robe.

35-36 that it might be fulfilled which was spoken by the prophet, They parted my garments among them, and upon my vesture did they cast lots. And sitting down they watched him there;

His enemies gloating their cruel eyes with the sight of his sufferings; his friends with many tears watching his amazing griefs. It is for us, with humble faith and grateful love, to mark the incidents connected with his painful death.

37-38 And set up over his head his accusation written, THIS IS JESUS THE KING OF THE JEWS. Then were there two thieves crucified with him, one on the right hand, and another on the left.

Giving him the place of honour, which means, in this case, the place of dishonour. He was the apex of that terrible triangle.

39-40 And they that passed by reviled him, wagging their heads, And saying, Thou that destroyest the temple, and buildest it in three days, save thyself. If thou be the Son of God, come down from the cross.

This is the cry of the Socinians today: 'Come down from the cross. Give up the atoning sacrifice, and we will be Christians.' But, by rejecting his vicarious atonement, they practically un-Christ the Christ, as those mockers at Golgotha did.

41-42 Likewise also the chief priests mocking him, with the scribes and elders, said, He saved others; himself he cannot save. If he be the King of Israel, let him now come down from the cross, and we will believe him.

Just so. Get rid of a crucified Saviour, then they will believe in him. Atonement, substitution, vicarious sacrifice, this staggers them. They will have Christ if they can have him *without* his cross.

43-46 He trusted in God; let him deliver him now, if he will have him: for he said, I am the Son of God. The thieves also, which were crucified with him, cast the same in his teeth. Now from the sixth hour there was darkness over all the land unto the ninth hour. And about the ninth hour Jesus cried with a loud voice, saying, Eli, Eli, lama sabachthani? that is to say, My God, my God, why hast thou forsaken me?

Every word in this terrible cry from the cross is emphatic; every syllable cuts and pierces to the heart.

47 Some of them that stood there, when they heard that, said, This man calleth for Elias.

They knew better, yet they jested at the Saviour's prayer.

48 And straightway one of them ran, and took a sponge, —

It always seems to me very remarkable that the sponge, which is the very lowest form of animal life, should have been brought into contact with Christ, who is at the top of all life. In his death, the whole circle of creation was completed.

48-50 and filled it with vinegar, and put it on a reed, and gave him to drink. The rest said, Let be, let us see whether Elias will come to save him. Jesus, when he had cried again with a loud voice, yielded up the ghost.

Christ's strength was not exhausted. His last word was uttered 'with a loud voice', like the shout of a conquering warrior. He need not have died on account of any infirmity in himself. But voluntarily, for *your* sake, for your sake and mine, he 'yielded up the ghost'. Blessed be his holy name!

MATTHEW 27:50-66

Matt. 27:50   Jesus, when he had cried again with a loud voice, yielded up the ghost.

Christ's strength was not exhausted; his last word was uttered 'with a loud voice', like the shout of a conquering warrior. And what a word it was, 'It is finished' [John 19:30]! Thousands of sermons have been preached upon that little sentence, but who can tell all the meaning that lies compacted, length and height altogether unmeasurable. Christ's life being finished, perfected, completed, he yielded up the ghost — willingly dying, laying down his life as he said he would: 'I lay down my life for the sheep... I lay it down of myself. I have power to lay it down, and I have power to take it again' [John 10:15,18].

51-53   And, behold, the veil of the temple was rent in twain from the top to the bottom; and the earth did quake, and the rocks rent; And the graves were opened; and many bodies of the saints which slept arose, And came out of the graves after his resurrection, and went into the holy city, and appeared unto many.

Christ's death was the end of Judaism: 'The veil of the temple was rent in twain from the top to the bottom.' As if shocked at the sacrilegious murder of her Lord, the temple rent her garments, like one stricken with horror at some stupendous crime. The body of Christ being rent, 'the veil of the temple was torn in twain from the top to the bottom'. *Now* was there an entrance made into the holiest of all by the blood of Jesus, and a way of access to God was opened for every sinner who trusted in Christ's atoning sacrifice. See what marvels accompanied and followed the death of Christ: 'The earth did quake, and the rocks rent; and the graves were opened.' Thus did the material world pay homage to him whom man had rejected, while nature's convulsions foretold what will happen when Christ's voice once more shakes not the earth only, but also heaven. These first miracles wrought in connection with the death of Christ were typical of spiritual wonders that will be continued till he comes again — rocky hearts are rent, graves of sin are opened. Those who have been dead in trespasses and sins and buried in sepulchres of lust and evil are quickened and come out from among the dead and go unto the holy city, the new Jerusalem.

54 Now when the centurion, and they that were with him, watching Jesus, saw the earthquake, and those things that were done, they feared greatly, saying, Truly this was the Son of God.

These Roman soldiers had never witnessed such scenes in connection with an execution before, and they could only come to one conclusion about the illustrious prisoner whom they had put to death: 'Truly this *was* the Son of God.' It was strange that those men should confess what the chief priests and scribes and elders denied. Yet, since their day, it has often happened that the most abandoned and profane have acknowledged Jesus as the Son of God, while their religious rulers have denied his divinity.

55-56 And many women were there beholding afar off, which followed Jesus from Galilee, ministering unto him: Among which was Mary Magdalene, and Mary the mother of James and Joses, and the mother of Zebedee's children.

We have no record of any unkindness to our Lord from any woman, though we have many narratives of the loving ministry of women at various periods in his life. It was meet, therefore, that even at Calvary 'many women were there beholding afar off'. The ribald crowd and the rough soldiers would not permit these timid yet brave souls to come near; but we learn from John 19:25 that some of them edged their way through the throng till they 'stood by the cross of Jesus'. Love will dare anything.

57-58 When the even was come, there came a rich man of Arimathaea, named Joseph, who also himself was Jesus' disciple: He went to Pilate, and begged the body of Jesus. Then Pilate commanded the body to be delivered.

This rich man of Arimathaea, named Joseph, a member of the Jewish Sanhedrim, was Jesus' disciple, 'but secretly for fear of the Jews' [John 19:38]. Yet when his Lord was actually dead, extraordinary courage nerved his spirit, and boldly he went to Pilate and begged the body of Jesus. Joseph and Nicodemus are 'types' of many more who have been emboldened by the cross of Christ to do what, without that mighty magnet, they would never have attempted. When night comes, the stars appear; so in the night of Christ's death these two bright stars shone forth with blessed radiance. Some flowers bloom only at night; such a blossom was the courage of Joseph and Nicodemus.

59-60 And when Joseph had taken the body, he wrapped it in a clean linen cloth, And laid it in his own new tomb, which he had hewn out in the rock: and he rolled a great stone to the door of the sepulchre, and departed.

Our King, even in the grave, must have the best of the best; his body was 'wrapped in a clean linen cloth', and laid in Joseph's own new tomb, thus completing the fulfillment of Isaiah 53:9. Some see in this linen shroud an allusion to the garments in which priests were to be clothed. Joseph's was a virgin sepulchre wherein up to that time no one had been buried, so that, when Jesus rose, none could say that another came forth from the tomb instead of him. That rock-hewn cell in the garden sanctified every part of God's acre where saints lie buried. Instead of longing to live till Christ comes, as some do, we might rather pray to have fellowship with Jesus in his death and burial.

61 And there was Mary Magdalene, and the other Mary, sitting over against the sepulchre.

Love and faith were both typified by these two Marys sitting over against the sepulchre. They will be the last to leave their Lord's resting-place, and the first to return to it when the Sabbath is past. Can we cling to Christ when his cause seems to be dead and buried? When truth is fallen in the streets or is even buried in the sepulchre of skepticism or superstition, can we still believe in it and look forward to its resurrection? That is what some of us are doing at the present time. O Lord, keep us faithful!

62-64 Now the next day, that followed the day of the preparation, the chief priests and Pharisees came together unto Pilate, Saying, Sir, we remember that that deceiver said, while he was yet alive, After three days I will rise again. Command therefore that the sepulchre be made sure until the third day, lest his disciples come by night, and steal him away, and say unto the people, He is risen from the dead: so the last error shall be worse than the first.

Those punctilious priests and Pharisees, who were so scrupulous about keeping the Sabbath, did not mind profaning the day of rest by holding a consultation with the Roman governor. They knew that Christ was dead and buried, but they still stood in dread of his power. They called him a 'deceiver', and they even pretended to 'remember' what 'he said, while he was yet alive'. At his trial, their false witnesses gave another meaning to his words, but they knew all the while that he was speaking of his resurrection, not of the temple on Mount Zion. Now they are afraid that, even in the sepulchre, he will bring to naught all their plans for his destruction. They must have known that the disciples of Jesus would not steal him away and say unto the people: 'He is risen from the dead'; so, they probably feared that he *really would* come forth from the tomb. Whatever conscience they had made great cowards of them. So they begged Pilate to do what he could to prevent the rising of their victim.

65-66 Pilate said unto them, Ye have a watch: go your way, make it as sure as ye can. So they went, and made the sepulchre sure, sealing the stone, and setting a watch.

The chief priests and Pharisees wanted Pilate to make the sepulchre sure, but he left them to secure it. There seems to have been a grim sort of irony about the governor's reply: 'Ye have a watch; go your way, make it as sure as ye can.' Whether he mean it as a taunt or as a command to secure the sepulchre, they became, unconsciously, witnesses that

Christ's resurrection was a supernatural act. The tomb in the rock could not be entered except by rolling away the stone, and they guarded that by sealing the stone and setting a watch. According to the absurd teaching of the rabbis, rubbing ears of corn was a kind of threshing and, therefore, was unlawful on the Sabbath — yet here were these men doing what, by similar reasoning, might be called furnace and foundry work, and calling out a guard of Roman legionaries to assist them in breaking the Sabbath. Unintentionally, they did honour to the sleeping King when they obtained the representatives of the Roman emperor to watch his resting-place till the third morning, when he came forth, Victor over sin and death and the grave. Thus once more was the wrath of man made to praise the King of glory, and the remainder of that wrath was restrained.

MATTHEW 28:1-15

Matt. 28:1-2 In the end of the sabbath, as it began to dawn toward the first day of the week, came Mary Magdalene and the other Mary to see the sepulchre. And, behold, there was a great earthquake: for the angel of the Lord descended from heaven, and came and rolled back the stone from the door, and sat upon it.

See what concern angels have about our Lord. Are they here tonight? Do they make a habit of coming where the saints meet together? I think they do. We have intimations in Scripture that that is the case. Let us behave ourselves aright tonight 'because of the angels'; and as they worship and count it their highest honour to serve the Son of man, let us also worship Jesus and adore him. What a picture this scene would make!

3-4 His countenance was like lightning, and his raiment white as snow: And for fear of him the keepers did shake, and became as dead men.

He said nothing as he rolled back the stone; he did not shake a sword at them, or over them, to fill them with terror. The presence of perfect purity, the presence of heavenly things, is a terror to ungodly men. May you and I be such that our very presence in company will cast a hush over it! 'It was e'en as though an angel shook his wings', they said of one good man, when he spake in common conversation. May there be about us enough of the heavenly to make the powers of evil quail (or flinch) before us!

5 And the angel answered and said unto the women, Fear not ye: —

But I notice that they *did* fear, although the angel said, 'Fear not'. Neither men nor angels can so speak as to silence fears in trembling hearts — but Jesus can, as we shall see farther on. One word from his lips has infinitely more power than all the words of angels or of saints.

5 for I know that ye seek Jesus, which was crucified.

And if you and I can truly say that we are on the side of Jesus, that we seek him who was crucified, then we can bear all the shame with which philosophy would fain cover the cross, and we have no cause for fear. Ridicule and all that it brings from this ungodly generation will not hurt you.

6 He is not here: for he is risen, as he said. —

'As he said.' A few words, but what a world of meaning! 'As he said.' He always does 'as he said'. He always gives 'as he said'. He always reveals himself 'as he said', not otherwise. He never fails to fulfill a promise or forgets even the mode of promising. Not only does he do *what* he said, but *as* he said: 'He is risen, as he said.'

6 Come, see the place where the Lord lay.

For even the place where he lay is hallowed to you. And, beloved, if there is a place where you have ever had communion with Christ, you will remember it. You might bless the spot of ground where Jesus met with you. Here, tonight, I hope that some of you can see the place where the Lord appeared to you.

7 And go quickly, and tell his disciples that he is risen from the dead; —

Such good news ought to be spread quickly. 'Go and tell his disciples' — they are trembling, they have fled — 'that he is risen from the dead.'

7 and, behold, he goeth before you into Galilee; there shall ye see him: lo, I have told you.

Brethren, this is good news for us tonight, though all may not, perhaps, feel the power of it. 'He is risen.' We have no dead Christ; we serve a living Saviour! He is risen, and therefore he can come to us tonight in the power of his resurrection life, and he can make us glad. 'Behold, he goeth before you into Galilee.' There is a great deal about Galilee in Matthew's Gospel; it is the Gospel of the Kingdom, and yet it often talks about Galilee, that border-land which touches Gentiles as well as the chosen seed of Abraham. There is the place where Jesus will meet his people, in the border-land between Jew and Gentile. There the risen Christ will hold the first general assembly of his church.

8 And they departed quickly from the sepulchre with fear and great joy; —

What a mixture — fear and joy! But notice that the fear was not great, and the joy was: 'fear and *great* joy'. Observe the proportions of the mixture; and if tonight you have some fear, yet I hope you will have great joy, and then the bitterness of the fear will pass away. A holy fear, mixed with great joy, is one of the sweetest compounds we can bring to God's altar. Some of us have brought those spices with us tonight. These holy women brought other spices to the sepulchre, but these were the spices that they took away from it, 'fear and great joy'.

8-9 and did run to bring his disciples word. And as they went to tell his disciples, behold, Jesus met them, saying, All hail. And they came and held him by the feet, and worshipped him.

He would not let Mary Magdalene do that when they were alone, but he said to her: 'Touch me not; for I am not yet ascended to my Father: it is more needful for you to go now and tell my disciples that I have risen from the dead. There will be time by and by for further fellowship with me.' But now Jesus permits these godly women to hold him by the feet. It was an act of humility, worshipping and holding; and holding not his hands, but his feet. They must have seen the nail-prints before Thomas did, as they held him by the feet and worshipped him. I do not find that these women ran to the angels, they rather shrank back from them; but they came to Jesus, for we are told that they came and held him by the feet. I think that there must have been a new attraction about Christ after he had risen from the dead, something more sweet about the tones of his voice, something more charming about the countenance that had been so maimed at Gethsemane and Gabbatha and Golgotha.

10   Then said Jesus unto them, —

As he saw their palpitating hearts and perceived that they were still all in a flurry, for the angel had not dispelled their fears.

10   Be not afraid: go tell my brethren that they go into Galilee, and there shall they see me.

The angel talked of 'disciples'; Christ talks of 'brethren'. He always has the sweeter word.

11   Now when they were going, behold, some of the watch came into the city, and shewed unto the chief priests all the things that were done.

While good people were active, bad people were active too. It is wonderful to think of how much good and evil is being done at the same time. While we are thankful that holy women are running with holy messages for Christ, here come the soldiers of the watch, and they are going in to those vile priests.

12   And when they were assembled with the elders, and had taken counsel, —

They ought at once to have repented when the watch came and told them that Jesus was risen. Ought they not to have gone and fallen at his feet and begged for mercy? But instead of that

12   they gave large money unto the soldiers,

Money, wherever it comes in, seems to do mischief. For money Christ was betrayed, and for money the truth about his resurrection was kept back as far as it could be. Money has had a hardening effect on some of the highest servants of God, and all who have to touch the filthy lucre have need to pray for grace to keep them from being harmed by being brought into contact with it.

13 Saying, Say ye, His disciples came by night, and stole him away while we slept.

If they were asleep, how did they know what happened? How could they know it if they were asleep? Evidence which is borne by men who were asleep at the time is evidently not worth regarding. But when you have to tell a lie, I suppose that any stick is good enough to beat a dog with, and any lie will do to slander one whom you hate.

14-15 And if this come to the governor's ears, we will persuade him, and secure you. So they took the money, and did as they were taught: —

No doubt you have heard of the man who said that he did not believe all the articles of his church because his salary was so small that he could not be expected to believe them all for the money. Oh, the depraving and debasing power of the whole system of bribery and falsehood! May none of us ever be affected by considerations of profit and loss in matters of doctrine, matters of duty and matters of right and wrong!

15 and this saying is commonly reported among the Jews until this day.

You may start a lie, but you cannot stop it; there is no telling how long it will live. Let us never teach even the least error to a little child, for it may live on and become a great heresy long after we are dead. There is scarcely any limit to its life and to its power.

MATTHEW 28

Matt. 28:1 In the end of the sabbath, as it began to dawn toward the first day of the week, came Mary Magdalene and the other Mary to see the sepulchre.

While the Jewish Sabbath lasted, they paid to it due respect. They did not even go the sepulchre to perform the kindly offices of embalmment; but when the old Sabbath was dying away and the new and better Sabbath began to dawn, these holy women found their way back to their Lord's tomb. Woman must be first at the sepulchre as she was last at the cross. We may well forget that she was first in the transgression; the honour which Christ put upon her took away that shame. Who but Mary Magdalene should be the first at the tomb? Out of her, Christ had cast seven devils, and now she acts as if into her he had sent seven angels. She had received so much grace that she was full of love to her Lord. 'In the end of the sabbath, as it began to dawn toward the first day of the week, came Mary Magdalene and the other Mary to see the sepulchre.' You can just see them in the gray light of the dawn: it is not clear enough to make out their form and shape, but in the twilight they are coming into the garden and finding their way to the new sepulchre.

2 And, behold, there was a great earthquake: —

The women must have wondered as they felt that tremor beneath their feet. If you have ever felt an earthquake, you will never forget it; and this was a great one, not one of an ordinary kind: 'a *great* earthquake'. Death was being upheaved, and all the bars of the sepulchre were beginning to burst. When the King awoke from the sleep of death, he shook the world; the bedchamber in which he rested for a little while trembled as the heavenly Hero arose from his couch: 'Behold, there was a great earthquake.' Nor was the King unattended in his rising —

2 for the angel of the Lord —

It was not merely one of the angelic host, but some *mighty* presence: 'the angel of the Lord' —

2 descended from heaven, and came and rolled back the stone from the door, and sat upon it.

Jesus was put in the prison of the tomb as a hostage for his people;

therefore, he must not break out by himself, but the angelic sheriff's officer must bring the warrant for his deliverance and set the captive at liberty. He was immured because of human debt; but the debt is paid, so he must go free. Like a flash of fire, the angel descends from the right hand of God. He stands at the mouth of the tomb; he touches the great stone, sealed as it was and guarded by the soldiery, and it rolls back. And when he has rolled back the stone from the door, he sits upon it, as if to defy earth and hell ever to roll it back again. That great stone seems to represent the sin of all Christ's people, which shut them up in prison — it can never be laid again over the mouth of the sepulchre of any child of God. Christ has risen, and all his saints must rise too. The angel 'rolled back the stone from the door, and sat upon it'. I think I see there one of the grandest sights that ever man beheld, for one greater than an earthly king is sitting on something better than a throne.

3 His countenance was like lightning, and his raiment white as snow:
Dazzling in its purity, like the raiment worn by Christ upon the Mount of Transfiguration, whiter than any fuller can make it.

4 And for fear of him the keepers did shake, and became as dead men.
First a palsy of fear and then a stiffening of fright fell upon them, for they had never seen such a sight as this before. They were Roman soldiers who knew nothing of the meaning of cowardice. Yet at the sight of this messenger of God, 'the keepers did shake, and became as dead men'.

5 And the angel answered and said unto the women, —
We had almost forgotten them; we had been thinking of the earthquake and the angel and the flaming lightning and the frightened soldiers, but this angel's thought is all about the women. He whose countenance was like lightning, and whose garments were white as snow, said to the women —

5-7 Fear not ye: for I know that ye seek Jesus, which was crucified. He is not here: for he is risen, as he said. Come, see the place where the Lord lay. And go quickly, and tell his disciples that he is risen from the dead;

Notice the angel's words; first 'see' and then 'go'. You cannot *tell* the message till you *know* it. You who would serve God, must first be instructed yourselves. 'Come, see the place where the Lord lay', and then 'go quickly'. If you have seen, then go. Do not sit down and admire the sight and forget the thousands who have never seen it. But come, see the place where the Lord lay, and then go, and 'go quickly'.

7 and, behold, he goeth before you into Galilee; there shall ye see him: lo, I have told you.

That is a very beautiful touch of condescension on the Saviour's part — that he would go before his disciples into Galilee. Why, Galilee was the very opposite of a classic region; it was a district that was much despised. The clod-hoppers, the boors, the illiterate people of no account lived in 'Galilee of the Gentiles'. 'Yet', says Christ, 'I will meet you there.' It was the King's own rendezvous — not in the courts of earthly monarchs nor in the palaces of the priests, but away down in Galilee. What cares he for the grandeur of men and their empty pomp and boasted wisdom? He goes to places that are despised, that he may lift them up by the glory of his light: 'Behold, he goeth before you into Galilee; there shall ye see him: lo, I have told you.'

8 And they departed quickly from the sepulchre with fear and great joy; —

That seems a strange mixture: 'fear and great joy'. Yet there was plenty of reason for both emotions. Who would not fear that had felt an earthquake and seen an angel and marked the tomb broken open? Yet who would not rejoice that had had such a cheering message and such an assurance that the crucified Christ had risen from the dead? Experience is the best explanation of experience. You must feel for yourself these two emotions working together, before you can understand how they can live in anyone at the same time. 'They departed quickly from the sepulchre with fear and great joy.'

8 and did run to bring his disciples word.

Good women! 'They did run.' These staid matrons did run, and who would not run to tell of a risen Lord?

9 And as they went to tell his disciples, behold, Jesus met them, —

Happy are the ministers who meet their Lord when they are going up the pulpit stairs! Blessed are the teachers who meet Jesus when they are going to the class. They will be sure to preach and teach well when that is the case: 'As they went to tell his disciples, behold, Jesus met them' —

9 saying, All hail. And they came and held him by the feet, and worshipped him.

These holy women were not Unitarians; knowing that Jesus was the Son of God, they had no hesitation in worshipping him. Perhaps these timid souls clung to their Lord through fear that he might be again taken from them. So 'they held him by the feet, and worshipped him', fear and faith striving within them for mastery.

10 Then said Jesus unto them, Be not afraid: go tell my brethren that they go into Galilee, and there shall they see me.

Note how Jesus dwells upon this despised district of Galilee; I should like to dwell upon it, too. He said nothing about classic Corinth or imperial Rome or proud Jerusalem. But his message is: 'Tell my brethren that they go into Galilee, and there shall they see me.' If we will be humble, if we will cast aside the pride of life, there shall we meet him who is meek and lowly of heart.

11-13 Now when they were going, behold, some of the watch came into the city, and shewed unto the chief priests all the things that were done. And when they were assembled with the elders, and had taken counsel, they gave large money unto the soldiers, Saying, Say ye, His disciples came by night, and stole him away while we slept.

You must often have noticed what a mixture of falsehood this was. 'You were asleep; you are sure that you were asleep?' 'Yes.' 'Yet you say that the disciples came; you knew they were the disciples though you were asleep. And they stole him away? You know how they did it; you can describe the stealthy way in which they took away the body of Jesus; you were the witnesses of it, although you were sound asleep all the while.' Go, sirs, it is worse than trifling to listen to the lying of a witness who begins by swearing that he was fast asleep all the time. Yet this was the tale that the soldiers were bribed to tell, and many a worse lie than this has been told to try to put the truth of God out of countenance. The modern philosophy which is thrust forward to cast a slur upon the great truths of revelation, is no more worthy of credence than this lie put into the mouths of the soldiers, yet common report gives it currency, and among a certain clique it pays. But the soldiers naturally said, 'We shall be put to death for sleeping while on duty.' So the chief priests said —

14   And if this come to the governor's ears, we will persuade him, and secure you.

'We can give some more of those arguments that have been so telling in your hands, and they will prevail with the governor as they have prevailed with you.'

15   So they took the money, and did as they were taught: —

Plenty do this still, and I have no doubt they will continue to do so as long as the world is what it is: 'They took the money, and did as they were taught.'

15-17   and this saying is commonly reported among the Jews until this day. Then the eleven disciples went away into Galilee, into a mountain where Jesus had appointed them. And when they saw him, they worshipped him: but some doubted.

Where will not Mr Doubting and other members of his troublesome family be found? We can never expect to be quite free from doubters in the church, since even in the presence of the newly risen Christ some doubted. Yet the Lord revealed himself to the assembled company, although he knew that some among them would doubt that it was really their Lord who was risen from the dead.

18-20 And Jesus came and spake unto them, saying, All power is given unto me in heaven and in earth. Go ye therefore, and teach all nations, baptizing them in the name of the Father, and of the Son, and of the Holy Ghost: Teaching them to observe all things whatsoever I have commanded you: and, lo, I am with you always, even unto the end of the world. Amen.

We say, 'Amen', too. May he be most manifestly with us here even now, for his sweet love's sake! Amen.

Charles Haddon Spurgeon

MARK

MARK 1:14-35

Mark 1:14   Now after that John was put in prison, Jesus came into Galilee, preaching the gospel of the kingdom of God,

When one servant of God is laid aside, it is a call to the rest to be the more earnest. So after John the Baptist was put into prison, 'Jesus came into Galilee.' Sometimes a loss may be a gain, and if the loss of John was the means of bringing out Jesus, certainly both the church and the world were the gainers: 'Jesus came into Galilee, preaching the gospel of the kingdom of God' —

15 And saying, The time is fulfilled, and the kingdom of God is at hand: repent ye, and believe the gospel.

It is clear, from this passage, that our Lord exhorted men to repent and to believe the gospel. There are some, who profess to be his followers, who will not suffer us to do this. They say we may teach men and warn them, but we must not exhort them to repent and believe. Well, as the contention of these people is not in accordance with the Scriptures, we are content to follow the Scriptures and to do as Jesus did, so we shall say to sinners, 'Repent ye, and believe the gospel.'

16-18   Now as he walked by the sea of Galilee, he saw Simon and Andrew his brother casting a net into the sea: for they were fishers. And Jesus said unto them, Come ye after me, and I will make you to become fishers of men. And straightway they forsook their nets, and followed him.

The gospel minister is like the fisherman with a net. I have sometimes heard the comparison drawn as though the gospel fisherman had a hook and a line, which he has not. His business is not to entice a fish to swallow his bait, but to cast the net all round him and lift him, by God's grace, out of the element in which he lies in sin, into the boat where Christ still sits, as he sat in the olden days, in the boat on the Sea of Galilee. To shut the sinner up to faith in Jesus Christ — that is the main work of the true gospel fisherman.

19-20 And when he had gone a little farther thence, he saw James the son of Zebedee, and John his brother, who also were in the ship mending their nets. And straightway he called them: and they left their father Zebedee in the ship with the hired servants, and went after him.

They never had cause to regret that they did so. Whatever they left, they were abundantly rewarded. They had a rich reward here on earth; and they have a far richer reward in heaven. Whatever a man gives up for Christ is a blessed investment, which will, sooner or later, bring him good interest.

21-22 And they went into Capernaum; and straightway on the sabbath day he entered into the synagogue, and taught. And they were astonished at his doctrine: for he taught them as one that had authority, and not as the scribes.

He did not do as the scribes did, who made a great parade of learning, by quoting this rabbi and the other, but Jesus said, 'Verily, verily, I say unto you.' He spoke as One who felt that he had authority to speak in his own name, and in the name of God his Father. This method of teaching quite astonished the Jews. I wish that those who *now* hear the gospel, might be astonished at it and be astonished into the belief of it by the power with which it comes home to their consciences and hearts.

23-24 And there was in their synagogue a man with an unclean spirit; and he cried out, Saying, Let us alone; —

How often that is still the cry of sinners, 'Let us alone. Why do not you hold your own views, and let us alone?' Yes the devils and those whom they control still say, 'Let us alone.' But it is a part of the gospel to attack that which is not the gospel, and it is as much the duty of the minister of the gospel to denounce error as to proclaim truth. If we do so, the old cry will still be heard, 'Let us alone. Let us alone.'

24-25 what have we to do with thee, thou Jesus of Nazareth? art thou come to destroy us? I know thee who thou art, the Holy One of God. And Jesus rebuked him, —

He did not want any testimony from the devil. When a man of ill character once praised Plato, the philosopher said, 'What can I have done wrong that such a fellow as that speaks well of me?' So when the devil bore testimony to the divinity of Christ, 'Jesus rebuked him.'

25-26 saying, Hold thy peace, and come out of him. And when the unclean spirit had torn him, and cried with a loud voice, he came out of him.

For, if Satan must come out of a man, he will do him as much mischief as ever he can before he departs. His wrath is all the greater because his time is so short.

He worries whom he can't devour,
With a malicious joy.

27 And they were all amazed, insomuch that they questioned among themselves, saying, What thing is this? what new doctrine is this? for with authority commandeth he even the unclean spirits, and they do obey him.

It was the authority of his preaching which first astonished them; and then the authority with which he wrought this miracle and subdued the world of demons. Blessed be God! Christ has not abdicated his authority. He is still the great Messenger of God, full of divine authority to save men and to deliver them from the power of Satan.

28-30 And immediately his fame spread abroad throughout all the region round about Galilee. And forthwith, when they were come out of the synagogue, they entered into the house of Simon and Andrew, with James and John. But Simon's wife's mother lay sick of a fever, and anon they tell him of her.

Christ was a house-to-house missionary, as well as an open-air preacher.

There is much good to be done by those who know how to visit and to look after individual cases; there is great good to be done in that way, as well as by dealing with mankind in the bulk.

31-35 And he came and took her by the hand, and lifted her up; and immediately the fever left her, and she ministered unto them. And at even, when the sun did set, they brought unto him all that were diseased, and them that were possessed with devils. And all the city was gathered together at the door. And he healed many that were sick of divers diseases, and cast out many devils; and suffered not the devils to speak, because they knew him. And in the morning, rising up a great while before day, he went out, and departed into a solitary place, and there prayed.

His hard day's work probably ran on far into the night. Yet, 'a great while before day', he was up at the sacred work of supplication. The more work we have to do with men for God, the longer we ought to be at work with God for men. If you plead with men, you cannot hope to prevail unless you first plead with God. And, inasmuch as our Lord had great success the day before, it teaches us that the greatest success does not release us from the necessity of still waiting upon God. If God has given you much, my brother, go with thy basket, and ask for more. Never stay thy prayer. Increase thy spiritual hunger, and God will increase the richness of the gift he will bestow upon thee.

MARK 1:28 – 2:12

Mark 1:28 And immediately his fame spread abroad throughout all the region round about Galilee.

'Immediately' — that is, as soon as Jesus had healed the man with an unclean spirit, his fame spread like wildfire! The miracle was reported from mouth to mouth till everybody in that region knew of it. It was said that the words and writings of Martin Luther were carried as by the wings of angels, so speedily was everything that he said and wrote made known far and wide. On this occasion, it was so with our Lord's wondrous deed of mercy and power: 'Immediately his fame spread abroad throughout all the region round about Galilee.'

29 And forthwith, when they were come out of the synagogue, they entered into the house of Simon and Andrew, with James and John.

'Forthwith', or again, 'immediately'. Simon and Andrew and James and John were intimately connected. We are told that they were 'partners' in their fishing business. James and John, the sons of Zebedee, seem to have been in a good position in life; we read that their father had 'hired servants' employed in the boats. So James and John went with Simon and Andrew into their partners' house when Christ went there after performing that notable miracle in the synagogue.

30 But Simon's wife's mother lay sick of a fever, and anon they tell him of her.

There were at least four of Christ's followers in the house, yet the mother of the wife of one of them lay sick of a fever. Grace does not prevent suffering in the body; there will still be physical diseases even though in the soul there is spiritual health.

31 And he came and took her by the hand, and lifted her up; and immediately the fever left her, and she ministered unto them.

Jesus was very calm; he was not afraid of catching the fever. See how deliberately and with what solemn, kindly dignity he deals with this sick woman: 'He came and took her by the hand.' I think I see him doing it. 'And lifted her up' — he gently raises her, and she yields to his tender uplifting hand and suddenly finds herself cooled of the burning fever and perfectly restored to health and strength. So, she rises from her bed, and the first thing she does is to minister unto them. I am sure that, whenever the Lord helps any of his people out of their temporal or spiritual distresses, they feel at once that they must say, 'What shall we render unto the Lord for all his benefits towards us?' Her ministering unto them proved that the fever was quite gone, and gone in a way in which it does not ordinarily go; for, as you all know, fever usually leaves behind it extreme weakness. It seems to burn up the strength that is in one; and after it is gone, one is not fit even to wait at table for a long while. But Peter's wife's mother immediately, when the fever was gone, rose and 'ministered unto them'. Christ's cures are always complete. If he saves us from the burning fever, he saves us from the weakness that follows it, and when he deals with soul maladies, his cures are equally complete. There are no after-affects to the soul, as there are in many diseases that afflict the body. When the great Physician restores the soul, he restores it completely.

32 And at even, when the sun did set, they brought unto him all that were diseased, and them that were possessed with devils.

It was the Sabbath, and they would not even bring out their sick folk until the day of rest was over. The Jewish Sabbath ended at the setting of the sun, so these people were all watching and waiting until the sun dipped below the horizon, and then, straightaway, they brought their suffering ones to Jesus. What a mass of misery filled the streets of Capernaum that memorable night! The whole city was turned into a hospital.

33 And all the city was gathered together at the door.

It seemed as if everybody had come either to be healed or to witness the healing of others: 'All the city was gathered together at the door.' Oh, when shall we see our places of worship thronged in this fashion with the spiritually sick? When will this great city of London begin to turn towards the Lord Jesus Christ? Will any of us live to see all our fellow citizens gathered together around the Saviour to be healed by him of all the wounds that sin hath made?

34 And he healed many that were sick of divers diseases, and cast out many devils; and suffered not the devils to speak, because they knew him.

They would persist in acknowledging him; perhaps with the design of injuring his cause, for nothing hurts the cause of Christ more than to have it praised by bad men or evil spirits. I do not know that an outrageous sinner, if he will not repent, can do Christ a better turn than to abuse him, for then he is speaking after his own natural manner. But when the devil or his servants go into the pulpit and begin to speak in praise of Christ, then is Christ's cause in an evil case indeed. So he 'suffered not the devils to speak, because they knew him'; or even, as the margin puts it, 'to say that they knew him'.

35   And in the morning, rising up a great while before day, —

While it was yet dark, he stole away even from his favoured disciples that he might be alone with his Father.

35-37   he went out, and departed into a solitary place, and there prayed. And Simon and they that were with him followed after him. And when they had found him, —

For he had endeavoured to conceal himself in the loneliest spot that he could find. Possibly, the disciples overheard his groans, his cries, his supplications, as he poured out his very soul in prayer to his Father: 'when they had found him' —

37-38   they said unto him, All men seek for thee. And he said unto them, Let us go into the next towns, that I may preach there also: for therefore came I forth.

Jesus Christ came forth from God the Father that he might proclaim throughout the land the message of redeeming grace and dying love.

39-40   And he preached in their synagogues throughout all Galilee, and cast out devils. And there came a leper to him, beseeching him, and kneeling down to him, and saying unto him, If thou wilt, thou canst make me clean.

It is a pity that he could not go further than to say to Christ, 'If thou wilt' — but it is a great mercy that he could go as far as that. So, if you, dear friend, cannot pray a prayer that is *full* of faith, pray one that has at least *some* faith in it. If you cannot go as far as some do, go as far as you can. I have often told you to bless God for moonlight, and then he will give you sunlight. But for anyone to say, 'I will not pray at all because I cannot pray as I would like to pray', is a very foolish thing. Say what you can, even as this poor leper said to Jesus, 'If thou wilt, thou canst make me clean.'

41 And Jesus, moved with compassion, —

This is a wonderful expression: 'moved with compassion'. The face of Jesus and his whole person showed that his very soul was stirred by an intense fellow-feeling for this poor leper: 'Jesus, moved with compassion' —

41 put forth his hand, and touched him, and saith unto him, I will; be thou clean.

If you or I were to touch a leper, his uncleanliness would at once be communicated to us, but when Christ touches a leper, his cleanliness is communicated to the leper. Oh, how high our blessed Lord stands above us! When we have to deal with certain peculiarly sad cases, we ought to go to the work with much earnest prayer that we ourselves may not be contaminated by contact with gross sinners, but Christ has such virtue in himself that he can even touch the fevered and the leprous, and yet sustain no injury.

42 And as soon as he had spoken, immediately the leprosy departed from him, and he was cleansed.

This was another very wonderful miracle. All that dryness of the skin, that scurf, that peeling, that inward foulness that eats into the bones and pollutes the very current of the blood — all this was quite gone. The Lord Jesus Christ made this foul, unclean leper perfectly clean and whole in a single moment.

43-44 And he straitly charged him, and forthwith sent him away; And saith unto him, See thou say nothing to any man: but go thy way, shew thyself to the priest, and offer for thy cleansing those things which Moses commanded, for a testimony unto them.

That was all he was to do — to go and show himself to the priest, so that it might be officially known and certified that he was clean, and he was not to tell anyone else of his cure. He was disobedient to Christ; perhaps you will think that he was very naturally and excusably so, but we must never make excuses for doing what Christ tells us not to do. Our duty is not to judge whether such-and-such a course will be profitable or beneficial, but to consider whether such-and-such a course is in accordance with the Word of the Lord. This man ought to have held his tongue, for Christ had told him to do so. I have no doubt that he said within himself, 'The more I talk about this miracle, the more good I shall do, and the more famous Christ's name will become.' But he had no business to think that, his business was to obey Christ's command.

45   But he went out, and began to publish it much, and to blaze abroad the matter, insomuch that Jesus could no more openly enter into the city, —

There were such crowds that he could not work his miracles of healing. The disobedient man was no doubt moved by gratitude, which seems a very proper motive; yet his disobedience caused Christ serious inconvenience and hindered his work; and I have no doubt that there are many things done in the church of God today of which many say, 'They are very proper and very nice'; yes, but are they scriptural? Did the Master command them? If not, they will cause him and his kingdom serious inconvenience and loss, at some time or other. We cannot too fully realize that, as Christ's disciples, we are to obey him implicitly; and the best proof of our gratitude is to do *exactly* as Christ bids us. This man blazed abroad the news of his cure, so that 'Jesus could no more openly enter into the city' —

45 – Mark 2:1-2   but was without in desert places: and they came to him from every quarter. And again he entered into Capernaum after some days; and it was noised that he was in the house. And straightway many were gathered together, insomuch that there was no room to receive them, no, not so much as about the door: and he preached the word unto them.

He could not be hid; the healed leper had made his name so famous that men crowded to see him, and he took advantage of their curiosity, and 'preached the word unto them'.

3-5   And they come unto him, bringing one sick of the palsy, which was borne of four. And when they could not come nigh unto him for the press, they uncovered the roof where he was: and when they had broken it up, they let down the bed wherein the sick of the palsy lay. When

Jesus saw their faith, he said unto the sick of the palsy, Son, thy sins be forgiven thee.

Those who brought this man to Jesus believed that he could and would heal him, and Christ delighted to honour their faith and, perhaps also, the faith of the man himself.

6-9 But there were certain of the scribes sitting there, and reasoning in their hearts, Why doth this man thus speak blasphemies? who can forgive sins but God only? And immediately when Jesus perceived in his spirit that they so reasoned within themselves, he said unto them, Why reason ye these things in your hearts? Whether is it easier to say to the sick of the palsy, Thy sins be forgiven thee; or to say, Arise, and take up thy bed, and walk?

It was just as easy to say either the one or the other.

10-12 But that ye may know that the Son of man hath power on earth to forgive sins, (he saith to the sick of the palsy,) I say unto thee, Arise, and take up thy bed, and go thy way into thine house. And immediately he arose, took up the bed, and went forth before them all; insomuch that they were all amazed, and glorified God, saying, We never saw it on this fashion.

MARK 2

Mark 2:1-2 And again he entered into Capernaum after some days; and it was noised that he was in the house. And straightway many were gathered together, insomuch that there was no room to receive them, no, not so much as about the door: and he preached the word unto them.

It is a very singular feat that, although man in his natural state of heart is opposed to the gospel, yet he is drawn to hear it. Even though he abhors it, yet oftentimes he cannot help listening to it. Wherever Jesus Christ is, whether he is present in person or in the preaching of the Word, it will be certain to be noised abroad, and multitudes will come to hear. The grandest attraction, either in or out of heaven, is still the Saviour, the Lord Jesus Christ.

3-5 And they come unto him, bringing one sick of the palsy, which was borne of four. And when they could not come nigh unto him for the press, they uncovered the roof where he was: and when they had broken it up, they let down the bed wherein the sick of the palsy lay. When Jesus saw their faith, he said unto the sick of the palsy, Son, thy sins be forgiven thee.

In Luke's account of this gathering, we read that 'the power of the Lord was present to heal them' [Luke 5:17], and when we ask, 'Why was that power so remarkably present?' We think that one reason was because there were persons present who were anxious about the good of others; and today, wherever four persons come together praying for some poor soul, you may rest assured that the power of the Lord will there be present to heal. I do not think that so much of the success of sermons depends upon the preacher as upon those model hearers who are all the while praying for a blessing and who are making other members of the congregation — those who are converted — the constant subject of their supplication. Christ blessed this man because of the faith of the four who carried him and, possibly, because of his own faith. Notice that our Lord did not at first say to the sick man, 'Thou art healed of thy palsy'; but he said, 'Thy sins be forgiven thee.' This was laying the axe at the root, because sin is at the bottom of sorrow; and where sin is pardoned, even the effects of sin will be removed.

6-9 But there was certain of the scribes sitting there, and reasoning in their hearts, Why doth this man thus speak blasphemies? who can forgive sins but God only? And immediately when Jesus perceived in his spirit that they so reasoned within themselves, he said unto them, Why reason ye these things in your hearts? Whether is it easier to say to the sick of the palsy, Thy sins be forgiven thee; or to say, Arise, and take up thy bed, and walk?

Whichever is spoken, omnipotence is implied. The presence and power of God alone could give efficacy to either sentence; but to him, the one is as easy as the other.

10-14 But that ye may know that the Son of man hath power on earth to forgive sins, (he saith to the sick of the palsy,) I say unto thee, Arise, and take up thy bed, and go thy way into thine house. And immediately he arose, took up the bed, and went forth before them all; insomuch that they were all amazed, and glorified God, saying, We never saw it on this fashion. And he went forth again by the sea side; and all the multitude resorted unto him, and he taught them. And as he passed by, he saw Levi the son of Alphaeus sitting at the receipt of custom, and said unto him, Follow me. And he arose and followed him.

There is a change in the method of displaying Christ's power, but his power is always the same. To the palsied man, he said 'Arise, and take up thy bed, and walk'; but to the man engaged in a calling which degraded him, Christ said, 'Follow me', and 'he arose and followed him'. Blessed be God, still we have in our midst the living Lord, who is as able to work miracles of mercy today as when he was upon the earth; and we have not merely to exhort, to persuade, and to entreat, though we have to do all that, but we have also to speak with authority in the name of this glorious Son of God, and to command men to repent and believe in him. He is with us, by his Spirit, to make his Word mighty, so that, to this day, palsied men do arise and walk, and sinful men are led to turn from evil and to follow Christ.

15-17 And it came to pass, that, as Jesus sat at meat in his house, many publicans and sinners sat also together with Jesus and his disciples: for there were many, and they followed him. And when the scribes and Pharisees saw him eat with publicans and sinners, they said unto his disciples, How is it that he eateth and drinketh with publicans and sinners? When Jesus heard it, he saith unto them, They that are whole have no need of the physician, but they that are sick: I came not to call the righteous, but sinners to repentance.

For ordinary Christians to associate with those who are like the publicans and sinners of Christ's day might be dangerous, for 'evil communications corrupt good manners' [1 Corinthians 15:33], and Christians should be careful as to the company in which they are found. But for Christians to go among such people to try to do them good, is Christlike. The church of Christ always fails in her duty when she looks upon any class of persons as being beneath her observation or too far gone for her to reach. Our Lord's mission was to find out, and to supply the needs of mankind, and he seems to have paid particular attention to the very worst of men because they needed him most! His church should always be guided in her choice of work by the necessity of the objects that need her care. Brethren, you and I, who are in the ministry, will do well to choose, not that sphere in which we may be most happy and comfortable, but that one in which we are most needed. If I were a lamp, and had my choice of where I would be hung, I should prefer to be hung up in the darkest place in London, where I could be of most service, and I think that every one of us would make just such a choice if we judged rightly and desired to be where we were wanted and to do as the Saviour did when he was on the earth.

18-20 And the disciples of John and of the Pharisees used to fast: and they come and say unto him, Why do the disciples of John and of the Pharisees fast, but thy disciples fast not? And Jesus said unto them, Can the children of the bridechamber fast, while the bridegroom is with them? as long as they have the bridegroom with them, they cannot fast. But the days will come, when the bridegroom shall be taken away from them, and then shall they fast in those days.

While Christ was with his people in person, they could not help having joy and gladness, but when he was gone from them, they must lament his absence.

21-22 No man also seweth a piece of new cloth on an old garment: else the new piece that filled it up taketh away from the old, and the rent is made worse. And no man putteth new wine into old bottles: else the new wine doth burst the bottles, and the wine is spilled, and the bottles will be marred: but new wine must be put into new bottles.

The bottles were made of skin, and the wine put into them must be of a suitable port. To prescribe fasting to his disciples, while he was making them glad with his personal presence, would have been incongruous and absurd; and there are some things that we ought not to expect from young Christians, and other things that we ought not to expect from old and mature Christians. We should not expect to find new wine in old bottles nor old wine in new bottles. 'A place for everything and everything in its place', is not only a rule for the home and the merchant's counting-house, but it is also a rule which should be observed in the church of Christ; for God, as a God of order, always puts things in their proper places and in due order.

23 And it came to pass, that he went through the corn fields on the sabbath day; and his disciples began, as they went, to pluck the ears of corn.

They had offended the Pharisees by not fasting, and now they were offending them again in a similar way, though with reference to a different matter.

24 And the Pharisees said unto him, Behold, why do they on the sabbath day that which is not lawful?

According to some rabbis, you might pick an ear of wheat on the Sabbath day, but if you rubbed it between your hands, they said that was a sort of threshing which was a kind of labour that must not be performed on the Sabbath. They made all sorts of ingenious restrictions, too ridiculous for us to quote. These disciples were therefore, according to them, chargeable with sin, because they had plucked ears of corn and had performed the operation of threshing them on the Sabbath day. We have some of that sort of folk living now, who take the smallest matter, which is altogether insignificant and in which there is neither good nor harm, and magnify and distort it, and then make a man a grave offender all for next to nothing. We have learned not to be very much troubled by anything that they choose to say.

25-28 And he said unto them, Have ye never read what David did, when he had need, and was an hungred, he, and they that were with him? How he went into the house of God in the days of Abiathar the high priest, and did eat the shewbread, which is not lawful to eat but for the priests, and gave also to them which were with him? And he said unto them, The sabbath was made for man, and not man for the sabbath: Therefore the Son of man is Lord also of the sabbath.

He has made it to be no longer a day of bondage, but a day of blessed rest and holy service for God. Works of necessity, works of piety, and works of mercy, are not only allowed to be done, but are commanded to be done upon the Sabbath day.

MARK 4:1-25

Mark 4:1 And he began again to teach by the sea side: and there was gathered unto him a great multitude, so that he entered into a ship, and sat in the sea; and the whole multitude was by the sea on the land.

You can easily picture that scene — the Master sitting down in the vessel, with a little breathing space of water between himself and the crowd, and then the multitude on the rising bank, standing one above another, and all gazing upon the Teacher, who sat down and taught them. It ought to reconcile any of you who have to stand in the crowd here when you remember that the hearers all stood in those days, and only the preacher sat down.

2-3 And he taught them many things by parables, and said unto them in his doctrine, Hearken; Behold, there went out a sower to sow:

He did not go out to show himself, to let people see how dexterous he was at the art of sowing seed; but he 'went out to sow'. And every true preacher should go out with this one design — to scatter abroad the good seed of the kingdom, and to try to obtain for it an entrance into the hearts of their hearers.

4 And it came to pass, as he sowed, some fell by the way side, and the fowls of the air came and devoured it up.

He could not help that; it was not his fault, but the fault of the way side and of the fowls. So, when the Word of God is denied entrance into men's hearts, if it be faithfully preached, the preacher shall not be blamed by his Master — the fault shall lie between the hard heart that will not let the seed enter in and the devil who came and took it away.

5 And some fell on stony ground, where it had not much earth; and immediately it sprang up, because it had no depth of earth:

Persons with shallow characters are often very quick in receiving religious impressions, but they also lose them just as quickly. Those who are hasty and impulsive are as easily turned the wrong way as the right way.

6-8 But when the sun was up, it was scorched; and because it had no root, it withered away. And some fell among thorns, and the thorns grew up, and choked it, and it yielded no fruit. And other fell on good ground, and did yield fruit that sprang up and increased; and brought forth, some thirty, and some sixty, and some an hundred.

Thank God for that! There were three failures, but there was one success; or, perhaps we might more correctly say, three successes. There were three sorts of ground that yielded nothing, but at last the sower came to a piece of soil that had been well prepared and, therefore, was good ground, which yielded fruit, though the quantity varied even there: 'some thirty, and some sixty, and some an hundred'.

9 And he said unto them, He that hath ears to hear, let him hear.

Some people have ears, but they have not 'ears to hear'. They have ears, but they close them to that which they ought to hear. When a man is really willing to listen to the truth, then may God help him to listen with all his heart and spiritually!

10-12 And when he was alone, they that were about him with the twelve asked of him the parable. And he said unto them, Unto you it is given to know the mystery of the kingdom of God: but unto them that are without, all these things are done in parables: That seeing they may see, and not perceive; and hearing they may hear, and not understand; lest at any time they should be converted, and their sins should be forgiven them.

This judicial blindness had happened to the Jews; they had so long closed their eyes to the light that, at last, God closed them, and they were blinded. They had refused to heed so many messages sent to them from the great God that, at last, this sentence was pronounced as the punishment of their sin — that they should die in their sins, and that even the preaching of the Word by the mouth of the Lord Jesus himself should be of no use to them. That is one of the most awful judgements that can ever happen to anyone, when God puts a curse even on a man's blessings; and when the gospel, which should be a savour of life unto life, becomes a savour of death unto death.

13 And he said unto them, Know ye not this parable? and how then will ye know all parables?

'For this is one of the simplest of them all; if you do not understand this parable, what will you understand?'

14-15 The sower soweth the word. And these are they by the way side, where the word is sown; but when they have heard, Satan cometh immediately, and taketh away the word that was sown in their hearts.

There is always a bird where there is a seed lying on the road, and there is always a devil where there is a sermon heard but not received into the heart. 'Satan cometh immediately'— he is very prompt; we may delay, but the devil never does: 'When they have heard, Satan cometh immediately, and taketh away the word that was sown in their hearts.'

16-17 And these are they likewise which are sown on stony ground; who, when they have heard the word, immediately receive it with gladness; And have no root in themselves, and so endure but for a time: afterward, when affliction or persecution ariseth for the word's sake, immediately they are offended.

These are the people that trouble and grieve the hearts of earnest ministers; and there are some revivalists who never go to a place without getting quite a lot of persons to come forward and say that they are converted. Why, I know a town where, according to the accounts that were put forth by certain preachers, there were so many professed converts every night that all the people in the town must have been converted, and a good many more from the surrounding villages; but, nobody can find them now. Were they converted, then? I trow (or believe) not; but that is the style in which much has been done by some whom I might name. Yet, there is some good even in their work. The sower in the parable is not blamed because his work was so evanescent; how could he prevent it? As the soil was so shallow, the apparent result was very quick, and the disappointment was equally quick. I do trust, dear friends, that you will never be satisfied with temporary godliness, with slight impressions, soon received and soon lost. Beware of what is not the work of the Holy Ghost. There must be a breaking up of the iron pan of the heart; there must be a tearing out of the rocks that underlie the soil, or else there will be no harvest unto God.

18-19 And these are they which are sown among thorns; such as hear the word, And the cares of this world, and the deceitfulness of riches, and the lusts of other things entering in, choke the word, and it becometh unfruitful.

The seed cannot grow in such soil as that. The man is too busy, or he is wholly taken up with pleasure; the women are too proud of themselves, or even of the clothes that cover them. How can there be room for Christ in the inn when it is crowded with other guests?

20   And these are they which are sown on good ground; such as hear the word, and receive it, and bring forth fruit, some thirtyfold, some sixty, and some an hundred.

All converts are not equally good. I am afraid that, in our churches, there is a large number of the thirtyfold people. We are glad to have them, but they are not very brilliant Christians. Oh, for some sixtyfold converts — some who are fit to be very leaders in the church of God! And when we get up to 100-fold — when it is not merely 100 per cent, but 100 gathered for every one sown — then are we indeed rejoiced. When everything that is good is multiplied over and over and over and over and over again, 100 for one, and when each one of that 100 bears another 100, that is the blessing we long to see. This 100-fold seed has in it the capacity for almost boundless multiplication; at the first sowing, we get a 100-fold return; but what comes of the next sowing, and the next, and the next? God send us this style of wheat. May we have a great quantity of it!

21   And he said unto them, Is a candle brought to be put under a bushel, or under a bed? and not to be set on a candlestick?

So this wheat, then, is meant to be sown; the Word of God is intended to be spread. 'Is a candle brought to be put under a bushel, or under a bed?' If it were put under a bed, it would set the bed on fire; and so, if you have true grace in your heart, there is nothing that can smother its light; the fire and the light together will force their way out.

22-23   For there is nothing hid, which shall not be manifested; neither was any thing kept secret, but that it should come abroad. If any man have ears to hear, let him hear.

Tell out, then, what God has told to you; and let everybody hear from you the truth as you yourself have heard it. See the compound interest that there is to be in this blessed trading for Christ.

24-25 And he said unto them, Take heed what ye hear: with what measure ye mete, it shall be measured to you: and unto you that hear shall more be given. For he that hath, to him shall be given: and he that hath not, from him shall be taken even that which he hath.

When the gospel is not received, when a man refuses it, it becomes a positive loss to him. There is a way by which it so works that, what a man thought he had, disappears. Some have been made worse by the preaching of that Word which ought to have made them better. May it not be so with any one of us!

MARK 4:35-41

Mark 4:35-36 And the same day, when the even was come, he saith unto them, Let us pass over unto the other side. And when they had sent away the multitude, —

Telling them that Christ would give them no more instruction that day, and that they had better go back to their homes. There are some preachers who have great gifts of dispersion — it does not take them long to scatter a congregation. But I expect that Christ's disciples found it to be no easy task to send away the crowds that had been listening to their Master's wondrous words. But, 'when they had sent away the multitude' —

36 they took him even as he was in the ship. And there were also with him other little ships.

Christ was Lord High Admiral of the Galilean lake that night, and he had quite a little fleet of vessels around his flagship.

37 And there arose a great storm of wind, —

Our friend, John MacGregor (Rob Roy), tells us that the lake is subject to very sudden and severe storms. It lies in a deep hollow, and down from the surrounding ravines and valleys the air comes with a tremendous rush seldom experienced even upon a real sea; for this was, of course, only a lake, though sometimes called a sea. I have been told that on some Scottish lochs the wind will occasionally come from three or four quarters at once, lifting the boat bodily out of the water and, sometimes, seeming to lift the water up towards heaven, with the boat and all in it; so was it, that night, when 'there arose a great storm of wind' —

37 and the waves beat into the ship, so that it was now full.

No doubt they baled out the boat with all their might, and did their best to prevent it from sinking, yet, 'It was now full of water.' But where was their Lord and Master, and what was *he* doing while the storm was raging?

38 And he was in the hinder part of the ship, asleep on a pillow: —

He was quite at home upon the wild waves,

> *Rocked in the cradle of the deep*

for winds and waves were but his Father's servants, obeying his commands. 'He was in the hinder part of the ship, asleep on a pillow'; doubtless weary and worn with the labours of the day. We do not always think enough of the weariness of Christ's human body. There was not only the effort of preaching, but his preaching was so full of high thought, and the expressions he used were so pregnant with meaning, that it must have taken much out of him to preach thus from the heart, with intense agony of spirit, and with his brain actively at work all the while. Remember that he was truly man as well as the Son of God, and that what he did was of so high an order, not to be reached by any of us, that it must have exhausted him, and therefore, he needed sleep to refresh him. And there he was wisely taking it, and serving God by sleeping soundly, and thus preparing himself for the toil of the following day.

38-39 and they awake him, and say unto him, Master, carest thou not that we perish? And he arose, and rebuked the wind, —

It was boisterous and noisy, and he bade it obey its Master's will.

39 and said unto the sea, Peace, be still. —

Can you not almost fancy that you can hear that commanding voice addressing the raging, roaring, tumultuous winds and waves?

39   And the wind ceased, and there was a great calm.

Not only was the wind quieted and the sea hushed to slumber, but a deep, dead, mysterious calm transformed the lake into a molten looking glass. When Christ stills winds and waves, it is 'a great calm'. Did you ever feel 'a great calm'? It is much more than ordinary peace of mind; it is to your heart as if there were no further possibilities of fear. Your troubles have so completely gone that you can scarcely recollect them. There is no one but the Lord himself who can speak so to produce 'a great calm'. Master, we entreat thee to speak such a calm for those of us who need it.

40   And he said unto them, —

When he had calmed the winds and the waves, he had to speak to another fickle set, more fickle than either winds or waves: 'and he said unto them' —

40-41   Why are ye so fearful? how is it that ye have no faith? And they feared exceedingly, —

They went from one fear to another, but this time it was the fear of awe — a hallowed dread of what might happen to a ship which had a mysterious Person on board. Though there was probably in their minds no fear of death, it seemed to them a fearsome thing to live in the presence of One who had such power over the raging elements. 'They feared exceedingly' —

41   and said one to another, What manner of man is this, that even the wind and the sea obey him?

Blessed God-man, we worship and adore thee!

MARK 5:1-24,35-43

Mark 5:1   And they came over unto the other side of the sea, into the country of the Gadarenes.

They had had a very eventful passage across that small but stormy sea, and Christ had proved himself to be the Lord High Admiral of the seas; but now that he steps ashore they are to see his power quite as distinctly displayed as upon the stormy wave.

2-3 And when he was come out of the ship, immediately there met him out of the tombs a man with an unclean spirit, Who had his dwelling among the tombs; and no man could bind him, no, not with chains:

Those ancient graveyards were in remote places, for the people were too wise to bury their dead inside their cities. Very often, the tombs were hewn in caverns in the sides of hills and rocks, and here the dead were laid. Of course, every man who touched a tomb was thereby ceremonially defiled, so that the tombs were fit places for an unclean person possessed by an unclean spirit. What a ghastly dwelling place! What a grim abode for the man, and yet most fitting, for he was dangerous to all who passed by — a raving lunatic, who could not be restrained by any bonds or chains that could be put upon him!

4-5 Because that he had been often bound with fetters and chains, and the chains had been plucked asunder by him, and the fetters broken in pieces: neither could any man tame him. And always, night and day, he was in the mountains, and in the tombs, crying, and cutting himself with stones.

Poor creature! His howlings must have made night hideous indeed. Those who passed that way were startled by his unearthly cries; he was a terror to the whole district; persons could not bear to live anywhere near the places where he resorted. 'Night and day' he was a misery to himself and a terror to all around him — sad type of some whom we know, to our sorrow, who have gone madly into sin. It certainly is madness, whatever else it may be; and when madness and badness go together, what a terror such a man becomes!

6 But when he saw Jesus afar off, he ran and worshipped him,

There is a wondrous attraction in the person of our divine Lord and Master. Though he was a long way off, yet a gracious magnetic influence proceeded from him by which he drew this poor object of pity to him:

'When he saw Jesus afar off, he ran and worshipped him.'

7 And cried with a loud voice, and said, What have I to do with thee, Jesus, thou Son of the most high God? I adjure thee by God, that thou torment me not.

Who was speaking then? The man himself, or the devil within him? It is very hard to tell; the man and the devil were two personalities, but they were so effectually blended into one that it is scarcely possible to tell when it was the man speaking and when it was the devil. So, when sin enters into a man, it gets so completely into his very nature that, sometimes, we feel it must be the evil spirit speaking in the man, and yet it is not easy to be quite sure that it is so, and we cannot free the man himself from the guilt of his words and actions.

8 For he said unto him, Come out of the man, thou unclean spirit.

Whenever Christ speaks to the devil, his message is a very short and very sharp one. The Lord treats him like the dog that he is: 'Come out of the man, thou unclean spirit.' Christ has no compliment for devils; and it is a pity that some of his servants have such soft words when they are dealing with unbelief, which is but a devil, or one of the devil's imps.

9 And he asked him, What is thy name? And he answered, saying, My name is Legion: for we are many.

The devil is obliged to tell his name when Christ treats him like a catechized child, and he is compelled to crouch before Christ like a whipped cur (or dog) at his master's feet.

10 And he besought him much that he would not send them away out of the country.

Satan clings to this world, and to any place where he has had a signal triumph, as he had among those tombs and those rocky ravines.

11-12 Now there was there nigh unto the mountains a great herd of swine feeding. And all the devils besought him, saying, Send us into the swine, that we may enter into them.

Such is the malice of these evil spirits, that they would rather do mischief among swine than nowhere. But notice their unanimity; with all the faults that can be laid at the door of demons, you cannot find them divided and quarrelling. They are unanimous in evil, and it is a shame that those who are the followers of Christ should often be divided, whereas the kingdom of Satan is not divided against itself. Let us learn from our great enemy at least this one lesson.

13   And forthwith Jesus gave them leave. And the unclean spirits went out, and entered into the swine: and the herd ran violently down a steep place into the sea, (they were about two thousand;) —

It was strange that there should be so many swine in the country where lived God's people Israel, and as they had no right to be there, and were there contrary to Jewish law, it was well that they should be destroyed.

13-15   and were choked in the sea. And they that fed the swine fled, and told it in the city, and in the country. And they went out to see what it was that was done. And they come to Jesus, and see him that was possessed with the devil, and had the legion, sitting, and clothed, and in his right mind: and they were afraid.

Ah, me! How variously different people look upon the same thing! If you and I, who are Christ's disciples, had gone there and seen this poor lunatic fully restored, we should have been filled with holy joy, and we would have composed new hymns of praise in honour of the great Physician who had cured him. But these people, in their alienation of heart from the Lord Jesus Christ, 'were afraid'. They feared and trembled in the presence of almighty mercy; omnipotent love awoke no joy in their hearts, but the spirit of bondage was upon them.

16   And they that saw it told them how it befell to him that was possessed with the devil, and also concerning the swine.

You may be sure that they dwelt upon the latter part of the story, for the loss of the swine touched them more than the healing of the demoniac.

17   And they began to pray him to depart out of their coasts.

O dear friends, let none of us ever get into such a state of mind and heart as to pray Christ to go away from us! Yet we have known people act in such a dreadful way as that; a person troubled in conscience has said, 'I will never go and hear that preacher again; I cannot sleep at nights after listening to him. I will never read such and such a book again; it disturbs me so that I cannot enjoy myself.' This is, in effect, to pray Christ to depart out of your coasts. What? Is salvation worth so little that you have no care to possess it? Is Christ himself so small a blessing that you even tremble lest he should change your nature and save you? I think there were more lunatics than one on that Gadarene shore; the people were all as mad at heart as that one poor man was mad in brain.

18   And when he was come into the ship, —

Christ will go from you if you want him to go. He forces himself upon no man; the grace of God does not violate the will of man. It acts in accordance with man's nature and achieves the divine purpose without disturbing the individuality of the man. So Christ went from Gadara: 'And when he was come into the ship' —

18   he that had been possessed with the devil prayed him that he might be with him.

Was not that a proper prayer? I think, dear friends, that not only nature, but the man's *new* nature must have suggested this petition; he prayed Christ that he might be with him. In our day, it is very natural that as soon as we are converted we should wish to go home to heaven; but what is the reason that we should not do so? It is in order that we may bear witness for Christ here on earth and gather in others unto him.

19   Howbeit Jesus suffered him not, but saith unto him, Go home to thy friends, and tell them how great things the Lord hath done for thee, and hath had compassion on thee.

That is one of the chief points on which we ought always to speak, not only to tell of the greatness of the change which the grace of God has wrought in us but especially to testify to the *tenderness* of God to us. Oh, how gently did he handle our broken bones! That good Physician of ours has a lion's heart, but he has a lady's hand; he does not spare us needful pain, but he never inflicts even a twinge that is unnecessary.

And, oh! The pity of his heart toward us when he sees the sorrow which our sin has brought upon us.

20   And he departed, and began to publish in Decapolis —

In the ten little cities that were in that region: 'he departed, and began to publish in Decapolis' —

20   how great things Jesus had done for him: and all men did marvel.

This is the kind of ready-made preacher whose service for his Lord is usually most effectual. The man who, though he has studied little on many points, yet knows by *experience* what the grace of God has done for him, and keeps to that one theme, and tells out the story with simple untrained eloquence, is the man who will do much for his Master, as we read here: 'all men did marvel'. If he had plunged into deep doctrinal subjects, it may be that men would have ridiculed him; but inasmuch as he spoke of what he did know, and told of the greatness and graciousness of God, 'All men did marvel.'

21-22   And when Jesus was passed over again by ship unto the other side, much people gathered unto him: and he was nigh unto the sea. And, behold, —

Wherever we see that word, 'behold', it is saying to us, 'Mark well what is coming.' 'Behold' —

22-24; 35-36   there cometh one of the rulers of the synagogue, Jairus by name; and when he saw him, he fell at his feet, And besought him greatly, saying, My little daughter lieth at the point of death: I pray thee, come and lay thy hands on her, that she may be healed; and she shall live. And Jesus went with him; and much people followed him, and thronged him. ... While he yet spake, there came from the ruler of the synagogue's house certain which said, Thy daughter is dead: why troublest thou the Master any further? As soon as Jesus heard the word that was spoken, he saith unto the ruler of the synagogue, Be not afraid, only believe.

I can imagine that, if Jairus had not been a man of much faith, he would have looked at the Saviour with a meaning glance, as much as to say, 'Only believe?' Couldst thou ask more of me when my child is dead? Yet thou biddest me, 'Only believe.' But, brethren, here is the very sphere of faith. Where there is no wading, there must be swimming; and where there is no hope in the creature, then we must throw ourselves upon the Creator. So, the child's death made room for the father's faith.

37-39 And he suffered no man to follow him, save Peter, and James, and John the brother of James. And he cometh to the house of the ruler of the synagogue, and seeth the tumult, and them that wept and wailed greatly. And when he was come in, he saith unto them, Why make ye this ado, and weep? the damsel is not dead, but sleepeth.

She was dead, but not dead as far as Christ's intention was concerned; she was not so dead as to remain dead. He meant soon to bring her back again to life, and therefore, to him it was as if she were but sleeping.

40 And they laughed him to scorn. —

What a wonderful picture this must have been — the Lord of glory in the centre of a ribald crew who laughed him to scorn! But it is not the man who is laughed at who is necessarily contemptible, it is often the laughers who are the most deserving of scorn. It was so here in Christ's day, and it has often been so since.

40 But when he had put them all out, —

They were not worthy to be answered in any other fashion.

40-42 he taketh the father and the mother of the damsel, and them that were with him, and entereth in where the damsel was lying. And he took the damsel by the hand, and said unto her, Talitha cumi; which is, being interpreted, Damsel, I say unto thee, arise. And straightway the damsel arose, and walked; for she was of the age of twelve years. And they were astonished with a great astonishment.

How very often persons were 'astonished' in Christ's day! Sometimes it is put, 'they marvelled'; at other times, 'they were amazed', or, 'they wondered'. It would have been well if wonder had always turned to faith; but sometimes it corrupted into hate. God grant that our wonder at Christ may always be of that kind which crystallizes into love!

43 And he charged them straitly that no man should know it; and commanded that something should be given her to eat.

Life must be nourished; young life especially needs frequent food. If Christ has spiritually quickened your child, see that you feed the child with food convenient. If you have won a convert to Christ in the Sunday school, take care that the unadulterated milk of the Word is brought forth, that the newborn child may be fed and nourished till it comes unto the perfect stature of a man in Christ Jesus.

MARK 5

Mark 5:1-5 And they came over unto the other side of the sea, into the country of the Gadarenes. And when he was come out of the ship, immediately there met him out of the tombs a man with an unclean spirit, Who had his dwelling among the tombs; and no man could bind him, no, not with chains: Because that he had been often bound with fetters and chains, and the chains had been plucked asunder by him, and the fetters broken in pieces: neither could any man tame him. And always, night and day, he was in the mountains, and in the tombs, crying, and cutting himself with stones.

What a pitiful object this poor creature must have been — a terror to the whole region! So far as man was concerned, he was in an utterly hopeless condition; yet there was hope for him, for Jesus had crossed the sea apparently with the special purpose of healing him. Our Saviour had proved his power over the winds and waves, and he was about to show that demons were equally subject to his control.

6-7 But when he saw Jesus afar off, he ran and worshipped him, And cried with a loud voice, and said, What have I to do with thee, Jesus, thou Son of the most high God? I adjure thee by God, that thou torment me not.

The voice was the voice of the man, but the devil so completely dominated the whole of him, being that he could only speak as the unclean spirit directed him.

8 For he said unto him, Come out of the man, thou unclean spirit.

So that the demon's adjuration was an answer to the Lord's command, 'Come out of the man, thou unclean spirit.'

9-13 And he asked him, What is thy name? And he answered, saying, My name is Legion: for we are many. And he besought him much that he would not send them away out of the country. Now there was there nigh unto the mountains a great herd of swine feeding. And all the devils besought him, saying, Send us into the swine, that we may enter into them. And forthwith Jesus gave them leave. And the unclean spirits went out, and entered into the swine: and the herd ran violently down a steep place into the sea, (they were about two thousand;) and were choked in the sea.

It is clear from this narrative that the demons knew that Jesus was the Son of the most high God, and that he had absolute power to do with them whatever he pleased. It is also clear that they believed in prayer, and that they were all agreed in their supplication to him; and it is significant that Jesus granted their request: 'Send us into the swine, that we may enter into them.' There was a certain congruity in the unclean spirit entering into the unclean animals, so 'forthwith Jesus gave them leave'.

14-15 And they that fed the swine fled, and told it in the city, and in the country. And they went out to see what it was that was done. And they come to Jesus, and see him that was possessed with the devil, and had the legion, sitting, and clothed, and in his right mind: and they were afraid.

What a wonderful sight that was for them to see! Yet they need not have been afraid, they ought rather to have rejoiced to see the poor demoniac 'sitting, and clothed, and in his right mind'.

16-17 And they that saw it told them how it befell to him that was possessed with the devil, and also concerning the swine. And they began to pray him to depart out of their coasts.

Here is a second prayer in which many united — a very foolish and wicked prayer — yet the Saviour did as these people wished. He would not force his company upon those who wanted him to go, so he at once turned his face to the ship that he might 'depart out of their coasts'.

18-19 And when he was come into the ship, he that had been possessed with the devil prayed him that he might be with him. Howbeit Jesus suffered him not, but saith unto him, Go home to thy friends, and tell them how great things the Lord hath done for thee, and hath had compassion on thee.

This is the third prayer in this chapter; not like the two previous ones, the petition of many who were not Christ's followers; it was the earnest supplication of one who was so grateful for what Jesus had done for him that he longed to be always with him. Yet it was not granted, because Jesus saw that the man could serve him better by bearing testimony among those who knew him to the great things the Lord had done for him.

20　And he departed, and began to publish in Decapolis how great things Jesus had done for him: and all men did marvel.

His testimony not only made men marvel, but it helped to prepare the people to welcome the Saviour when he returned to that region.

21　And when Jesus was passed over again by ship unto the other side, much people gathered unto him: and he was nigh unto the sea.

How many missionary voyages Jesus made, sometimes to one side of the sea, sometimes to the other side! What an example of holy diligence he is to us! So long as he lived here below, he never ceased to labour, for he never ceased to love.

22　And, behold, there cometh one of the rulers of the synagogue, Jairus by name; and when he saw him, he fell at his feet,

It was an unusual thing for a ruler of the synagogue to be at the feet of Jesus, yet that is the best place for us all. If God has placed any of you in an eminent position, it will well become you to fall at the feet of Jesus as Jairus did. There is no place more suitable, no place more honourable, no place more profitable, than at the feet of Jesus. What brought Jairus there? It was his great necessity; and that is what will bring us there, a sense of our great need.

23　And besought him greatly, saying, My little daughter lieth at the point of death: I pray thee, come and lay thy hands on her, that she may be healed; and she shall live.

This was great faith, yet it was also little faith, for he limits Christ's power to his bodily presence, and he stipulates about the way in which the cure is to be wrought: 'I pray thee, come and lay thy hands on her, that she may be healed.' Yet we never like to criticize faith, there is so little of it, and it is so precious a thing that we are glad to see it anywhere, and especially in a ruler of the synagogue. Oh, that we all prayed thus for our little daughters and our little sons: 'Lord, come and lay thy hands on them! There is sin in them, and sin means spiritual death, come and lay thy hands on them, that they may be healed, and live for ever.'

24   And Jesus went with him; —

He will always regard true prayer; if we can believe, Jesus will come.

24-25   and much people followed him, and thronged him. And a certain woman, —

There were many in the throng around Jesus who did not touch him, and there were many who touched him, but not as she did; so she is singled out from the crowd: 'A certain woman' —

25-28   which had an issue of blood twelve years, And had suffered many things of many physicians, and had spent all that she had, and was nothing bettered, but rather grew worse, When she had heard of Jesus, came in the press behind, and touched his garment. For she said, If I may touch but his clothes, I shall be whole.

Was this woman sent, do you think, to encourage the faith of Jarius? It has been well said that the child of Jairus had been twelve years living, but this woman had been twelve years dying. So, if Christ could heal the woman who had been twelve years dying, he could raise the child who had been twelve years living. It is significant that there should have been this equalization of the number of years in the two cases. Although Jairus seemed strong in faith, he was not really so. He put the best side of his faith forward; while this woman, who was strong in faith, yet coming behind Christ, and touching him as it were by stealth, put the worst side of her faith forward. We have known this to be the case in others; some who seem to be strong in faith are none too strong, and some who seem to be very weak in faith are much stronger than they seem.

29-31   And straightway the fountain of her blood was dried up; and she felt in her body that she was healed of that plague. And Jesus, immediately knowing in himself that virtue had gone out of him, turned him about in the press, and said, Who touched my clothes? And his disciples said unto him, Thou seest the multitude thronging thee, and sayest thou, Who touched me?

They spoke too fast, as we also sometimes do. It would have been well if they had said nothing which looked like questioning their Master's word.

32-33 And he looked round about to see her that had done this thing. But the woman fearing and trembling, knowing what was done in her, came and fell down before him, and told him all the truth.

The miracle had been wrought in her, yet she was fearing and trembling because she perceived the imperfection of her way of approaching the Saviour. Probably, after we are saved, we see more of our mistakes than we did before; and when the blessing really comes to us, we begin to be anxious lest we should lose Christ because of some misapprehension in our way of finding him. The woman 'fell down before him, and told him all the truth'.

34 And he said unto her, Daughter, —

This was a very unusual way for Christ to speak to a woman, so careful was he in his speech, but then she was a very exceptional woman: 'Daughter' —

34-35 thy faith hath made thee whole; go in peace, and be whole of thy plague. While he yet spake, there came from the ruler of the synagogue's house certain which said, Thy daughter is dead: why troublest thou the Master any further?

This ruler of the synagogue was on the brink of getting the blessing he sought, and then the very worst news comes to him. It may be that just now some of you have seemed to receive the sentence of death to all your hopes, yet you are on the very verge of getting the blessing. It is often so; just when the devil knows that the blessing is near, he struggles the hardest with the soul that is seeking it. Do not be cast down if that sentence of death comes to you, but still believe.

36-39 As soon as Jesus heard the word that was spoken, he saith unto the ruler of the synagogue, Be not afraid, only believe. And he suffered no man to follow him, save Peter, and James, and John the brother of James. And he cometh to the house of the ruler of the synagogue, and seeth the tumult, and them that wept and wailed greatly. And when he was come in, he saith unto them, Why make ye this ado, and weep? the damsel is not dead, but sleepeth.

Jesus knew what he was about to do, and, speaking with the knowledge of the miracle he was about to perform, he said, 'The damsel is not dead but sleepeth.' A charlatan, who wanted to make himself famous, and in order to increase the clat of the miracle, would have said, 'The damsel is really dead', but the Saviour, in his infinite modesty of heart, puts it thus: 'The damsel is not dead, but sleepeth.'

40   And they laughed him to scorn. —

Can you picture the scene? These people, who had been hired to weep and wail, had not much of the spirit of mourning in them, for they laughed directly and derisively; they turned upon the mighty Master of life and death, and 'laughed him to scorn'.

40   But when he had put them all out, —

That was the best way to answer the scorners. It is no good arguing with people who can cry or laugh to order: 'when he had put them all out' —

40-42   he taketh the father and the mother of the damsel, and them that were with him, and entereth in where the damsel was lying. And he took the damsel by the hand, and said unto her, Talitha cumi; which is, being interpreted, Damsel, I say unto thee, arise. And straightway —

Notice how this word 'straightway' comes in again. It is the characteristic word in reference to Christ's miracles; they are usually wrought at once. We read, in verse 29: 'Straightway the fountain of her blood was dried up.' Now we read: 'Straightway' —

42   the damsel arose, and walked; —

Oh, that the Lord Jesus Christ would work some 'straightway' miracles in our midst just now! He can do it if he pleases; before this service ends, there may be some who shall have passed from death unto life, out of the darkness of sin into the marvelous light of grace. Blessed be God for this. Who will it be?

42-43   for she was of the age of twelve years. And they were astonished with a great astonishment. And he charged them straitly that no man should know it; —

He did not want to blaze abroad the story of these wondrous deeds of his. The crowd was already inconveniently large, so that 'he charged them straitly that no man should know it'.

43 and commanded that something should be given her to eat.

She might have continued to live by a miracle as she had been miraculously raised from the dead; but it was needless, and Christ never wrought an unnecessary miracle. Do not look for miracles when ordinary means will suffice. 'He commanded that something should be given her to eat.' When life is given or restored, the next thing needed is nourishment; when you are made spiritually to live, be sure to attend a soul-feeding ministry — and diligently read the Word, that you may get all needful nourishment for your soul out of it.

MARK 8:1-30

Mark 8:1-4   In those days the multitude being very great, and having nothing to eat, Jesus called his disciples unto him, and saith unto them, I have compassion on the multitude, because they have now been with me three days, and have nothing to eat: And if I send them away fasting to their own houses, they will faint by the way: for divers of them came from far. And his disciples answered him, From whence can a man satisfy these men with bread here in the wilderness?

Why did they not ask their Master what he could do in such an emergency as that. After so much experience of his power as they had already had, it is a wonder that they did not refer the matter to him, and say, 'Lord, thou canst feed the multitude; we beseech thee do it.' But they did not act so wisely; instead, they began questioning about ways and means. 'From whence can a man satisfy these men with bread here in the wilderness?'

5-9   And he asked them, How many loaves have ye? And they said, Seven. And he commanded the people to sit down on the ground: and he took the seven loaves, and gave thanks, and brake, and gave to his disciples to set before them; and they did set them before the people. And they had a few small fishes: and he blessed, and commanded to set them also before them. So they did eat, and were filled: and they took up of the broken meat that was left seven baskets. And they that had eaten were about four thousand: and he sent them away.

Christ is the great Master of the art of multiplication. However small is the stock with which we begin, we have only to dedicate it all to him, and he will multiply and increase it until it will go far beyond our utmost expectations, and there will be more left after the feast is over than there was before it began. Bring your small talents, bring the little grace you have, to Christ, for he can so increase your store that you will never know any lack, but shall have all the greater abundance the greater the demand that is made upon that store. Had these 4,000 people not been miraculously fed by Christ, the seven loaves and the few small fishes would have remained just as they were; but now that the 4,000 have to be fed, the loaves and fishes are multiplied by Christ in a very extraordinary manner, so that, in the end, there is far more provision than they had at the beginning. Expect, beloved, to be enriched by your losses, to grow by that which looks as if it would crush you, and to become greater by that which threatens to annihilate you. Only put yourself into Christ's hands, and he will make good use of you, and leave you better than you were before he used you as the means of helping and blessing others.

10-12 And straightway he entered into a ship with his disciples, and came into the parts of Dalmanutha. And the Pharisees came forth, and began to question with him, seeking of him a sign from heaven, tempting him. And he sighed deeply in his spirit, and saith, Why doth this generation seek after a sign? verily I say unto you, There shall no sign be given unto this generation.

Unbelief always pricked him to the heart, and greatly grieved him. When men trusted him, he delighted to exhibit his matchless grace; but when they cavilled and questioned, his heart was heavy, and he turned away from them.

13 And he left them, and entering into the ship again departed to the other side.

But, alas! Even on board that little ship there was unbelief; and from the small and select circle of his own disciples he had fresh reason for sorrow from the same cause.

14-21   Now the disciples had forgotten to take bread, neither had they in the ship with them more than one loaf. And he charged them, saying, Take heed, beware of the leaven of the Pharisees, and of the leaven of Herod. And they reasoned among themselves, saying, It is because we have no bread. And when Jesus knew it, he saith unto them, Why reason ye, because ye have no bread? perceive ye not yet, neither understand? have ye your heart yet hardened? Having eyes, see ye not? and having ears, hear ye not? and do ye not remember? When I brake the five loaves among five thousand, how many baskets full of fragments took ye up? They say unto him, Twelve. And when the seven among four thousand, how many baskets full of fragments took ye up? And they said, Seven. And he said unto them, How is it that ye do not understand?

Can we not learn from past experience? If the Lord has helped us before, is he not equally ready to help us again? What? When there are only a few of you disciples on board ship, do you begin to distrust your Lord because you have only one loaf, when he found enough food for 5,000 and for 4,000 out of a few scanty loaves? O ye unbelieving children of God, what infinite patience your gracious God has with you, though you so often and so shamefully doubt him! 'Do ye not remember?' 'How is it that ye do not understand?' Can it be that all your Lord's lessons of love and deeds of kindness have taught you nothing? Do you still doubt him — still distrust him? Has he delivered you in six troubles, and can you not trust him in the seventh? Has he kept you, by his grace, till you are seventy years of age, and can you not trust him for the few remaining years of your earthly pilgrimage? Oh, shame upon us that we are such dull scholars in the school of Christ!

22-26   And he cometh to Bethsaida; and they bring a blind man unto him, and besought him to touch him. And he took the blind man by the hand, and led him out of the town; and when he had spit on his eyes, and put his hands upon him, he asked him if he saw aught. And he looked up, and said, I see men as trees, walking. After that he put his hands again upon his eyes, and made him look up: and he was restored, and saw every man clearly. And he sent him away to his house, saying, Neither go into the town, nor tell it to any in the town.

'Your house is outside Bethsaida, so go round-about, and get home without going into the town; and if any of your neighbours call to see you, say nothing about me to them, for I wish to remain concealed for the present.'

27 And Jesus went out, and his disciples, into the towns of Caesarea Philippi: and by the way he asked his disciples, saying unto them, Whom do men say that I am?

It was Christ's usual way, when he took a walk with his disciples, to beguile the time with holy conversation. It would be well if we always did the same. We might do much good, and we might get much good, if we made our Lord Jesus the theme of our talks 'by the way'. It was an important question that he put to his disciples, 'Whom do men say that I am?'

28-29 And they answered, John the Baptist; but some say, Elias; and others, One of the prophets. And he saith unto them, But whom say ye that I am? —

'That is the main point. It matters little to you what other men say about me — whether they are right, or wrong, may not concern you — but what is your own opinion? What do you know about me? 'Whom say ye that I am?''

29 And Peter answereth and saith unto him, Thou art the Christ.

'Thou art the Messiah.' We know, from Matthew's Gospel, that it was this confession of which our Lord said to Peter, 'Blessed art thou, Simon Barjona (son of Jonas), for flesh and blood hath not revealed it unto thee, but my Father which is in heaven' [Matthew 16:17].

30 And he charged them that they should tell no man of him.

He wished, at that time, to remain in comparative retirement; he was not anxious that his miracles should be blazoned abroad. By and by, he was to die; and he preferred to derive his fame from his death rather than from his life, and to gather his honours from his cross rather than from his miracles. He never bade any man to be silent about his death on the cross; but when honour was likely to come to him among men from his miracles, he frequently 'charged them that they should tell no man of him'. That restriction is no longer in force; it was entirely abrogated after our Lord's resurrection, when he said to his disciples, 'All power is given unto me in heaven and in earth. Go ye therefore, and teach all nations, baptizing them in the name of the Father, and of the Son, and of the Holy Ghost: teaching them to observe all things whatsoever I have commanded you: and, lo, I am with you alway, even unto the end of the world. Amen' [Matthew 28:18-20].

MARK 9:2-21

Mark 9:2-7 And after six days Jesus taketh with him Peter, and James, and John, and leadeth them up into an high mountain apart by themselves: and he was transfigured before them. And his raiment became shining, exceeding white as snow; so as no fuller on earth can white them. And there appeared unto them Elias with Moses: and they were talking with Jesus. And Peter answered and said to Jesus, Master, it is good for us to be here: and let us make three tabernacles; one for thee, and one for Moses, and one for Elias. For he wist not what to say; for they were sore afraid. And there was a cloud that overshadowed them: and a voice came out of the cloud, saying, This is my beloved Son: hear him.

You and I have sometimes wished that we could see Christ in his earthly glory. We need not however wish it; for, if such a sight were permitted to us, in all probability we should be more full of fear than of joy. These three men, the elect out of the elect, the very choicest of the apostles, yet had little delight in what they saw at the time, for the glory was too bright for their overwhelmed natures.

> *At the too transporting sight,*
> *Darkness rushes o'er my sight.*

We had better wait awhile until these eyes shall have been cleansed, and our whole fabric shall be fit for such a weight of glory as the sight of our exalted Lord will be.

8 And suddenly, when they had looked round about, they saw no man any more, save Jesus only with themselves.

Unhappy, indeed, would they have been if they had looked about and seen none but Moses, for poor comfort could Moses bring. Or if, looking around, they had seen none but Elias, for the stern prophet of fire would have been but a poor consolation to them in their life struggles. But Moses may go, and Elijah may go. Lawgiver and prophet may vanish so long as Jesus Christ remains, it is enough. Jesus only is enough for all our wants — for all our desires.

9-10 And as they came down from the mountain, he charged them that they should tell no man what things they had seen, till the Son of man were risen from the dead. And they kept that saying with themselves, questioning one with another what the rising from the dead should mean.

For they did not understand the Master's words — not even these apostles — for the Spirit of God was not yet fully given. Happy indeed is he upon whom the spirit of God resteth, and in whom he dwells, for as John says 'Ye have an anointing from the Holy One, and ye know all things' [1 John 2:20], and these men without that measure of anointing did not know at that time even such a simple word as this — that the Son of man should rise again from the dead. Brethren, we must be taught of the Holy Spirit, or we shall never know anything profoundly. We might go to school to Christ himself — now, mark this word — we might go to school to Christ himself and yet learn nothing until the Holy Ghost should come upon us to write the truth upon our *heart* which Christ has spoken to the ear. Oh, if ye lack wisdom, ask of God, and he will give you of his Spirit.

11-13 And they asked him, saying, Why say the scribes that Elias must first come? And he answered and told them, Elias verily cometh first, and restoreth all things; and how it is written of the Son of man, that he must suffer many things, and be set at nought. But I say unto you, That Elias is indeed come, —

John the Baptist was he.

13   and they have done unto him whatsoever they listed, as it is written of him.

It is rather singular that the disciples should begin to ask about the scribes, for this was, as it were, a sort of warning note for a battle into which they were about to plunge. They talked about the scribes, but the scribes were down below in conflict with the rest of the apostolic brotherhood, and now, while they are talking about them, they find themselves immediately in their presence.

14-15   And when he came to his disciples, he saw a great multitude about them, and the scribes questioning with them. And straightway all the people, when they beheld him, were greatly amazed, and running to him saluted him.

The probability is that the face of Jesus Christ was shining like the face of Moses when he came down from the mount, and the people were amazed, though not with that same amazement which seized upon Israel when they saw the face of Moses, for Moses had to cover his face with a veil. But they ran to him and saluted him. The glory of Christ attracts, whereas the glory of Moses repels. The glory of the law is terrible, but the glory of the gospel is cheering and attractive.

16   And he asked the scribes, What question ye with them?

Like some great commander stepping into the field when his under followers are being beaten, he comes right to the front and charges the foe boldly. Christ said, 'What question ye with them?' — as much as to say, 'Why did ye not wait a bit and ask me? I could have answered you if they cannot.'

17-18   And one of the multitude answered and said, Master, I have brought unto thee my son, which hath a dumb spirit; And wheresoever he taketh him, he teareth him: and he foameth, and gnasheth with his teeth, and pineth away: —

A case of dreadful epilepsy accompanied with satanic possession.

18-19   and I spake to thy disciples that they should cast him out; and they could not. He answereth him, and saith, O faithless generation, how long shall I be with you? how long shall I suffer you? bring him unto me.

That is a grand piece of advice, and a blessed word of permit: 'Bring him unto me.' There is no case so bad but, if you bring it to Jesus, he can meet it. 'Bring him unto me.' Now, good woman, bring your daughter's case to Christ tonight in prayer while you are sitting in the pew. Now, come, brother, bring the case of your son who seems utterly to be abandoned to vice. Bring the case before Christ tonight. 'Bring him unto me.' Oh, who would not bring his friend — his wife? Who would not bring her husband or her child unto Jesus Christ? 'Bring him unto me.'

20 And they brought him unto him: —

Some came to help the father, probably the bringing of the young man was too much an effort for one alone. 'They brought him unto him.' Two or three of you with united prayer can do what, peradventure, one man's prayer would not. Come, help one another. 'Bear ye one another's burdens' in prayer. I would suggest that, if one of you should have an ungodly son who causes you trouble, you should communicate with some few of your brethren and sisters in Christ, and say, 'Let us conjointly make this case a matter of prayer till God hears us.' And then you must take up a case of theirs — you know, turn and turn about — and see whether God does not in answer to prayer bless one after another that you thus bring to Christ. I know what the result will be, if it be honestly tried in simple confidence in the power of Jesus.

20-21 and when he saw him, straightway the spirit tare him; and he fell on the ground, and wallowed foaming. And he asked his father, How long is it ago since this came unto him? And he said, Of a child.

A terrible case.

MARK 9:2-29

Mark 9:2-4 And after six days Jesus taketh with him Peter, and James, and John, and leadeth them up into an high mountain apart by themselves: and he was transfigured before them. And his raiment became shining, exceeding white as snow; so as no fuller on earth can white them. And there appeared unto them Elias with Moses: and they were talking with Jesus.

In the midst of all his sorrow and humiliation, our Lord let out some gleams of his glory, to remind us who he was even while he was here in the depths of his grief. He was still none other than the all-glorious Lord of heaven and earth, whose raiment, if he chose to make it so, would be whiter than snow, and brighter than the sun. Let us think of

287

him with great love and gratitude as we see what glory he willingly laid aside for our sakes, and see how low he stooped, who was in himself immeasurably high.

5-6 And Peter answered and said to Jesus, Master, it is good for us to be here: and let us make three tabernacles; one for thee, and one for Moses, and one for Elias. For he wist not what to say; for they were sore afraid.

Peter had enough wit left to wish to keep where he was; and, sometimes, when we are with our Lord in the mount, we can only say, 'Master, it is good for us to be here; let us stay where we are! Let our union and communion with thyself continue for evermore!'

7-8 And there was a cloud that overshadowed them: and a voice came out of the cloud, saying, This is my beloved Son: hear him. And suddenly, when they had looked round about, they saw no man any more, save Jesus only with themselves.

Moses is gone, and Elias is gone, but Jesus remains; and it is much the same with us now, and we are quite content that all others should go that we may have 'Jesus only'. If he be with us, we have the best company in the world.

9-10 And as they came down from the mountain, he charged them that they should tell no man what things they had seen, till the Son of man were risen from the dead. And they kept that saying with themselves, questioning one with another what the rising from the dead should mean.

You see the great modesty and patience of our Lord. Though these three favoured apostles might see his glory and, afterwards, bear witness concerning it, yet for the time being they must hold their tongues. All this glory, and only three men to see it, and these three must be quite silent! Our Lord seeketh not honour from men; neither ought we to do so. His mind was even then occupied with thoughts of his great sacrifice. When he spoke to Moses and Elias, his theme was, 'his decease which he should accomplish at Jerusalem' [Luke 9:31], and when he spoke with these three eye-witnesses of his majesty, the subject of his converse was his own death and resurrection. That was the object on which his heart's affection was set.

11-13 And they asked him, saying, Why say the scribes that Elias must first come? And he answered and told them, Elias verily cometh first, and restoreth all things; and how it is written of the Son of man, that he must suffer many things, and be set at nought. But I say unto you, That Elias is indeed come, and they have done unto him whatsoever they listed, as it is written of him.

Notice that, even when our Saviour was answering his disciples' question about Elias and John, the ruling passion being strong upon him, he introduced into that answer something about his own death. That subject is ever before his eye; he never forgets it; he is, in a sense, undergoing his passion even as he descends the Mount of Transfiguration.

14 And when he came to his disciples, he saw a great multitude about them, and the scribes questioning with them.

What a descent for Christ, from the peace and quiet of the hill of communion with the glorified, to the noise and tumult of a surging multitude, and the mocking question of the jeering scribes!

15 And straightway all the people, when they beheld him, were greatly amazed, and running to him saluted him.

I think there must be some truth in the common tradition that the face of our Lord Jesus still shone with the light of the transfiguration. It does appear so to me from these words: 'All the people, when they beheld him, were greatly amazed.' Surely, it was not an amazement at the mere fact of seeing him whom they had so often seen, but his face, I doubt not, glowed as the face of Moses did when he came down from the mount. Only observe that, when the face of Moses burned with the reflected glory of God's presence, the people could not bear to look upon him, but when the face of Christ shone with supernatural splendour, they 'were greatly amazed, and running to him saluted him.' There is an attractive glory about the Christ of God. Oh, for such a sight of his face at this moment that we should all run to him, and salute him!

16 And he asked the scribes, What question ye with them?

There had been a skirmish between the scribes and the disciples of

Christ, and the scribes were winning the day; but when the Captain had come, the tide of battle was soon turned.

17-18 And one of the multitude answered and said, Master, I have brought unto thee my son, which hath a dumb spirit; And wheresoever he taketh him, he teareth him: and he foameth, and gnasheth with his teeth, and pineth away: and I spake to thy disciples that they should cast him out; and they could not.

It was an aggravated case of epilepsy, attended with possession by an evil spirit. The disciples could not cast out this devil, and the scribes had therefore attacked their faith in the Master himself while he was away.

19 He answereth him, and saith, O faithless generation, how long shall I be with you? how long shall I suffer you? bring him unto me.

Unbelief is a great trouble to Christ. I never read that he said to the poor or to the sick, 'How long shall I be with you? how long shall I suffer you?' I never read that he expressed any weariness of human ignorance, or scarcely even of human sin, but when it is a matter of unbelief, then it stings him, and he cries, 'O faithless generation, how long shall I be with you? how long shall I suffer you? Bring him unto me.'

20-21 And they brought him unto him: and when he saw him, straightway the spirit tare him; and he fell on the ground, and wallowed foaming. And he asked his father, How long is it ago since this came unto him? And he said, Of a child.

And having begun with that sorrowful subject, the father, with the painful eloquence of pity, went on to tell the tale of woe.

22 And ofttimes it hath cast him into the fire, and into the waters, to destroy him: but if thou canst do any thing, have compassion on us, and help us.

Here was unbelief, it is true; but there was with it a pitying entreaty that meant more faith than it could express. Men do not usually beg where they expect nothing, and they do not make pitiful entreaties with tears unless they have some hope. Even though it was almost covered up, still the Saviour fastened on that one utterance of unbelief: 'if'.

23 Jesus said unto him, If thou canst believe, all things are possible to him that believeth.

It is not, 'If I can'; but, 'If thou canst'.

24   And straightway the father of the child cried out, and said with tears, Lord, I believe; help thou mine unbelief.

There was faith, even though it was mixed with unbelief. It was a faith that made him pray, as I have already told you, and the Lord Jesus Christ found out where the faith was. He had, as it were, broken the great black lump of dead coal that looked to be nothing but unbelief, and there was the living light of faith burning in the very centre of it.

25   When Jesus saw that the people came running together, he rebuked the foul spirit, saying unto him, Thou dumb and deaf spirit, I charge thee, come out of him, and enter no more into him.

That is Christ's way of curing. Our Lord does not save sinners as some say that he does, just for a short time, and then let his work all rumble back to nothingness. This would be unworthy of himself and unworthy of that gracious Spirit by whom he works. No, if he casts out a devil, he shall enter no more into the one he formerly tormented.

26   And the spirit cried, and rent him sore, and came out of him: and he was as one dead; insomuch that many said, He is dead.

As old Thomas Fuller says, 'The devil knew that he had to go out, so, like a bad tenant, he did all the mischief he could before he left.' Satan often acts in this fashion; just when Christ has come to cast him out, he drives the poor soul into deeper despair, and perhaps into greater sin than he ever fell into in all his life before.

27   But Jesus took him by the hand, and lifted him up; and he arose.

He was not dead, though many thought he was, and said so. Christ does not cure and then kill; he cures so that we shall never die. No, no, poor sinner, the last pangs of despair shall not destroy you; the fiercest, bitterest assaults of Satan shall not cause you to die. Christ will take you by the hand, and you shall arise.

28-29   And when he was come into the house, his disciples asked him privately, Why could not we cast him out? And he said unto them, This kind can come forth by nothing, but by prayer and fasting.

MARK 9:14-32,43-48

Our Lord had been absent from the people, and transfigured on the top of the mountain; when he came down from this manifestation of his glory, he was brought face to face with Satan's work at almost the first step he took. Let us read about what he did.

Mark 9:14-15   And when he came to his disciples, he saw a great multitude about them, and the scribes questioning with them. And straightway all the people, when they beheld him, were greatly amazed, and running to him saluted him.

There was a glory about his face not altogether unlike that of Moses when he came down from the other mountain, so that the people were struck with wonder when they looked upon him.

16   And he asked the scribes, What question ye with them?

The battle had been raging between Christ's enemies and his disciples but now that their Captain has come, he rallies his forces, and at once attacks his foes: 'What question ye with them?'

17   And one of the multitude answered and said, Master, I have brought unto thee my son, which hath a dumb spirit;

We do not know if the scribes gave any answer to Christ's question; and it does not signify at all. What does always signify is practical, living, earnest prayer. So what the scribes may have said is not recorded, but the prayer of the poor father is: 'Master, I have brought unto thee my son, which hath a dumb spirit.' If any of you have come here to cavil, we shall take no notice of that; but if there is a soul that has come here to pray, the recording angel will write it down in the eternal book.

18   And wheresoever he taketh him, he teareth him: and he foameth, and gnasheth with his teeth, and pineth away: and I spake to thy disciples that they should cast him out; and they could not.

No, it was no use going to the disciples. It is of no avail to pray to saints and angels. Go to the Master himself. 'Straightforward makes the best runner.' There is nothing like carrying your case to headquarters. Get to the Court of King's Bench as soon as you can, for there the matter will be finally settled.

19 He answereth him, and saith, O faithless generation, how long shall I be with you? how long shall I suffer you? bring him unto me.

Grand words: 'Bring him unto me.' Lord, he has a dumb spirit. 'Bring him unto me.' It is the devil who is his enemy. 'Bring him unto me.'

20 And they brought him unto him: and when he saw him, straightway the spirit tare him; and he fell on the ground, and wallowed foaming.

What a dreadful sight! He struggled on the ground, like one in a fit of epilepsy.

21-22 And he asked his father, How long is it ago since this came unto him? And he said, Of a child. And ofttimes it hath cast him into the fire, and into the waters, to destroy him: but if thou canst do any thing, have compassion on us, and help us.

'Help us', he cries, identifying himself with his child. Father, mother, when you pray, use the plural, as this man did: 'Have compassion on us and help us.' That is the way to pray for every sinner whom you bring before Christ. Join yourself to the poor soul for whom you are pleading and say, 'Have compassion on us, and help us.'

23 Jesus said unto him, If thou canst believe, all things are possible to him that believeth.

Hear that, any of you who have come in here desiring to be delivered from sin, to be made holy, to break off old habits and to become new men in Christ Jesus. 'All things are possible to him that believeth.' So, take courage, trust in Christ, and cry unto him to save you.

24 And straightway the father of the child cried out, and said with tears, Lord, I believe; help thou mine unbelief.

There were within him two men, as it were, a believing man, and an unbelieving man, and the two struggled for mastery; 'Lord, I do believe; but there is so much unbelief in me, I pray thee to drive it out, that I may believe in thee wholly.'

25-26 When Jesus saw that the people came running together, he rebuked the foul spirit, saying unto him, Thou dumb and deaf spirit, I charge thee, come out of him, and enter no more into him. And the spirit cried, and rent him sore, and came out of him: —

It must obey Christ. The Master bids that dog of a devil to lie down, and he must do so. It shows what an abject creature, after all, the prince of darkness is — he must obey the voice of Christ. Lord, speak to him at this moment, and drive him out of other souls by thine omnipotent Word!

26 and he was as one dead; insomuch that many said, He is dead.

It was not a case of 'kill or cure', but it seemed to be one of 'cure and kill', and, sometimes, poor sinners in their struggles with sin and Satan are brought to such despair that they are afraid that they will die before they get a glimpse of hope. 'Many said, He is dead', but he was not.

27 But Jesus took him by the hand, and lifted him up; and he arose.

So may the Lord come, and take by the hand any here who seem to be dead in despair! A touch of his hand will enable them to stand.

28-29 And when he was come into the house, his disciples asked him privately, Why could not we cast him out? And he said unto them, This kind can come forth by nothing, but by prayer and fasting.

The watchword for Christ's disciples is 'intensity'. Here was the devil in an intensely terrible form, and he could only be driven out by *intense grace*. There must be prayer and fasting. Even Christ himself must exert the greatness of his power to work a cure in such a case as this. Oh, for more intensity in us all! Carry that word in your ear as we read on.

30-32 And they departed thence, and passed through Galilee; and he would not that any man should know it. For he taught his disciples, and said unto them, The Son of man is delivered into the hands of men, and they shall kill him; and after that he is killed, he shall rise the third day. But they understood not that saying, and were afraid to ask him.

See how intense he was; always thinking of his approaching death, that cruel, bitter death, yet he hasted towards it, longed for that baptism to be accomplished, for the great redeeming price to be paid. Oh, that you and

I were as fully absorbed in the service of God as our great Master was! Now let us see what intensity he requires of us.

43 And if thy hand offend thee, cut it off: it is better for thee to enter into life maimed, than having two hands to go into hell, into the fire that never shall be quenched:

Anything is better than the loss of your soul. It is better to lose the greatest joy, skill, comfort, honour, that you ever had, than to lose your soul for ever.

44-46 Where their worm dieth not, and the fire is not quenched. And if thy foot offend thee, cut it off: it is better for thee to enter halt into life, than having two feet to be cast into hell, into the fire that never shall be quenched: Where their worm dieth not, and the fire is not quenched.

That is the second time he said these words. Our Lord was not fond of dreadful metaphors and terrible language, but he knew that they must be used, though some of his servants shrink from the use of them. Are they more loving than he is? Is it, after all, a greater love for souls that makes men keep back terrible truths? Is it not more honest and loving to tell the *whole* truth, whatever it may be? It is harder to speak, but does it not show a tenderer heart to be able to speak so as to warn men of their peril? If anything should seem as necessary to you as your foot, so that you can make no progress in life without it, yet if it would cost you your soul, give it up. Just as it would be better to live without a foot than to die, so is it better to go to heaven without even the necessaries of life on the road than to perish everlastingly.

47 And if thine eye offend thee, pluck it out: —

Notice how severe our Saviour is, how deep he goes. He does not say, 'Shut it, cover it up with a green shade', but 'Pluck it out.'

47-48 it is better for thee to enter into the kingdom of God with one eye, than having two eyes to be cast into hell fire: Where their worm dieth not, and the fire is not quenched.

That is the third time he has uttered those terrible words; then they must mean something. What do they mean? Can they mean anything less than everlasting destruction away from the presence of the Lord?

Oh, that we might be prepared to sacrifice everything rather than be lost for ever! Dear hearts, are you saved or not? If you are not saved, see first to this all-important business; let everything else go, sooner than that, in eternity, you should find yourself for ever shut in where hope can never come.

MARK 9:20-29,38-41

This miracle is one that shows the transforming power of the Saviour in a remarkable fashion.

Mark 9:20-21 And they brought him unto him: and when he saw him, straightway the spirit tare him; and he fell on the ground, and wallowed foaming. And he asked his father, How long is it ago since this came unto him? And he said, Of a child.

A terrible case.

22-25 And ofttimes it hath cast him into the fire, and into the waters, to destroy him: but if thou canst do any thing, have compassion on us, and help us. Jesus said unto him, If thou canst believe, all things are possible to him that believeth. And straightway the father of the child cried out, and said with tears, Lord, I believe; help thou mine unbelief. When Jesus saw that the people came running together, he rebuked the foul spirit, saying unto him, Thou dumb and deaf spirit, I charge thee, come out of him, and enter no more into him.

That is one way in which Christ cures. When he drives the devil out of a man, he adds, 'Enter no more into him.' I believe in the final perseverance of the saints, because I believe in the omnipotent ejection of Satan out of men, when Christ speaks the word, 'Come out of him, and enter no more into him.'

26-29 And the spirit cried, and rent him sore, and came out of him: and he was as one dead; insomuch that many said, He is dead. But Jesus took him by the hand, and lifted him up; and he arose. And when he was come into the house, his disciples asked him privately, Why could not we cast him out? And he said unto them, —

According to another evangelist, it was from want of faith. Howbeit, he added:

29 This kind can come forth by nothing, but by prayer and fasting.

God does not give us everything in answer to one prayer. It may be necessary for some blessings that the prayer should be reiterated — that it should deepen — that it should grow into an aching. It may be even necessary, in order that a blessing should come, that fasting should be used with prayer in order to show the intense eagerness and earnestness of the petitioner.

Now notice verse 38.

38 And John answered him, saying, Master, we saw one casting out devils in thy name, and he followeth not us: and we forbad him, because he followeth not us.

John in this case was like a good many people at the present day. You notice it. They could not cast out the devils themselves, and when they found somebody else that did it, they forbade his doing it because he did not follow with them. I have known learned, eloquent, respectable ministers who cannot save sinners. And they hear that certain poor, illiterate, uneducated men have snatched sinners 'like brands from the burning', and they forbid them to do what they cannot do themselves. It is insanity that would stop any man from doing what God enables him to do; and we ought to be the very last to forbid others from doing it.

39 But Jesus said, Forbid him not: for there is no man which shall do a miracle in my name, that can lightly speak evil of me.

These people were dissenters, we may say — a sort of outsiders. And John puts forth the whole power of his apostolical authority to put them down; and then Jesus Christ puts forth the full power of his divine authority to give them liberty to go on.

40-41 For he that is not against us is on our part. For whosoever shall give you a cup of water to drink in my name, because ye belong to Christ, verily I say unto you, he shall not lose his reward.

MARK 10:13-27,32-52

Mark 10:13   And they brought young children to him, that he should touch them: and his disciples rebuked those that brought them.

They thought them too little, too insignificant, and that the Master had greater things to do; but he thinketh not so. None are too little for him. He receiveth even childish honours to himself.

14   But when Jesus saw it, he was much displeased, and said unto them, Suffer the little children to come unto me, and forbid them not: for of such is the kingdom of God.

Many of them come into that kingdom, and all who some think must be like them. The child is not the hardest subject of conversion; nay, rather:

15   Verily I say unto you, Whosoever shall not receive the kingdom of God as a little child, he shall not enter therein.

Instead of growing wiser, in order to be fit for Christ, we must be more conscious of ignorance, more trustful towards him, more dependent upon him, more childlike.

16-18   And he took them up in his arms, put his hands upon them, and blessed them. And when he was gone forth into the way, there came one running, and kneeled to him, and asked him, Good Master, what shall I do that I may inherit eternal life? And Jesus said unto him, Why callest thou me good? there is none good but one, that is, God.

He did not here unveil his deity to that young man; but, if he had thought a while, he might have seen it. However, he answered his question: 'If you are to be saved by your doings, this is what you have to do — not attend to sacraments and go through performances, but this.'

19-20   Thou knowest the commandments, Do not commit adultery, Do not kill, Do not steal, Do not bear false witness, Defraud not, Honour thy father and mother. And he answered and said unto him, Master, all these have I observed from my youth.

And he probably had very cautiously and anxiously done so; yet, for all that, he had not really kept all those commands without a flaw. We are right well sure of that, but as yet his eyes were not open to see his own shortcomings.

21   Then Jesus beholding him loved him, —

There was so much that was amiable about him.

21   and said unto him, One thing thou lackest: go thy way, sell whatsoever thou hast, and give to the poor, and thou shalt have treasure in heaven: and come, take up the cross, and follow me.

He knew that there was a weak point in the young man's character — that he did not yet supremely love God, but loved his wealth — that he was living for this world, after all. And are there not many such — most correct in character? No one could point to a single flaw in their morals, but they are living purely for self — altogether that they may buy and sell and get gain — no thought of God, except a fear lest they should come under his rod, but no thought of serving him and laying themselves out for his glory nor much thought, either, for their fellow men. Christ had hit the blot and marked it out for him.

22-24   And he was sad at that saying, and went away grieved: for he had great possessions. And Jesus looked round about, and saith unto his disciples, How hardly shall they that have riches enter into the kingdom of God! And the disciples were astonished at his words. —

For the rabbis had pretty well taught that money would answer everything — that if you could give so much, and pay so much, it was all well with you. Christ went against all such teaching and showed that, in this respect, money was of no service, in fact, that it often was a hindrance.

24   But Jesus answereth again, and saith unto them, Children, how hard is it for them that trust in riches to enter into the kingdom of God!

It is an impossibility. Only God can do it.

25-27,32-34   It is easier for a camel to go through the eye of a needle, than for a rich man to enter into the kingdom of God. And they were astonished out of measure, saying among themselves, Who then can be saved? And Jesus looking upon them saith, With men it is impossible, but not with God: for with God all things are possible. ... And they were in the way going up to Jerusalem; and Jesus went before them: and they were amazed; and as they followed, they were afraid. And he took again the twelve, and began to tell them what things should happen unto him, Saying, Behold, we go up to Jerusalem; and the Son of man shall be delivered unto the chief priests, and unto the scribes; and they shall condemn him to death, and shall deliver him to the Gentiles: And they shall mock him, and shall scourge him, and shall spit upon him, and shall kill him: and the third day he shall rise again.

From the number of these sentences it is clear that our Saviour entered into a very detailed account of his sufferings, dwelling upon each particular which he plainly foresaw, wherein we see his prophetic character. But it is more to our point to see that he knew beforehand what it would cost him to redeem our souls.

> *When the Saviour knew the price of pardon was his blood,*
> *His pity ne'er withdrew.*

He knew not only that he must die, but he knew all the circumstances of pain and shame with which that death should be attended. They should condemn him; should deliver him to the Gentiles; mock him; scourge him; spit upon him; kill him. Thus we learn that we also should dwell in holy, grateful meditation upon every point of our Lord's passion. There is something in it. He would not himself thus have divided it out, and laid it, as it were, piece by piece, if he had not intended us to do with it as they did with the burnt offering of old, when they divided it — a picture of what every intelligent, instructed believer should do with the passion of his Master. He should try to look into the details of the great sacrifice and have communion with God therein. Now, albeit that this revelation of his coming shame and sorrow and death afflicted the hearts of his disciples, yet, for all that, observe what they did.

35 And James and John, the sons of Zebedee, come unto him, saying, Master, we would that thou shouldest do for us whatsoever we shall desire.

Strange request! First of all, read those words, 'We would that thou shouldest do for us.' Now the genuine spirit of a Christian is not to ask that something should be done to him, but to ask his Master, especially in such a time as that, what they could do for him. Christ was all unselfishness, but his disciples had not yet learned the lesson. 'We would that thou shouldest do for us.' And then see how much they indulged their ambition. 'We wouldest that thou shouldest do for us *whatsoever we desire.*' And yet I question whether we are, any of us, free from this spirit, for when the Lord reproves us a little, and we have not everything our own way, how apt we are to rebel! The fact is, we have got this tincture — this gall — in us: we would that he should do for us whatsoever we shall desire. Should it be according to *thy* mind? Should the disciple dictate to his Master? Should the child be lord of the family?

36-39 And he said unto them, What would ye that I should do for you? They said unto him, Grant unto us that we may sit, one on thy right hand, and the other on thy left hand, in thy glory. But Jesus said unto them, Ye know not what ye ask: can ye drink of the cup that I drink of? and be baptized with the baptism that I am baptized with? And they said unto him, We can. —

Again, he might have said, 'Ye know not what ye say.'

39-40 And Jesus said unto them, Ye shall indeed drink of the cup that I drink of; and with the baptism that I am baptized withal shall ye be baptized: But to sit on my right hand and on my left hand is not mine to give; but it shall be given to them for whom it is prepared.

They are not content, you see, with being ambitious themselves: they would fire him with ambition — that humble, lowly servant of God, who had laid aside for a while the power to distribute crowns and thrones. But he does not forget himself, nor the position which he had taken up in reference to the Father, but said, 'It is not mine to give.'

41-43 And when the ten heard it, they began to be much displeased with James and John. But Jesus called them to him, and saith unto them, Ye know that they which are accounted to rule over the Gentiles exercise lordship over them; and their great ones exercise authority upon them. But so shall it not be among you: —

However, how sad the contrast is — the Master's thoughts all taken up with his death for others, and their thoughts occupied with little petty jealousies as to who should be the greatest! It is a sad thing when this creeps into Christian churches (and it still does), when souls are perishing, and this poor world wants our weeping eyes and our labourious hands, and we get quarrelling about points of precedence. This brother thinks the other too forward. This one has not enough respect paid to him. This one has spoken sharply, and the other cannot bear it. Oh! What poor disciples we are! What a blessing it is we have a patient. Master, who still bears with us and will not leave us until he has infused his own spirit into us, which spirit is the spirit of self-denial, self-abnegation — the spirit which desireth not its own, but looketh on the things of others. God grant us all to be full of it.

43 but whosoever will be great among you, shall be your minister:

Your servant.

44 And whosoever of you will be the chiefest, shall be servant of all.

And that is the way to be truly great in the church of God. It is to be less and less in your own esteem and willing to be nothing. The way up is downward. That is not a contradiction, but it is a paradox. Sink, and you shall rise. Be willing to serve the very least, and you shall have honour among your brethren. Remember that the King of kings was the servant of servants. 'Whosoever of you will be the chiefest, shall be servant of all.'

45-49 For even the Son of man came not to be ministered unto, but to minister, and to give his life a ransom for many. And they came to Jericho: and as he went out of Jericho with his disciples and a great number of people, blind Bartimaeus, the son of Timaeus, sat by the highway side begging. And when he heard that it was Jesus of Nazareth, he began to cry out, and say, Jesus, thou son of David, have mercy on me. And many charged him that he should hold his peace: but he cried the more a great deal, Thou son of David, have mercy on me. And Jesus stood still, and commanded him to be called. And they call the blind man, saying unto him, Be of good comfort, —

'Cheer up' — that would be a very exact translation.

49-51 rise; he calleth thee. And he, casting away his garment, rose, and came to Jesus. And Jesus answered and said unto him, What wilt thou that I should do unto thee? —

Do you notice here a sort of gentle rebuke that the Saviour gives to James and John? Read verse 36, and then read this again. 'He said unto them, What would ye that I should do for you?' And now here is a blind beggar, and he sweetly puts the same question to him, 'What wilt thou that I should do unto thee?'

51   The blind man said unto him, —

And here he might well have shamed John and James. He asked for no thrones or kingdoms.

51   Lord, that I might receive my sight.

'Lord, that I might look up.' That was the word he used exactly; for no doubt he had been conscious that the light came from the sun as he felt its warmth upon him as he sat by the wayside; and, therefore, he thought that seeing must be looking up towards the place whence the sunlight came. 'Lord, that I might look up.'

52   And Jesus said unto him, Go thy way; thy faith hath made thee whole. And immediately he received his sight, and followed Jesus in the way.

It is a very remarkable thing that you will not often find the Lord Jesus Christ granting a favour without ascribing it to some excellency in that person to whom he grants it. It is generally, 'Great is thy faith,' or something of that sort — 'I have not seen such faith.' Now this is a very remarkable thing, because we know there really was nothing whatever in the persons that they should deserve his great favour.

MARK 10:17-45

Mark 10:17-18   And when he was gone forth into the way, there came one running, and kneeled to him, and asked him, Good Master, what shall I do that I may inherit eternal life? And Jesus said unto him, Why callest thou me good? there is none good but one, that is, God.

This was a hint that Christ was more than man. If he was really worthy of the title that the inquirer gave him, he was God as well as man, for 'there is none good but one, that is God'.

19-20   Thou knowest the commandments, Do not commit adultery, Do not kill, Do not steal, Do not bear false witness, Defraud not, Honour thy father and mother. And he answered and said unto him, Master, all these have I observed from my youth.

Possibly, in the ordinary sense of the words, he had observed these commandments, but Christ tested the reality of his declaration.

21-22 Then Jesus beholding him loved him, and said unto him, One thing thou lackest: go thy way, sell whatsoever thou hast, and give to the poor, and thou shalt have treasure in heaven: and come, take up the cross, and follow me. And he was sad at that saying, and went away grieved: for he had great possessions.

Thus he proved that he had not kept either table of the law perfectly, for he did not love the Lord with all his heart, nor did he love his neighbour as himself.

23-27 And Jesus looked round about, and saith unto his disciples, How hardly shall they that have riches enter into the kingdom of God! And the disciples were astonished at his words. But Jesus answereth again, and saith unto them, Children, how hard is it for them that trust in riches to enter into the kingdom of God! It is easier for a camel to go through the eye of a needle, than for a rich man to enter into the kingdom of God. And they were astonished out of measure, saying among themselves, Who then can be saved? And Jesus looking upon them saith, With men it is impossible, but not with God: for with God all things are possible.

It is impossible for man, unaided by the Spirit of God, to enter the kingdom of heaven, but that which is impossible to man by himself is made possible by the grace and power of God.

28 Then Peter began to say unto him, Lo, we have left all, and have followed thee.

He spoke as if they had done what the rich man had failed to do, and evidently he thought they should be rewarded, for, according to Matthew, he added, 'What shall we have therefore?'

29-31 And Jesus answered and said, Verily I say unto you, There is no man that hath left house, or brethren, or sisters, or father, or mother, or wife, or children, or lands, for my sake, and the gospel's, But he shall receive an hundredfold now in this time, houses, and brethren, and sisters, and mothers, and children, and lands, with persecutions; and in the world to come eternal life. But many that are first shall be last; and the last first.

In the final account, it shall be found that no man has been a loser through giving up anything for the Lord Jesus Christ though he has his own method of deciding who are to be first and who are to be last.

32 And they were in the way going up to Jerusalem; —

It was well known to them all that the crisis of our Saviour's history was close at hand and a sort of indefinable dread was upon them all. The bravest spirit in the whole company was their blessed Lord and Master. He knew that he was going up to Jerusalem to die, so you may view him as the Sacrifice going to the altar, or as the Hero going to the conflict in which he would die and yet conquer. 'They were in the way going up to Jerusalem' —

32   and Jesus went before them: —

The disciples might well have been filled with holy courage as their Leader was in the front. This is true concerning the whole life of all the saints: 'Jesus went before them.' What if trials lie beyond, and the dark river itself is in front of them, yet Jesus goes before them, so they need not fear to follow.

32   and they were amazed; and as they followed, they were afraid. —

They did not know much about what was to happen, but a great depression was upon their spirits. They must have wondered at the cheerful bravery of their Master when all of them were ready to turn back from this mournful march.

32-34   And he took again the twelve, and began to tell them what things should happen unto him, Saying, Behold, we go up to Jerusalem; and the Son of man shall be delivered unto the chief priests, and unto the scribes; and they shall condemn him to death, and shall deliver him to the Gentiles: And they shall mock him, and shall scourge him, and shall spit upon him, and shall kill him: and the third day he shall rise again.

He thought it right that the twelve, who led the way, should be better acquainted than the rest with the sad history that was so soon to be enacted. So he tells them about it in private, and I want you to notice how he dwells in detail upon his sufferings. He does not describe them in general terms, but he brings out into strong relief each separate set of infamy: 'they shall mock him, and shall scourge him, and shall spit upon him and shall kill him' — from which we learn that our Saviour knew all that he had to endure, yet he went bravely forward to bear it for our sakes. For this reason, we should admire his divine courage and complete self-sacrifice. Mere men may promise to do a certain thing without knowing what it will involve, but —

This was compassion like a God,
  That when the Saviour knew
The price of pardon was his blood,
  His pity ne'er withdrew.

I think, too, that as our Lord thus dwells upon each point, he means us also to dwell upon the details of his redeeming griefs. We should not be strangers at the cross-foot, nor in Gethsemane; but should hear each one of these notes ring out its sorrowful yet joyful music: 'They shall mock him, and shall scourge him, and shall spit upon him, and shall kill him.' But what a glad note that concluding one is: 'And the third day he shall rise again.' Death cannot hold him in her bands; the sepulchre cannot continue to enclose him in her gloomy prison. This is the glory and boast of our Christianity, our hope and our joy, for —

As the Lord our Saviour rose,
So all his followers must.

35-36 And James and John, the sons of Zebedee, come unto him, saying, Master, we would that thou shouldest do for us whatsoever we shall desire. And he said unto them, What would ye that I should do for you?

Our Saviour's question suggests to us the prudent lesson never to promise in the dark. If anyone shall say to you, 'Promise that you will do whatever I ask', follow the example of Christ and first ask, 'What would you that I should do for you?' Otherwise, you may entangle yourself with your own words. These young men evidently needed to have this question put to them, for they had not themselves thoroughly considered what they were asking their Lord to do for them.

37   They said unto him, Grant unto us that we may sit, one on thy right hand, and the other on thy left hand, in thy glory.

There was, undoubtedly, much that was wrong about this request, and you have often heard that view of the matter dwelt upon, so I will call your attention to that which was right about it. These disciples showed their faith that this same Jesus, who was to be mocked, and scourged, and spit upon, and killed, would yet *reign*; and I think it was wonderful faith that, after they had heard from his own lips, in sorrowful detail, the description of how he should die, yet nevertheless they so fully believed in his kingdom that they asked to have a share in its honours. It is true that they were ambitious, but their ambition was to be near the Saviour. It would be well if all those, who ask for right hand and left hand places, wanted them at the right hand and the left hand of the Saviour.

38   But Jesus said unto them, Ye know not what ye ask: —

Has the Lord ever said to us, when we have been praying, 'Ye know not what ye ask'? I suppose that is usually true in a certain sense; we do not fully understand the compass of the most of our prayers, and sometimes we ask so unadvisedly that we prove that we know not what we are asking.

38   can ye drink of the cup that I drink of? and be baptized with the baptism that I am baptized with?

'Can ye share my drinking in Gethsemane and my sinking on Golgotha?'

39   And they said unto him, We can. —

They knew not what they said, but they felt that such was the strength of their love, that they could share anything that had to do with Christ! His throne? Yes, they would like to sit at the right hand of it. His cup? Yes, they can drink of it. Immersion into his suffering? Yes, they can endure that baptism.

39   And Jesus said unto them, Ye shall indeed drink of the cup that I drink of; and with the baptism that I am baptized withal shall ye be baptized:

And so they were, for James was soon put to death, and John lived the last and longest of the apostles — a life-long martyrdom for the Master's sake.

40-41 But to sit on my right hand and on my left hand is not mine to give; but it shall be given to them for whom it is prepared. And when the ten heard it, they began to be much displeased with James and John.

Why were they displeased? Because they were of the same spirit as James and John. As they were displeased with James and John, it is evident that they wanted those places themselves, and many a man is thus displeased with his own faults. Did you ever see a dog bark at himself in a glass? You and I have often done that; we have even grown very angry with what was, after all, only our own image.

42-45 But Jesus called them to him, and saith unto them, Ye know that they which are accounted to rule over the Gentiles exercise lordship over them; and their great ones exercise authority upon them. But so shall it not be among you: but whosoever will be great among you, shall be your minister: And whosoever of you will be the chiefest, shall be servant of all. For even the Son of man came not to be ministered unto, but to minister, and to give his life a ransom for many.

Christ instituted bishops, that is, overseers, but never prelates. He never had any idea of setting some men in his church over the heads of others, but he put all his servants upon an equality. They are to exercise no lordship the one over the other, nor to seek it, for the truest honour in the church of God is found in *service*. He that serves most is the greatest. He that will occupy the lowest office, he that will bear patiently to be the most put upon, he that is readiest to be despised, and to be the servant of all, shall be the chiefest of all. The way to rise in the kingdom of heaven is to descend, for even so was it with our Lord himself. God give to all of us the humble and lowly spirit that will make us willing to be the least of all!

MARK 10:46-52; JOHN 9:1-7

We have several records of blind men being cured by the Lord Jesus Christ. One of them is in Mark 10:46-52.

Mark 10:46   And they came to Jericho: and as he went out of Jericho with his disciples and a great number of people, —

For, now, his march to the battle was like a triumphal march, which was by and by to be attended with the waving of palms and the shout of hosannas: 'as he went out of Jericho with his disciples and a great number of people' —

46-47   blind Bartimaeus, the son of Timaeus, sat by the highway side begging. And when he heard that it was Jesus of Nazareth, —

That is all that the crowd called him, 'Jesus of Nazareth'.

47   he began to cry out, and say, Jesus, thou son of David, have mercy on me.

He had advanced much further than the mass of the people. To him it was not 'Jesus of Nazareth', but it was 'Jesus, thou son of David'.

48-50   And many charged him that he should hold his peace: but he cried the more a great deal, Thou son of David, have mercy on me. And Jesus stood still, and commanded him to be called. And they call the blind man, saying unto him, Be of good comfort, rise; he calleth thee. And he, casting away his garment, rose, and came to Jesus.

Blind as he was, he found his way to the Saviour. I suppose the ear directed by the voice helped him to do so.

51   And Jesus answered and said unto him, What wilt thou that I should do unto thee? The blind man said unto him, Lord, that I might receive my sight.

His request was plainly put, but it was most respectfully and even adoringly addressed to Christ.

52   And Jesus said unto him, Go thy way; thy faith hath made thee whole. —

You will find that it is often the Saviour's way thus to give the credit of his own work, to the patient's faith. 'Thy faith', saith he, 'hath made thee whole.' Whereas, you and I, if we do a good thing, are very anxious that nobody else should take the credit for it. We are very willing to have all the honour put upon ourselves, but Jesus does not say, 'I have made thee whole', though that was true enough; but, 'Thy faith hath made thee whole.' And why is it, think you, that Christ takes the crown off his own head to put it on the head of faith? Why? Because he loves faith, and because faith is quite certain not to wear that crown, but to lay it at his feet. For, of all the graces, faith is the surest to deny herself, and ascribe all to him in whom she trusts.

52   And immediately he received his sight, and followed Jesus in the way.

Another of these records is in John 9:1-7.

John 9:1-7   And as Jesus passed by, he saw a man which was blind from his birth. And his disciples asked him, saying, Master, who did sin, this man, or his parents, that he was born blind? Jesus answered, Neither hath this man sinned, nor his parents: but that the works of God should be made manifest in him. I must work the works of him that sent me, while it is day: the night cometh, when no man can work. As long as I am in the world, I am the light of the world. When he had thus spoken, he spat on the ground, and made clay of the spittle, and he anointed the eyes of the blind man with the clay, And said unto him, Go, wash in the pool of Siloam, (which is by interpretation, Sent.) He went his way therefore, and washed, and came seeing.

I will not say anything now about this miracle, as it will form the subject of my discourse.

MARK 12:12-44

Mark 12:12   And they sought to lay hold on him, but feared the people: for they knew that he had spoken the parable against them: and they left him, and went their way.

Christ's enemies could not injure him then, partly because the people heard him gladly and were ready to protect him, but still more because the appointed time for his suffering and death had not fully come.

13-14   And they send unto him certain of the Pharisees and of the Herodians, to catch him in his words. And when they were come, they say unto him, Master, we know that thou art true, and carest for no man: for thou regardest not the person of men, but teachest the way of God in truth: —

They meant 'to catch him in his words' if they could, so they baited their trap with flattery. Whenever a man begins to flatter you, be on your guard against him. If he tries to commence a conversation with you by uttering words of excessive admiration, depend upon it that he admires something that you have got more than he admires you; and therefore, be on the watch against him. Our Saviour must, in his heart, have utterly despised men who were so foolish as to imagine that they could entrap him by their flattering words. After that preface, they asked the questions which they thought would impale him upon the horns of a dilemma:

14-15 Is it lawful to give tribute to Caesar, or not? Shall we give, or shall we not give? —

They knew very well that if Christ said, 'Do not give tribute to Caesar', the Romans would have taken him up, and imprisoned him for preaching sedition. But, on the other hand, if he said, 'Pay tribute to Caesar', the Jews would have said that he was their enemy and not a true patriot, or else he would not have admitted that the chosen people were bound to pay taxes to their Roman conquerors.

15-17 But he, knowing their hypocrisy, said unto them, Why tempt ye me? bring me a penny, that I may see it. And they brought it. And he saith unto them, Whose is this image and superscription? And they said unto him, Caesar's. And Jesus answering said unto them, Render to Caesar the things that are Caesar's, and to God the things that are God's. And they marvelled at him.

He had answered them with matchless wisdom without committing himself in any way.

18-23 Then come unto him the Sadducees, which say there is no resurrection; and they asked him, saying, Master, Moses wrote unto us, If a man's brother die, and leave his wife behind him, and leave no children, that his brother should take his wife, and raise up seed unto his brother. Now there were seven brethren: and the first took a wife, and dying left no seed. And the second took her, and died, neither left he any seed: and the third likewise. And the seven had her, and left no seed: last of all the woman died also. In the resurrection therefore, when they shall rise, whose wife shall she be of them? for the seven had her to wife.

No doubt they thought that they had completely entangled him this time. How could he answer such a difficult question as that? But, you see, they had based their enquiry upon the erroneous supposition that things are to be, in another state, as they are here. So Jesus was able at once to answer them as effectively as he had just answered the Pharisees and Herodians.

24-27 And Jesus answering said unto them, Do ye not therefore err, because ye know not the scriptures, neither the power of God? For when they shall rise from the dead, they neither marry, nor are given in marriage; but are as the angels which are in heaven. And as touching the dead, that they rise: have ye not read in the book of Moses, how in the bush God spake unto him, saying, I am the God of Abraham, and the God of Isaac, and the God of Jacob? He is not the God of the dead, but the God of the living: ye therefore do greatly err.

His answer carried the war into the enemies' camp. They professed to believe in Moses, yet they denied the existence of spirits and the fact of the resurrection; but Jesus Christ proved in a demonstration that God cannot be the God of the dead. If, therefore, he is the God of Abraham, Isaac, and Jacob, Abraham, Isaac, and Jacob are still alive; and if he be your God, and my God, dear friends, we need not fear extinction; we must live, and we must live for ever.

28-34 And one of the scribes came, and having heard them reasoning together, and perceiving that he had answered them well, asked him, Which is the first commandment of all? And Jesus answered him, The first of all the commandments is, Hear, O Israel; The Lord our God is one Lord: And thou shalt love the Lord thy God with all thy heart, and with all thy soul, and with all thy mind, and with all thy strength: this is the first commandment. And the second is like, namely this, Thou shalt love thy neighbour as thyself. There is none other commandment greater than these. And the scribe said unto him, Well, Master, thou hast said the truth: for there is one God; and there is none other but he: And to love him with all the heart, and with all the understanding, and with all the soul, and with all the strength, and to love his neighbour as himself, is more than all whole burnt offerings and sacrifices. And when Jesus saw that he answered discreetly, he said unto him, Thou art not far from the kingdom of God. And no man after that durst ask him any question.

He had so decidedly put all his questioners to the rout that no other man had the audacity to court defeat at his hands. The infallible wisdom of Christ had put all his accusers and tempters to flight.

35-36 And Jesus answered and said, while he taught in the temple, How say the scribes that Christ is the son of David? For David himself said by the Holy Ghost, —

In Psalm 110:1 —

36-37 The LORD said to my Lord, Sit thou on my right hand, till I make thine enemies thy foot-stool. David therefore himself calleth him Lord; and whence is he then his son? —

They could not answer that riddle, but we can. We know that Jesus is both David's Son and David's Lord; a man like ourselves, of the great human race, yet 'very God of very God', blessed be his holy name!

37-40 And the common people heard him gladly. And he said unto them in his doctrine, Beware of the scribes, which love to go in long clothing, and love salutations in the market-places, And the chief seats in the synagogues, and the uppermost rooms at feasts: Which devour widows' houses, and for a pretence make long prayers: these shall receive greater damnation.

We often hear foolish people say 'You must always preach in love, and not say anything against anybody; Jesus did not denounce anybody.' Oh, dear! Then what about this denunciation of the scribes? Were Jesus here today, he would not be the molluscus creature (or creature having no backbone) that some people want us to be. He had a backbone, and a conscience, and a very heavy right hand, and he brought that hand down, like a sledge hammer, upon cant (or insincere talk) and hypocrisy and error and, if we would be like Christ, we must be manly and bold and outspoken. They tell us this in order that we may easily glide through the world, and that all men may speak well of us. But so did their fathers to the false prophets; and do you suppose that we who preach God's Word are going to keep back any part of our testimony because it will bring us into ill repute with the ungodly? God forbid! We live for something higher and nobler than being fed upon the breath of evil men. If there be error in high places, if there be vice anywhere, it is the duty of the minister of Christ, in his Master's name, to attack it with all his might. Here we find our Lord and Master plainly declaring that the scribes, the great masters of the law, were a set of pretentious hypocrites who robbed even the widow and the fatherless, and who would, in due time, 'receive greater damnation'. Even so must the truth still be spoken, whoever may be offended by it.

41-42 And Jesus sat over against the treasury, and beheld how the people cast money into the treasury: and many that were rich cast in much. And there came a certain poor widow, —

Doubly poor because she was not only a widow but in poverty: 'a certain poor widow' —

42-44 and she threw in two mites, which make a farthing. And he called unto him his disciples, and saith unto them, Verily I say unto you, That this poor widow hath cast more in, than all they which have cast into the treasury: For all they did cast in of their abundance; —

Christ measures what we really give by what we have left — by the proportion which what we give bears to what we possess: 'For all they did cast in of their abundance' —

44 but she of her want did cast in all that she had, even all her living.

So she gave more than any or all the others did.

MARK 14:27-31,53-54,66-72; JOHN 18:15-18,25-27

Mark 14:27-29 And Jesus saith unto them, All ye shall be offended because of me this night: for it is written, I will smite the shepherd, and the sheep shall be scattered. But after that I am risen, I will go before you into Galilee. But Peter said unto him, Although all shall be offended, yet will not I.

There was love in that utterance, and so far it was commendable. But there was also much self-trust in it and great presumption, for Peter dared even to contradict his Master to his face. At the same time, he contradicted the inspired Scripture, for Jesus had told the disciples that it was written that the sheep should be scattered. Yet Peter boldly denied both what God had written and what Christ had said. Alas! There is nothing of evil which proud self-confidence will not make us do. God save us from such a spirit as that!

30-31 And Jesus saith unto him, Verily I say unto thee, That this day, even in this night, before the cock crow twice, thou shalt deny me thrice. But he spake the more vehemently, If I should die with thee, I will not deny thee in any wise. —

See how positive he was, how reliant upon the strength of his own love. It was well to feel such love, but it was ill to mix with it such self-confidence.

31 Likewise also said they all.

Whenever a man who is called to be a leader goes astray, others are pretty sure to follow him. It was so on this occasion, for when Peter made his boastful speech, 'Likewise also said they all' — all the rest of his brethren chimed in, and so shared in his sin, but he was chief in the wrongdoing, for he led them all. In verse 53, we read what happened after Christ's agony and betrayal in Gethsemane:

53-54 And they led Jesus away to the high priest: and with him were assembled all the chief priests and the elders and the scribes. And Peter followed him afar off, even into the palace of the high priest: and he sat with the servants, and warmed himself at the fire.

Meanwhile, Christ was being put to the utmost derision and contempt. In verse 66 we are told more concerning the boastful apostle:

66-70 And as Peter was beneath in the palace, there cometh one of the maids of the high priest: And when she saw Peter warming himself, she looked upon him, and said, And thou also wast with Jesus of Nazareth. But he denied, saying, I know not, neither understand I what thou sayest. And he went out into the porch; and the cock crew. And a maid saw him again, and began to say to them that stood by, This is one of them. And he denied it again. And a little after, they that stood by said again to Peter, Surely thou art one of them: for thou art a Galilaean, and thy speech agreeth thereto.

He could not hold his tongue, you see. He was always fast and forward in speech; and no sooner did he begin to speak than the people said, 'That is the Galilaean brogue; you come from that part of the country, your speech betrays you.'

71-72; John 18:15 But he began to curse and to swear, saying, I know not this man of whom ye speak. And the second time the cock crew. And Peter called to mind the word that Jesus said unto him, Before the cock crow twice, thou shalt deny me thrice. And when he thought thereon, he wept. ... And Simon Peter followed Jesus, and so did another disciple: —

That is John, of course; he never mentions his own name if he can help it.

15-16 that disciple was known unto the high priest, and went in with Jesus into the palace of the high priest. But Peter stood at the door without. Then went out that other disciple, which was known unto the high priest, and spake unto her that kept the door, and brought in Peter.

I always fancy that John had a greater tenderness for Peter because he was the means of getting him into the palace of the high priest. Peter could not have got in if he had been alone, but John was known to the high priest, and so secured his admission. He must always have felt sorry that he took Peter into a place where he was so strongly tried. Hence John sought him out after his great fall. When perhaps the other apostles were inclined to leave him by himself, John cheered him up and brought him back to the faith.

17-18 Then saith the damsel that kept the door unto Peter, Art not thou also one of this man's disciples? He saith, I am not. And the servants and officers stood there, who had made a fire of coals; for it was cold: and they warmed themselves: and Peter stood with them, and warmed himself.

That was a very dangerous place for Peter to be in; he would have been safer out in the cold.

25 And Simon Peter stood and warmed himself. —

Twice over, we are told that, while his Master was being buffeted, Peter stood in the midst of the ribald throng, and warmed himself.

25-27 They said therefore unto him, Art not thou also one of his disciples? He denied it, and said, I am not. One of the servants of the high priest, being his kinsman whose ear Peter cut off, saith, Did not I see thee in the garden with him? Peter then denied again: and immediately the cock crew.

Thus was Christ's prediction literally fulfilled, and thus, by what seems the humble instrumentality of a cock crowing, was Peter brought to repentance. There is many an eloquent divine who has missed the mark when he has been preaching, but God has spoken by a very humble voice. You, dear friend, though you have no gifts of speech, may go and tell the story of Jesus Christ to someone, and God may bring him to repentance through you, as he brought Peter back to himself through the agency of this bird. May God make us all useful, and keep us from falling into transgression as Peter did! Amen.

MARK 15:1-41; LUKE 8:1-3

Let us read again what we have often read before, that saddest of all stories which, nevertheless, is the fountain of the highest gladness — the story of our Saviour's death, as recorded by Mark.

Mark 15:1 And straightway in the morning the chief priests held a consultation with the elders and scribes and the whole council, and bound Jesus, and carried him away, and delivered him to Pilate.

'The whole council' would be there, so early in the morning, for such an evil purpose. Wicked men are very diligent in carrying out their sinful schemes; so, when Christ was to be murdered, his enemies were there, as Luke tells us, 'as soon as it was day'. How much more diligent ought the followers of Christ to be to give him their devoted service! It is a good thing to begin the day with united prayer and holy converse with his people. Let these wicked men, who were so early in the morning seeking to secure the death of Christ, make us ashamed that we are not more diligent in his blessed service.

2-3 And Pilate asked him, Art thou the King of the Jews? And he answering said unto them, Thou sayest it. And the chief priests accused him of many things: but he answered nothing.

Silence was the best answer, the most eloquent reply, that he could give to such accusers; they deserved no other answer. Moreover, by his silence, he was fulfilling the prophecy: 'As a sheep before her shearers is dumb, so he openeth not his mouth' [Isaiah 53:7].

4-5 And Pilate asked him again, saying, Answerest thou nothing? behold how many things they witness against thee. But Jesus yet answered nothing; so that Pilate marvelled.

You will often find that your highest wisdom, when you are slandered, will lie in the imitation of your Lord and Master. Live a blameless life, and it shall be the best reply to the false charges of the wicked.

6-10 Now at that feast he released unto them one prisoner, whomsoever they desired. And there was one named Barabbas, which lay bound with them that had made insurrection with him, who had committed murder in the insurrection. And the multitude crying aloud began to desire him to do as he had ever done unto them. But Pilate answered them, saying, Will ye that I release unto you the King of the Jews? For he knew that the chief priests had delivered him for envy.

And he therefore hoped that the people, who were not moved by the same envy, would have chosen to have Jesus set at liberty.

11-13 But the chief priests moved the people, that he should rather release Barabbas unto them. And Pilate answered and said again unto them, What will ye then that I shall do unto him whom ye call the King of the Jews? And they cried out again, Crucify him.

This was the very best reply to the charge of high treason; for, if Jesus had really set himself up as a king in the place of Caesar, the people, when they were thus publicly appealed to, would not have cried out: 'Crucify him.' If there had been any truth in the allegation that he was the ringleader of a sedition, the Jews would not have said again and again, 'Crucify him.' Thus Christ gave Pilate a much more effectual answer than if he had himself spoken.

14-16 Then Pilate said unto them, Why, what evil hath he done? And they cried out the more exceedingly, Crucify him. And so Pilate, willing to content the people, released Barabbas unto them, and delivered Jesus, when he had scourged him, to be crucified. And the soldiers led him away into the hall, called Praetorium; —

The hall of the Praetorian guard.

16-17 and they call together the whole band. And they clothed him with purple, —

The uniform of the Roman soldiers was purple, as if to indicate that they belonged to an imperial master. So, when these soldiers, in mockery, put on our Lord the old cloak of one of their comrades, it sufficed to clothe him with the royal purple to which, as King, he was fully entitled.

17-19 and platted a crown of thorns, and put it about his head, And began to salute him, Hail, King of the Jews! And they smote him on the head with a reed, and did spit upon him, and bowing their knees worshipped him.

All this homage was paid to him in mockery yet what stern reality there was in that mockery!

20   And when they had mocked him, they took off the purple from him, and put his own clothes on him, and led him out to crucify him.

They 'led him out to crucify him'. It seems as if Christ had to lean upon those who led him — the word almost signifies as much as that, at least, it can be the word employed concerning anyone leading a child or a sick man who needed support — for the Saviour's weakness must have been very apparent by that time. After the agony and bloody sweat in Gethsemane, and the night and morning trials, and scourging, and mockery, and the awful strain upon his mind and heart in being made a sacrifice for sin, it was no wonder that he was weak. Besides, he was not like the rough, brutal criminals that are often condemned to die for their crimes; he was a man of gentle mould and more delicate sensibilities than they were, and he suffered much more than any ordinary man would have done in similar circumstances.

21   And they compel one Simon a Cyrenian, who passed by, coming out of the country, the father of Alexander and Rufus, to bear his cross.

Christ would not bear it himself; the soldiers saw that he was faint and weary, so they laid the cross, or at least one end of it, on Simon's shoulders.

22   And they bring him —

Here the word almost implies that they lifted him, and carried him, for his faintness had increased. They 'led him out to crucify him', but now they bear him.

22   unto the place Golgotha, which is, being interpreted, The place of a skull.

We sometimes speak of it as mount Calvary, but it was not so; it was a little rising ground, the common place of execution — the Tyburn or Old Bailey of Jerusalem.

23   And they gave him to drink wine mingled with myrrh: but he received it not.

He did not wish to have his sufferings abated, but to bear them to the bitter end. Christ forbids not that pain should be alleviated in the case of others, wherever that is possible; but, in his own case, it was not fit that it should be so relieved, since he was to bear the full brunt of the storm of vengeance that was due on account of sin.

24   And when they had crucified him, they parted his garments, casting lots upon them, what every man should take.

Christ's garments must go to his executioners in order to carry out the full shame associated with his death, as well as to fulfill the prophecy: 'They part my garments among them, and cast lots upon my vesture' [Psalm 22:18].

25-27   And it was the third hour, and they crucified him. And the superscription of his accusation was written over, THE KING OF THE JEWS. And with him they crucify two thieves; the one on his right hand, and the other on his left.

As if, in carrying out that ordinary etiquette which gives the central place to the chief criminal, they gave to Christ the place of greatest contempt and scorn.

28   And the scripture was fulfilled, which saith, And he was numbered with the transgressors.

You could not count the 'transgressors' on those crosses without counting him. There were three, and the One in the middle could not be passed by as you counted the others.

29-32   And they that passed by railed on him, wagging their heads, and saying, Ah, thou that destroyest the temple, and buildest it in three days, Save thyself, and come down from the cross. Likewise also the chief priests mocking said among themselves with the scribes, He saved others; himself he cannot save. Let Christ the King of Israel descend now from the cross, that we may see and believe. —

That is the world's way: 'that we may see and believe'. But Christ's way is: 'Believe, and thou shalt see.' Christ off the cross is admired by worldlings, but Christ on the cross is our hope and stay, especially as we know that this same Christ is now on the throne waiting for the time when he should return to claim his own — all who have trusted in the Crucified.

32 And they that were crucified with him reviled him.

Out of their black hearts and mouths came words of obloquy (or abuse) and scorn even then.

33 And when the sixth hour was come, —

When the sun had reached the zenith, at high noon —

33-41; Luke 8:1-3   there was darkness over the whole land until the ninth hour. And at the ninth hour Jesus cried with a loud voice, saying, Eloi, Eloi, lama sabachthani? which is, being interpreted, My God, my God, why hast thou forsaken me? And some of them that stood by, when they heard it, said, Behold, he calleth Elias. And one ran and filled a sponge full of vinegar, and put it on a reed, and gave him to drink, saying, Let alone; let us see whether Elias will come to take him down. And Jesus cried with a loud voice, and gave up the ghost. And the veil of the temple was rent in twain from the top to the bottom. And when the centurion, which stood over against him, saw that he so cried out, and gave up the ghost, he said, Truly this man was the Son of God. There were also women looking on afar off: among whom was Mary Magdalene, and Mary the mother of James the less and of Joses, and Salome; (Who also, when he was in Galilee, followed him, and ministered unto him;) and many other women which came up with him unto Jerusalem. ... And it came to pass afterward, that he went throughout every city and village, preaching and shewing the glad tidings of the kingdom of God: and the twelve were with him, And certain women, which had been healed of evil spirits and infirmities, Mary called Magdalene, out of whom went seven devils, And Joanna the wife of Chuza Herod's steward, and Susanna, and many others, which ministered unto him of their substance.

The previous chapter tells how the woman in Simon's house manifested her love to the Saviour. She showed her love in one way, and in a very special way; but there were others, who had similar affection for him, who showed it in other ways. What is right for one person to do might not be a wise or right thing for everybody to do. Christ did not want his feet washed with tears every minute in the day nor to have them anointed with even precious ointment very often. There are some Christians who ought to do and, I trust, will do some extraordinary thing for Christ — something which shall need no apology from them, because they are extraordinary persons, who used to be extraordinary sinners. And it would not be right for them to run in the ruts made by others, but they ought to strike out a distinct pathway for themselves. Happy is the church that has any such members; happier still if it has many such. But there are others, who love Christ just as truly, yet who must be content to show their love to him in some other, and apparently more common but, perhaps in the long run, more useful way. These gracious women ministered to Christ of their substance. He was only a poor itinerant preacher who needed daily sustenance. Some people say that every preacher ought to earn his own bread by trade or profession and preach freely, yet the Lord Jesus Christ, the Prince of preachers, did not do this. 'Oh, but Paul did!' Yes, Paul attained to a very high honour; but, we may be perfectly satisfied, as the servants of the Lord Jesus Christ, to attain to as high a degree of honour as our Master did; and, inasmuch as he never did any carpentering after he began to preach, but gave his whole soul and being up to the work of preaching, he was fed and cared for by the kindness of these godly women who were glad to minister unto him of their substance. 'The disciple is not above his master, nor the servant above his lord. It is enough for the disciple that he be as his master, and the servant as his lord' [Matthew 10:24-25]. So, as ministers of Christ, we need not be ashamed to minister spiritual things to the people and to receive of their carnal things in return. These women, though they did not wash Christ's feet with their tears nor anoint them with precious ointment, did well, for they 'ministered unto him of their substance'. Let us all do for him all that we can.

MARK 15:15-39; LUKE 23:27-49

We will read two short passages from the Gospels this evening. May the blessed Spirit, who taught the evangelists to record the sad story of our Lord's sufferings and death, give us fully to enter into the blessed meaning of it while we read it! First, turn to Mark 15:15.

Mark 15:15-16 And so Pilate, willing to content the people, released Barabbas unto them, and delivered Jesus, when he had scourged him, to be crucified. And the soldiers led him away into the hall, called Praetorium; —

The guard room of Herod's palace, where the Praetorian guards were wont to gather.

16-20 and they call together the whole band. And they clothed him with purple, and platted a crown of thorns, and put it about his head, And began to salute him, Hail, King of the Jews! And they smote him on the head with a reed, and did spit upon him, and bowing their knees worshipped him. And when they had mocked him, —

To the utmost — and gone the full length of their cruel scorn.

20-23 they took off the purple from him, and put his own clothes on him, and led him out to crucify him. And they compel one Simon a Cyrenian, who passed by, coming out of the country, the father of Alexander and Rufus, to bear his cross. And they bring him unto the place Golgotha, which is, being interpreted, The place of a skull. And they gave him to drink wine mingled with myrrh: but he received it not.

They did for him what they did for others who were crucified, they gave him myrrhed wine, as a stupefying draught, 'But he received it not.' He came to suffer, and he would bear, even to the end, the full bale (or pain and misery) of his suffering.

24-27 And when they had crucified him, they parted his garments, casting lots upon them, what every man should take. And it was the third hour, and they crucified him. And the superscription of his accusation was written over, THE KING OF THE JEWS. And with him they crucify two thieves; the one on his right hand, and the other on his left.

They gave him the place of eminence, as if he were a greater offender than either of the two thieves.

28 And the scripture was fulfilled, which saith, And he was numbered with the transgressors.

Sinners to the right of him, sinners to the left of him, sinners all round him, compassed about with those who sinned in the very highest degree by putting him to death: 'He was numbered with the transgressors.' Oh, that sweet word! It is the hope of transgressors now that he was counted with them, and for his sake all the benefactions of heaven now descend upon transgressors who accept him as their Substitute and Saviour.

29   And they that passed by railed on him, —

Not only those who sat down to gloat their cruel eyes upon his miseries, but even the passers-by: 'They that passed by, railed on him.'

29-30   wagging their heads, and saying, Ah, thou that destroyest the temple, and buildest it in three days, Save thyself, and come down from the cross.

He never said he would destroy the literal temple. He did, however, say concerning the temple of his body: 'Destroy this temple, and in three days I will raise it up' — and he *did* raise it up in three days after they had destroyed it.

31   Likewise also the chief priests mocking said among themselves with the scribes, He saved others; himself he cannot save.

What they said in bitter scorn was true; for mighty love had bound his hands for self-salvation. Infinite in love, found guilty of excess of love to men: He saved others; himself he could not save.

32-33   Let Christ the King of Israel descend now from the cross, that we may see and believe. And they that were crucified with him reviled him. And when the sixth hour was come, there was darkness over the whole land until the ninth hour.

A supernatural darkness, which could not have occurred according to the laws of nature. It did, as it were, 'set a tabernacle for the sun' — the Sun of Righteousness was canopied a while in darkness, that no longer might those horrible eyes gaze upon his terrible anguish.

34   And at the ninth hour Jesus cried with a loud voice, saying, Eloi, Eloi, lama sabachthani? which is, being interpreted, My God, my God, why hast thou forsaken me?

There was a denser darkness over his spirit than was over all the land and out of that darkness came this cry of agony.

35   And some of them that stood by, when they heard it, said, Behold, he calleth Elias.

Ah, me! This was either a cruel jest upon our Saviour's prayer, or an utter misapprehension of it.

36 And one ran and filled a sponge full of vinegar, and put it on a reed, and gave him to drink, saying, Let alone; let us see whether Elias will come to take him down.

Jesus did receive this vinegar, and so fulfilled Psalm 69:21: 'In my thirst they gave me vinegar to drink.'

37-38 And Jesus cried with a loud voice, and gave up the ghost. And the veil of the temple was rent in twain from the top to the bottom.

Even as the flesh of Christ, which is the veil of the incarnate God, was rent, so now was the veil of mystery taken away. The temple in her sorrow rent her veil. The old ceremonial law passed away with this token of grief by the rending of the veil. It was a strong, I might say, a massive veil; it could not have been rent by any ordinary means. But when the hand of God takes hold upon the veil of Jewish types, it readily rends, and into the innermost mystery of the holy of holies we may gaze, yea, and through it we may enter.

39 And when the centurion, which stood over against him, saw that he so cried out, and gave up the ghost, he said, Truly this man was the Son of God.

Convinced by the cross! Oh, the triumphs of Christ! The last word he speaks won this testimony from the centurion in charge of the crucifixion. Now we will read part of Luke's narrative.

Luke 23:27-31 And there followed him a great company of people, and of women, which also bewailed and lamented him. But Jesus turning unto them said, Daughters of Jerusalem, weep not for me, but weep for yourselves, and for your children. For, behold, the days are coming, in the which they shall say, Blessed are the barren, and the wombs that never bare, and the paps which never gave suck. Then shall they begin to say to the mountains, Fall on us; and to the hills, Cover us. For if they do these things in a green tree, what shall be done in the dry?

Our Saviour, even amidst the greatest sufferings, seemed almost to forget them in the deep sympathy that he had for the people around him. He pictured in his mind's eye that awful siege of Jerusalem. Who can read it, as Josephus describes it, without feeling the deepest horror? Oh, the misery of the women and of the children in that dreadful day when the zealots turned against each other within the city, and fought to the death, and when the Roman soldiery, pitiless as wolves, at last stormed the place! Truly did the Saviour say of it that there should be no day like to it; neither was there the concentration of human misery; and our Lord wept because he foresaw what it would be, and he bade these poor women reserve their tears for those awful sorrows.

32-33 And there were also two other, malefactors, led with him to be put to death. And when they were come to the place, which is called Calvary, there they crucified him, and the malefactors, one on the right hand, and the other on the left.

O blessed Master, they did not spare thee any scorn! There was no mode of expressing their contempt, which their malignity did not invent. Truly, 'He was numbered with the transgressors.' You could not count the three sufferers on Calvary without counting him; he was so completely numbered with the others that he must be reckoned as one of them.

34 Then said Jesus, Father, forgive them; for they know not what they do. —

It was all that he could say in their favour, and he did say that. If there is anything to be said in thy favour, O my fellow sinner, Christ will say it; and if there is nothing good in thee that his eyes can light upon, he will pray on his own account: 'Father, forgive them for my sake.'

34 And they parted his raiment, and cast lots.

His garments were the executioners' perquisites; pitilessly they took them from him and left him naked in his shameful sorrow.

35 And the people stood beholding. —

There was no pity in their eyes. No one of them turned away his face because he could not look upon so disgraceful a deed.

35 And the rulers also with them derided him, saying, He saved others; let him save himself, if he be Christ, the chosen of God.

I have already reminded you that there was a deep truth hidden away in what these cruel mockers said, for Jesus must give himself up as a ransom if we were to be redeemed.

36-38 And the soldiers also mocked him, coming to him, and offering him vinegar, And saying, If thou be the king of the Jews, save thyself. And a superscription also was written over him in letters of Greek, and Latin, and Hebrew, —

For these were the three languages known to the throng, and Pilate invited them all to read in 'Greek, and Latin, and Hebrew':

38-39 THIS IS THE KING OF THE JEWS. And one of the malefactors which were hanged railed on him, saying, If thou be Christ, save thyself and us.

Poor man; even though he is dying a felon's death, he must be in the swim with the multitude; he must keep in with the fashion, so strong, so powerful, is the 'popular' current with all mankind.

40-42 But the other answering rebuked him, saying, Dost not thou fear God, seeing thou art in the same condemnation? And we indeed justly; for we receive the due reward of our deeds: but this man hath done nothing amiss. And he said unto Jesus, Lord, remember me when thou comest into thy kingdom.

It was strange that Christ should find a friend dying on the cross by his side. Nobody else spoke to him about a kingdom. I am afraid that even his former followers began to think that it was all a delusion; but this dying thief cheers the heart of Jesus by the mention of a kingdom, and by making a request to him concerning that kingdom even when the King was in his death agony.

43 And Jesus said unto him, Verily I say unto thee, Today shalt thou be with me in paradise.

The Master, you see, uses his old phraseology. In his preaching, he had been accustomed to say, 'Verily, verily', and here he is, even on the cross, the same Preacher still — for there was such assurance, such confidence, such verity, in all his words, that he never had to alter his style of speaking. 'Verily I say unto thee, Today shalt thou be with me in paradise.' Well does our poet put it:

He that distributes crowns and thrones,
Hangs on a tree, and bleeds and groans.

He was distributing these crowns and thrones even while hanging on the tree. 'Tell it out among the nations that the Lord reigneth from the tree' may not be an exact translation of the psalm, but it is true, psalm or no psalm.

44 And it was about the sixth hour, —

About noon, when the sun was at its height.

44 and there was a darkness over all the earth until the ninth hour.

Three o'clock in the afternoon.

45 And the sun was darkened, and the veil of the temple was rent in the midst.

As if the great light of heaven and the pattern of heavenly things were both disturbed. The sun puts on mourning, and the temple rends her veil in horror at the awful deed enacted on the cross.

46 And when Jesus had cried with a loud voice, he said, Father, —

Is it not sweet to see how Jesus begins and ends his prayers on the cross with 'Father'?

46-48 into thy hands I commend my spirit: and having said thus, he gave up the ghost. Now when the centurion saw what was done, he glorified God, saying, Certainly this was a righteous man. And all the people that came together to that sight, beholding the things which were done, smote their breasts, and returned.

A strange ending to that day, was it not? The three hours' darkness and the death-cry of the Christ had not converted them, but it had convicted them of sin. They felt that a great and heinous crime had been committed; and, though they had come together as to a mere show or sight, they went away from the spectacle impressed as they had never been before: 'All the people that came together to that sight, beholding the things which were done, smote their breasts, and returned.'

49 And all his acquaintance, and the women that followed him from Galilee, stood afar off, beholding these things.

In these doings on Calvary you and I have a share — in their guilt, or else in their merit. Oh, that we may not be condemned with those who were guilty of his death, but may we be cleansed by that precious blood which puts away the sin of all who believe on him!

MARK 16

Mark 16:1   And when the sabbath was past, Mary Magdalene, and Mary the mother of James, and Salome, had bought sweet spices, that they might come and anoint him.

True love had made a mistake; but it was true love for all that, and the Lord accepted it, although he had no need of the sweet spices that the women brought.

2   And very early in the morning the first day of the week, they came unto the sepulchre at the rising of the sun.

There had already been another rising of the sun that morning, for the Sun of Righteousness had risen; and, with his rising, our hopes had risen, and eternal life had come to light. These holy women proved their affection to their Lord by being there so early. Love will not wait — it delights to render its service as speedily as ever it can: 'They came unto the sepulchre at the rising of the sun.'

3-4   And they said among themselves, Who shall roll us away the stone from the door of the sepulchre? And when they looked, they saw that the stone was rolled away: for it was very great.

Take comfort from this verse, you who are seeking to serve your Lord. There will be sure to be stones in your way, and some of them may be very great ones; but they will be rolled away in the Lord's good time, and in the rolling away often you will have all the greater joy. If the effort shall need the strength of an angel, then an angel will be sent from heaven for the purpose. There might have been no angel if there had been no stone; and you might have no revelation of the power of heaven to help you if you had not first had a revelation of your own weakness and inability to roll away the stone.

5 And entering into the sepulchre, they saw a young man sitting on the right side, clothed in a long white garment; and they were affrighted.

An angel had assumed the appearance of a young man sitting inside the sepulchre.

6 And he saith unto them, Be not affrighted: —

Why should they be affrighted? They had come to serve their Lord, and so had the angel, so there was no cause for fear. Those who love Jesus need never be afraid of angels; nor, for the matter of that, of devils either; for the Lord, whom they serve, will take care of them.

6 Ye seek Jesus of Nazareth, which was crucified: —

This was the first gospel sermon preached after the resurrection, so note particularly how the angel describes Christ. He calls him by his lowly name, 'Jesus of Nazareth', and does not speak of him as the risen or reigning Christ, but as 'Jesus of Nazareth, which was crucified'. The angels are evidently not ashamed of the cross of Christ, they do not attempt to hide the shame of it; for this one speaks of 'Jesus of Nazareth, which was crucified'.

6 he is risen; he is not here: —

That is the epitaph inscribed on Christ's tomb: 'He is not here.' On other people's graves it is written, 'Here lies So-and-So.' But on Christ's sepulchre it is recorded: 'He is not here.' He is everywhere else, but, 'He is not here.' He is with us in our solitude; he is with us in our public assemblies, but there is one place where he is not, and that is, in the empty tomb. Thank God that he is not there! We do not worship a dead man lying in the grave. He, on whom we rely, has risen from the dead and gone up into the glory, where he ever liveth to carry out the great design of salvation. 'He is not here' —

6-8 behold the place where they laid him. But go your way, tell his disciples and Peter that he goeth before you into Galilee: there shall ye see him, as he said unto you. And they went out quickly, and fled from the sepulchre; for they trembled and were amazed: neither said they any thing to any man; for they were afraid.

There was a mixture of joy with their fear, and of fear with their joy, and that tended to keep them silent for a while. Some people tell all they know, even when it would be wiser not to speak; but these godly women waited till they reached those to whom they were bidden to speak. They said nothing to anybody by the way, but hurried on to find the disciples, that they might give them the blessed tidings of their Lord's resurrection.

9 Now when Jesus was risen early the first day of the week, he appeared first to Mary Magdalene, out of whom he had cast seven devils.

Where grace had wrought its greatest wonders, there Christ paid his first visit: 'He appeared first to Mary Magdalene, out of whom he had cast seven devils.'

10-11 And she went and told them that had been with him, as they mourned and wept. And they, when they had heard that he was alive, and had been seen of her, believed not.

I can imagine that scene: the weeping and mourning disciples, and this eager woman telling out her story, and telling it with evident truthfulness and deep pathos, but they believed her not. Do you expect to be believed whenever you tell the story of your Lord's resurrection, or any other part of the gospel message? You have to tell it, not to Christ's disciples, but to those who are aliens from the commonwealth of Israel; and, probably, you do not tell it as well as Mary Magdalene did. Marvel not, therefore, if many a time those who hear your message believe it not. Mind that you believe it yourself, and keep on telling it whether others believe it or not, and God will bless it to some of them by and by.

12-13 After that he appeared in another form unto two of them, as they walked, and went into the country. And they went and told it unto the residue: neither believed they them.

Unbelief is not easily driven out of even true disciples; but let none of us ever harbour it in our hearts. As we see how unbelieving these disciples were, and know how wrong their unbelief was, let us not be like them.

14-20 Afterward he appeared unto the eleven as they sat at meat, and upbraided them with their unbelief and hardness of heart, because they believed not them which had seen him after he was risen. And he said unto them, Go ye into all the world, and preach the gospel to every creature. He that believeth and is baptized shall be saved; but he that believeth not shall be damned. And these signs shall follow them that believe; In my name shall they cast out devils; they shall speak with new tongues; They shall take up serpents; and if they drink any deadly thing, it shall not hurt them; they shall lay hands on the sick, and they shall recover. So then after the Lord had spoken unto them, he was received up into heaven, and sat on the right hand of God. And they went forth, and preached every where, the Lord working with them, and confirming the word with signs following. Amen.

God bless to us the reading of his holy Word! Amen.

MARK 16

Mark 16:1   And when the sabbath was past, Mary Magdalene, and Mary the mother of James, and Salome, had bought sweet spices, that they might come and anoint him.

We know that 'him' whose name is not given here. There is scarcely need to mention that it was Jesus whom the women came to anoint. Oh, how gladly would we also anoint 'him' whose name is the Anointed One! But not as a dead Christ, for 'He is risen.' Our sweet spices must henceforth be for that living One whom we anoint with our living joy and consecration; or, rather, we must receive our anointing from him, for he is the Christ, and we the Christians who get our very name and life from him. As he was supposed to be dead, and still lying in the tomb, these holy women came to anoint him.

2   And very early in the morning the first day of the week, they came unto the sepulchre at the rising of the sun.

We often lose a great blessing by not rising early for devotion. While yet the flowers are wet with dew; it were well if our souls had the dew of heaven resting upon them.

3-4 And they said among themselves, Who shall roll us away the stone from the door of the sepulchre? And when they looked, they saw that the stone was rolled away: for it was very great.

Which was, I suppose, the reason for their thinking about the stone; but still, I cannot help reading it as a reason why it was rolled away. At all events, this was the argument that David used when he prayed, 'For thy name's sake, O Lord, pardon mine iniquity; for it is great' [Psalm 25:11]; as if the greatness of the sin had in it some reason for pardon. So the greatness of the care may be some reason why we might expect a great God to come to our relief. It was a very great stone, therefore God, who knew that poor feeble women could not move it, himself had it rolled away.

5-6 And entering into the sepulchre, they saw a young man sitting on the right side, clothed in a long white garment; and they were affrighted. And he saith unto them, Be not affrighted: —

They were afraid of an angel.

Conscience doth make cowards of us all.

and even good men and good women are apt to be afraid of anything celestial and bright. The angel said to the women, 'Be not affrighted.'

6-7 Ye seek Jesus of Nazareth, which was crucified: he is risen; he is not here: behold the place where they laid him. But go your way, tell his disciples and Peter that he goeth before you into Galilee: there shall ye see him, as he said unto you.

Does not that little clause drop out very sweetly? Yet there is somewhat of a rebuke in it: 'as he said unto you'. Did he not tell you that he would rise from the dead? Did he not say that he would meet you in Galilee? And the day shall come, beloved, when you also shall rejoice in your Deliverer and your deliverance, and you shall not wonder so much then as you do now, for you shall *see* that the deliverance was what you ought to have expected: 'as he said unto you'. Poor seeking sinner, if you have found the Saviour, you are full of wonder; but the day will come when you will see it in another light; you will be equally grateful, but you will say, 'I ought to have had faith to expect this, as he said to me.' It will always be so. Just as God says, so it is — in creation, in providence, in grace. And as he has said to you, so shall it be in your spiritual experience.

8 And they went out quickly, and fled from the sepulchre; for they trembled and were amazed: neither said they any thing to any man; for they were afraid.

There was no reason in Christ's resurrection for anything but delight, yet these dear women were overwhelmed, silenced, struck dumb, by that which made the angels sing.

9 Now when Jesus was risen early the first day of the week, he appeared first to Mary Magdalene, out of whom he had cast seven devils.

It has been a general tradition in the church of Christ that Mary Magdalene was a great sinner; I do not feel sure that she was, but still, she is the type of a great sinner. The seven devils that were within her do not represent actual guilt on her part, but they depict or symbolize the subjection of her nature to the power of Satan. It is very beautiful to notice that those people for whom Christ does most he seems to love best; yet this is also according to human nature, for if there be a child in the family that the mother loves most, it is the one that was the hardest to bring up, and who has cost her most of care and most of labour. The casting out of seven devils endears the Magdalene to Christ, and first of all he appears to her. Besides, she loved much, doubtless, and she was quick of sight, so she saw him first. O my soul, if thou hast been a great sinner, do not take any place but that of first in love and first in fellowship with Christ! Be thou content to be nothing, but be thou anxious to make him thy all in all.

10 And she went and told them that had been with him, as they mourned and wept.

It is a curious 'interior' that Mark here sketches, or rather stipples, with just a few touches. There are most of Christ's disciples, who had been with him, sitting mourning and weeping over his death,

and in comes Mary, and says that she has seen him alive.

11   And they, when they had heard that he was alive, and had been seen of her, believed not.

This was both cruel to the Magdalene and forgetful of their Master's word, but unbelief is a very cruel thing. It is not only grievous to ourselves, but it acts in a shameful manner to Christian brethren and sisters, and worst of all is its treatment of our divine Master himself. It says that he is dead, when truly he is alive. Unbelief has no good in it; it is altogether evil, only evil, and that continually. The Lord deliver us from it!

12-13   After that he appeared in another form unto two of them, as they walked, and went into the country. And they went and told it unto the residue: neither believed they them.

It is very hard to kill unbelief. It has more lives than a cat is supposed to possess. There is no end to it, and if men sit down and indulge in it, and look upon it as an infirmity, or as a painful trial, instead of regarding it as an abominable sin against the Lord, they are likely to sink deeper and deeper into this horrible mire.

14   Afterward he appeared unto the eleven as they sat at meat, and upbraided them with their unbelief and hardness of heart, —

Christ is full of love to them, yet he must upbraid them. He loves them, but he loves not their unbelief. Nay, he is more vexed with unbelief in them than in other people.

14-15   because they believed not them which had seen him after he was risen. And he said unto them, Go ye into all the world, and preach the gospel to every creature.

That commission of our Lord makes me smile, for it seems such a curious cure for unbelief — yet I have proved the usefulness of it many a time. There have I been sitting down, fretting and worrying, and my Master, instead of giving me some gracious promise, that I might sit there by myself and enjoy its sweetness, has said, 'Up with you; go into the world, and preach the gospel to every creature.' Those who preach most, if they preach with all their hearts, will believe most, and they will grow strong enough to tread their doubts beneath their feet. So ought it to be. In the lives of those who have brought many to Christ, I do not, as a rule, read long chapters about their doubts and fears. No, but God encourages them by the signs and seals which he gives them; they see his hand with them, they mark how the Lord works with them and by them, and they forget their unbelief. Does not this passage seem to run so? 'He upbraided them with their unbelief and hardness of heart, because they believed not them which had seen him after he was risen. And he said unto them, Go ye into all the world, and preach the gospel to every creature.'

16   He that believeth and is baptized shall be saved; but he that believeth not shall be damned.

This is a weighty message for us to carry, and we have need to carry it with due solemnity, with our hearts on fire with love.

17-18   And these signs shall follow them that believe; In my name shall they cast out devils; they shall speak with new tongues; They shall take up serpents; and if they drink any deadly thing, it shall not hurt them; they shall lay hands on the sick, and they shall recover.

The apostles and the early Christians had these miraculous signs; there was no need that they should be given over again. The seal was set upon the gospel at the first. A man buys a house, and on the first day when he takes possession, he gets the signature of the seller and the legal seal upon the conveyance. That matter is done; if he ever doubts his right to the property, he can always look back to that seal. He does not want a fresh lot of sealing wax every five minutes; neither do we need continual miracles. The church of Christ at first was like a ship going to sea, the tug takes her out of the harbour, but when she is fairly out at sea, she does not need the tug any longer; she is dependent then upon the wind from heaven and so she speeds on her way. Or, the church is like a young tree newly planted in the orchard. It has a stake stuck in the ground by the side of it, to which it is tied; but when it grows into a strong tree, where is the stake? The tree does not require it, for it stands fast by other means; it is just so with us and the miracles which were needed at the first.

19 So then after the Lord had spoken unto them, he was received up into heaven, and sat on the right hand of God.

The disciples were not at once received up into heaven, though they might have been if God had so willed it. There was work for them to do here below, so Christ alone 'was received up into heaven, and sat on the right hand of God'; and as for his followers:

20 And they went forth, and preached every where, the Lord working with them, and confirming the word with signs following. Amen.

These last verses of Mark's Gospel have, as some of you know, been questioned as to their inspiration and authenticity, but they are so like Mark that you cannot read them without feeling that they are part and parcel of what the evangelist wrote. Set any critic you please to work, and if he knows the idiom and style of Mark's writing, he will be bound to say that this is part of the Gospel according to Mark; and God the Holy Spirit, blessing these words to our hearts, as I trust he will, will set his seal to what we believe and know to be his inspired Word.

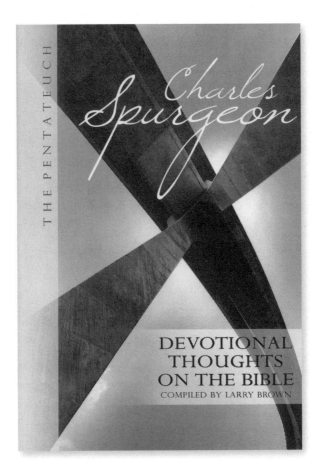

The book you have just read, Devotional thoughts on the Bible –
Matthew and Mark, *is part of a multi-volume collection that is
being published to eventually form a complete library of
Spurgeon's devotional expositions of the Bible.*

Visit our website to order other volumes in this series.

www.evangelicalpress.org